A Cook's Guide to
Asian Vegetables

A Cook's Guide to
Asian Vegetables

Wendy Hutton

illustrations by Sui Chen Choi
photos by Masano Kawana
Styling by Loretta Reilly and Christina Ong

PERIPLUS

Published by Periplus Editions with editorial offices
at 130 Joo Seng Road #06-01 Singapore 368357

http://www.periplus.com

ISBN 0 7946 0078 6
Printed in Singapore

Distributed by:
North America, Latin America and Europe
Tuttle Publishing, 364 Innovation Drive,
North Clarendon, VT 05759-9436, USA
tel (802) 773 8930; fax (802) 773 6993
email: info@tuttlepublishing.com

Asia Pacific
Berkeley Books Pte Ltd
130 Joo Seng Road #06-01,
Singapore 368357
tel (65) 6280 1330; fax (65) 6280 6290
email: inquiries@periplus.com.sg

Japan
Tuttle Publishing
Yaekari Building 3F, 5-4-12 Osaki,
Shinagawa-ku, Tokyo 141-0032, Japan
tel (813) 5437 0171; fax (813) 5437 0755
email: tuttle-sales@gol.com

contents

Discovering a new world of taste

Spices, ginger and other seasonings have been traded by Chinese, Indian and Arab merchants long before the Europeans began their own epic voyages of discovery at the end of the 15th century. The so-called Age of Discovery—when the Portuguese, Spanish, Dutch and British sailed across uncharted seas—led not only to the source of precious spices, and to treasure troves of gold and silver, but to the discovery of a host of previously unknown vegetables and fruits. Over the next few centuries, New World plants, such as tobacco, chilies, potatoes, sweet potatoes, pumpkin, peanuts, corn and tomatoes, spread throughout the world, to Asia as well as to Europe, while some Asian plants (particularly tea) became very popular in many parts of the world.

We are in the midst of another era of discovery today. Thanks to a growing interest in Asian cuisines as a result of large-scale Asian migration and increasing international travel, dozens of previously unknown vegetables from around Asia are now readily available. They are planted in the West or imported for sale in farmers' markets, supermarkets, Asian stores and specialty shops every-where from Seattle to Sydney, Berlin to Boston and London to Los Angeles.

Asian vegetables offer a new world of flavors and textures, as well as exciting possibilities in the kitchen. However, the challenge of identifying unfamiliar vegeta-bles, then knowing how to select, store and prepare them deters many cooks from experimenting with the exotic-looking produce now available. This timely book introduces cooks to everything they might need to know about all the major vegetables—fresh, dried, salted, or processed—used in Asia.

Major Asian cultures, particularly Indian and Chinese, have a strong tradition of using a wide range of vegeta-bles. Indeed, with the largest population of vegetarians worldwide, India has some of the most imaginative and delicious recipes for fresh vegetables, as well as for lentils and dried beans.

As a result of the Buddhist prohibition on killing animals, China and Japan have both had periods in their history where the eating of meat (although in the case of Japan, not chicken and fish) was banned, and when chefs and home cooks had to rely solely on vegetables to create imaginative meals. Many Chinese Buddhists today avoid meat on the 15th day of each lunar month, and meat is still not eaten in Buddhist monasteries—many of these (especially in China) have restaurants that serve excellent vegetarian food to the general public.

China first developed the art of making bean curd or tofu, a delicious meat substitute, from the dried soy bean, the plant with the richest protein content. Japan and Korea followed suit, and both countries now make a range of products from the soy bean. Tofu and other soy bean products are increasingly enjoyed by vegetarians and non-vegetarians around the world, and are described in detail in this book.

In many Asian countries, meat is expensive and is served mainly during festivals. Vegetables thus have a greater importance than they tend to in the West, where larger amounts of protein are eaten. Grain—generally rice—forms the staple food, accompanied by vegetables and fresh fish from the sea, rivers or lakes.

Home cooks in India, China and Japan, and to a lesser extent in Korea (where the climate limits the variety of vegetables cultivated), are skilled in preparing a variety of vegetable dishes, using them in soups and stews, stir-frying, braising, or making them into fritters, dumplings and pickles, or even using them in desserts. In the tropi-cal countries of Southeast Asia, vegetables are frequently blanched or eaten raw in salads, often accompanied by spicy dips or dressings.

For at least 2,000 years, major Asian cultures have been aware of the medicinal and nutritional benefits of vegetables. Now, it seems, Western science is catching up. Countless scientific reports confirm the powerful properties of many plants, and we are urged to have at least three servings of vegetables every day.

Many plants have been proven to help strengthen the immune system, thus protecting against disease. Some seem to have anti-cancer properties, while others help lower cholesterol levels and ease the symptoms of ailments such as arthritis or rheumatism. The nutritional and medicinal properties, as well as some of the traditional folk beliefs surrounding certain vegetables, are briefly described in this book.

The fact that they are, quite simply, "good for you" would be reason enough to start experimenting with unfamiliar Asian vegetables, but there is another compelling reason for eating them: they taste good, even superb, when prepared properly. This book offers sample recipes from around Asia for most of the vegetables described, as well as suggestions for using them. A whole new world of eating awaits you.

Stretching across a vast area and encompassing a wide range of climates, Asia's cuisines are naturally very diverse. However, some cooking styles are widely used and many utensils and techniques are shared.

When preparing the Asian recipes in this book, be sure never to use olive oil, which is not used in Asian cuisines and will alter the flavor of the dish. Light, non-flavored oils such as canola, sunflower, safflower or corn oil, or light, blended vegetable oils are recommended.

One of the healthiest ways and perhaps the most popular way of cooking vegetables is stir-frying, using a curved wok over high heat so that the vegetables are cooked quickly with minimum loss of nutrition. A wok allows for quick tossing of ingredients, which fall back into the wok and not outside as they would if a frying pan were used. It is important to select a heavy wok so that the heat is evenly distributed, and to avoid non-stick or aluminum woks. The wok should be heated, then oil is poured in and swirled around to coat the sides before adding the vegetables, often after some garlic and ginger have been briefly stir-fried as a seasoning. The vegetables should be constantly stirred over very high heat using a specially shaped wok spatula. For vegetables that need longer cooking, water or stock is often added after the initial stir-frying and the wok covered to allow the vegetables to cook in steam.

Asian cooks often steam food, using either a multi-tiered bamboo steaming basket that sits inside a wok, or placing the food in a bowl or plate on a metal rack or perforated disk set into the wok above boiling water. It is important for the water to be fully boiling before the steamer is set into the wok, and that the water be topped up from time to time if the steaming is lengthy.

Simmering food in coconut milk is a popular cooking method in tropical Asia. Although coconut milk is usually made from freshly grated coconut, cans of coconut cream, which can be diluted as required to make thick or thin coconut milk, are recommended as a substitute.

A Note to Vegetarian Readers

In most parts of Asia, fish products (especially fish sauce, dried shrimp paste and prawns), as well as meat and poultry are frequently cooked with vegetables for additional flavor and nutrition. However, it is possible to adapt some of the authentic Asian recipes in this book by using substitutes for fish, meat or poultry. The final result may be somewhat different, but the overall flavor will still be perfectly acceptable.

- Vegetable stock can replace chicken or beef stock.
- Oyster-flavored vegetarian sauce can be used instead of genuine oyster sauce.
- Instead of fish sauce, use soy sauce.
- Fermented bean curd squares, available in jars, can be used instead of dried shrimp paste.
- Twists of dried bean curd skin can often replace chicken or pork.
- Meat or poultry can be replaced with flavored gluten (which is often available in cans), deep-fried bean curd—either the sweetened Japanese version, *aburage*, or the unsweetened Chinese variety, *tau pok*—or *tempeh*.

BEANS, peas & pulses

All peas and beans are legumes, members of the botanical family, Leguminosae, and are among the most ancient foods enjoyed by man. The dried seeds of legumes are inexpensive and highly nutritious, containing both protein and oils. There is no scientific or culinary distinction between a pea and a bean, although many cooks consider a pea to be the fresh young seed of a legume, and a bean either as an edible green pod or the dried seed of a mature

legume. Both are enjoyed fresh in their immature state, and the mature seeds or pulses—known variously as beans, *dal*, grams, lentils and peas—are dried and eaten in countless ways, as are the leaves and sprouts of some legumes.

Some dried peas and beans need preliminary cooking to reduce any oligosaccharides, which may cause indigestion. Put in a pan covered with three times their volume of water. Bring to the boil, turn off the heat, cover and stand 1 hour. Drain, rinse and add fresh water to cover by about 1 in (2 cm)—some cooks may recommend adding salt, but this toughens the pulses—and simmer until soft.

Azuki, sometimes spelled adzuki, is also known as the red bean. This bean is particularly popular in China, Japan and Korea. It has a nutty, rather sweet flavor that makes it popular in cakes and desserts. According to the Chinese, foods can be classified either as *yin* ("cooling") or *yang* ("warming") to the body. Azuki beans are considered to be more *yang* than other pulses, and are frequently eaten by those following a macrobiotic diet rich in *yang* foods.

Appearance & Flavor These small, dark red beans, about $1/4$ in (50 mm) in length, are roughly oblong. The flavor lends itself well to sweet rather than savory dishes. **Nutritional & Medicinal Properties** Azuki beans contain as much as 25% protein. They are very low in oligosaccharides, and so are easily digested. In Japan, a type of soup made with azuki beans is believed to be good for helping kidney problems. **Culinary Uses** Azuki beans do not need soaking and preliminary cooking. They are very popular in cakes and desserts in northern Asia, where they are boiled and mashed with sugar to make a sweet filling for pancakes, Chinese mooncakes and many Japanese cakes. Azuki beans are simmered with water in China, Japan and Korea or with added coconut milk in parts of Southeast Asia to make a soupy snack or dessert. Boiled azuki beans are also added to various drinks and shaved ice concoctions (such as *ais kacang* in Malaysia and *halo halo* in the Philippines). Azuki beans are also cooked together with rice in Korea and Japan to make a savory and nutritious alternative to plain rice.

Black-eyed Beans are also called black-eyed peas, and are the mature, dried seeds of the long bean (an excellent vegetable when fresh, see page 17). Black-eyed beans are widely used in Asia, and are particularly popular among Punjabis in India and in parts of north Asia, including China. Black-eyed beans are also enjoyed in the southern states of the US, as well as in Mexico, where they are cooked in robust soups and hearty stews.

Appearance & Flavor These creamy colored beans are similar in shape to kidney beans, although somewhat smaller, and have a black patch at the side where they were attached inside the pod. They have a pleasant savory flavor and are very versatile in the kitchen. **Nutritional & Medicinal Properties** Black-eyed beans contain 22% protein and are rich in phosphorus. They also have appreciable amounts of iron and thiamine. **Culinary Uses** Black-eyed beans have a considerably higher level of oligosaccharides than most pulses, so be sure to soak and pre-cook them, as directed on page 11. Black-eyed beans are very good in soups, added to slow-cooked vegetable combinations, or simmered in a stew with meat and vegetables. Dried black-eyed beans are ground to make flour used for pancakes in India, and are also split to make *chowla dal*.

Black Gram or Urad Dal is eaten mostly in India, particularly in the south

where it is referred to as black gram or *ulundoo*. Black gram is available in two distinctly different forms. When sold whole, the black skin is left intact—hence the common name of this pulse. When skinned and split, however, the gram reveals a creamy white color, and is therefore sometimes known as "white lentil." Like its black counterpart, the husked white lentils are an essential ingredient in the cuisines of India as well as Sri Lanka.

Appearance & Flavor The appearance of the whole black gram—a small, oblong-shaped lentil with a shiny, black skin—is totally different to the skinned, creamy white split lentil. Black gram has a relatively pronounced flavor, and is therefore used as a seasoning in its skinned, split form, as well as eaten as a savory dish when used whole. **Nutritional & Medicinal Properties** Black gram is a good source of calories and is particularly high in phosphorus and calcium. **Culinary Uses** Whole, unskinned black gram is cooked in vegetable dishes and vegetarian curries. It does not require soaking and pre-cooking. The skinned black gram (white lentil) is often stir-fried with brown mustard seeds, dried chili and curry leaves to make a seasoning which is added during the final stages of cooking lentil stews, fish curries and soupy dishes in southern India. White lentils are also soaked for several hours and allowed to ferment slightly, ground to a paste and mixed with soaked ground rice to make a batter. This is used in steamed breads (*idli*), deep-fried savories (*vadai*) and savory pancakes (*dosai* and *appalam*) in southern India. Flour made from white lentils is also used in making *poppadum* or *papad*, a wafer-thin savory which puffs up to a crisp circle after brief deep-frying, and is often eaten as a snack with curries and rice.

Broad Beans originated in Europe and the Middle East and have been eaten in

China for several thousand years. The fresh young beans are enjoyed as a vegetable in cold areas of Asia, while elsewhere, dried broad beans are popular boiled, roasted or deep-fried and mixed with salt as a savory snack food.

Appearance & Flavor Broad beans are one of the largest pulses, measuring about 1 in (2$\frac{1}{2}$ cm) in length. When dried, they are reddish brown in color; the flavor is somewhat earthy and is improved when the beans are cooked with seasonings such as soy sauce. **Nutritional & Medicinal Properties** Broad beans are high in protein, iron and fiber and are a good source of vitamins A and C. They contain a high concentration of dopamine, a neuro-transmitter in the brain. Broad beans should not be eaten by anyone taking drugs containing monoamine inhibitors, which are found in some anti-depressants. **Culinary Uses** The dried beans should be soaked and pre-boiled as described on page 11. They can then be simmered in water to cover, with soy sauce and a little sugar and sesame oil and then served with rice and other dishes. Pre-boiled dried broad beans can also be left to dry thoroughly before being deep-fried in very hot oil. Sprinkle with salt and, if liked, a little ground red pepper before serving as a snack.

Channa Dal

Channa Dal is often known as Bengal gram, and is a variety of the common chickpea, reputed to make up more than half the production of pulses in India. *Channa dal*, like chickpeas, is used in savory stews and curries, although a large portion of the crop is dried and ground to make a widely used flour, *besan*, known as chickpea flour in English.

Appearance & Flavor When whole, *channa dal* is yellowish brown in color and somewhat wrinkled. *Besan*, or *channa dal* flour, is yellowish cream in color. *Channa dal* is most commonly sold split, and resembles yellowish beige lentils, with its somewhat oval shape. The flavor is nutty and pleasant. **Nutritional & Medicinal Properties** *Channa dal* is, like all other pulses, nutritious. It contains fiber and carbohydrates as well as protein, minerals and vitamins. It also contains lecithin and linoleic acid and is easily digested. **Culinary Uses** If using whole *channa dal*, soak and pre-cook as directed on page 11. It can be cooked in any vegetarian stew or curry, either alone or with fresh vegetables. *Channa dal*, should be soaked in water for about 30 minutes, then drained before being cooked in a lentil stew or simmered with vegetables. *Channa dal* is used as a seasoning in some regions of India, stir-fried with oil or ghee and added to various dishes such as simmered pumpkin. *Besan* is used to make batters, as a thickening or binding agent in many dishes and also used in some Indian sweetmeats. In Burma and parts of northern Thailand, this flour is used lightly toasted and sprinkled on some soup and noodle dishes.

Chickpeas

Chickpeas originated in the Middle East, where they have been cultivated for several thousand years. Most of the chickpea crop is dried before use. The Arabian armies which conquered northern Africa and southern Spain were reputedly fed on this nourishing pulse. Chickpeas have spread as far as the Americas (particularly South America) across to India and, in recent times, are even grown in Australia. They are also known as garbanzos.

Appearance & Flavor Chickpeas are hard and wrinkled, beige-brown in color, and are pointed at one end. Their nutty flavor is particularly appreciated in India and in other countries with a sizeable Indian population. **Nutritional & Medicinal Properties** Similar to *channa dal*. **Culinary Uses** Chickpeas are renowned for taking a long time to cook, so they should be soaked and pre-cooked as directed on page 11. After pre-cooking, the colorless, almost jelly-like skins covering the chickpeas will have been loosened. Skim the skins off the surface while they are still in the cooking liquid, then detach and discard the rest of the skins. This is not essential, but many cooks prefer the appearance of the finished dish without these skins. Although purées of chickpeas are popular in the Middle East, Indian cooks generally leave the chickpeas whole, usually cooking them with spices and other seasonings to make a type of stew. They are also cooked with vegetables such as tomatoes and carrots, or with leafy greens such as spinach.

Green Beans

Green Beans are probably the most widely eaten fresh bean in the world. Also known as haricot beans, French beans or, in the US, as string beans, they are native to Mexico and Guatemala. Green beans are now eaten throughout Asia, although in some countries they are less popular than long beans. If left to mature, the almost negligible seeds inside the young green pods will swell to form legumes. When these are dried, they turn red and are known as kidney beans (see page 17).

Appearance & Flavor There are many varieties of green bean, ranging from light to dark green in color, to pale yellow. Some fresh beans have wide, flat pods, while others may be rounded. Green beans are highly versatile, with a pleasant texture that makes them almost universally appealing. **Choosing & Storing** When buying the beans, look for those which snap rather than bend. Avoid those where the seeds are starting to swell, as the beans will be too mature. Keep refrigerated in a plastic bag for 3–4 days. **Preparing** Most varieties lack strings, although if they are present, they should be pulled away and the stem end cut off before cooking. The beans are usually sliced diagonally into 1-in ($2^1/_2$-cm) lengths, although some recipes may call for them to be finely chopped. **Nutritional & Medicinal Properties** Fresh green beans contain appreciable levels of calcium and phosphorus and are high in beta-carotene. **Culinary Uses** Green beans are eaten stir-fried, simmered, added to soups and used in salads. Very young beans are often eaten raw, accompanied with a dip in Thailand, or blanched before they are added to salads in Indonesia. To ensure the beans keep their texture and bright color, be sure not to overcook them; cook them briefly in boiling water, drain, then cool the beans in iced water before draining again.

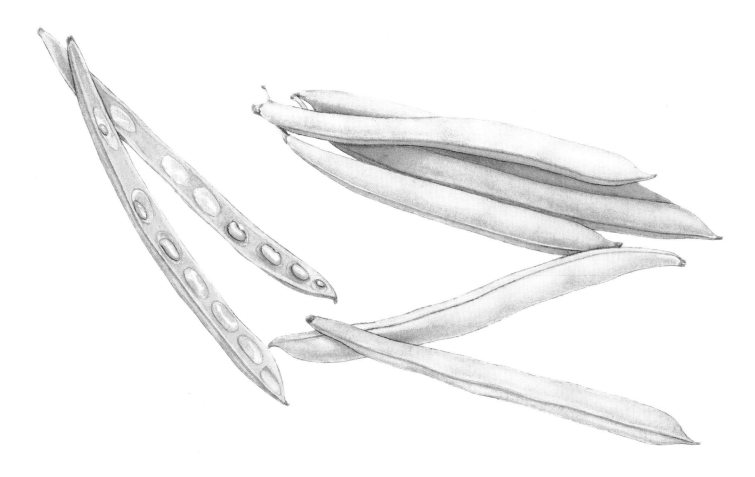

Drumsticks or Horseradish Tree Pods

Drumsticks or Horseradish Tree Pods is the common English name for the fruit of *Moringa oleifera*. The name derives from the fact that the pungent roots of this tree were used as a substitute for true horseradish by the British in India (the Thais, however, use the root to obtain an orange dye). The young seed pods—commonly referred to as as "drumsticks"—are a very popular vegetable in India and other parts of Asia with large Indian communities. In Southeast Asia, the young, fern-like green leaves are also eaten, and are particularly popular in the Philippines, where they are known as *malunggay*. The leaves are frequently plucked from horseradish trees growing in village gardens and are added to vegetable stews and soups.

Appearance & Flavor The young seed pods are long (at least 12 in/30 cm), pale green and thin, with small bumps revealing the seeds inside. The taste is pleasantly mild, with a touch of sweetness. The leaves of the horseradish tree are tiny and delicate, growing in feathery clusters somewhat like acacia leaves. **Choosing & Storing** If buying fresh drumsticks or seed pods, look for those which are narrow. Avoid buying those that contain well-developed seeds. They can be kept refrigerated for 2–3 days. The leaves are generally sold still on the stems. Wrap in kitchen paper and refrigerate for up to 2 days. **Preparing** Wash the drumsticks, cut into pieces and simmer until soft. Only the soft interior is eaten, and the fibrous skin of the pods is discarded at the table. The leaves should be rinsed thoroughly and drained before cooking. **Nutritional & Medicinal Properties** Drumsticks contain rather high levels of vitamin C as well as calcium, phosphorus and riboflavin. The leaves, which are very rich in vitamins A and C, stimulate digestion and are a diuretic. They are also traditionally used as a poultice for dog bites in India. **Culinary Uses** Although both the seed pods and leaves are edible, the various uses of the horseradish tree proves that what people eat is often determined by culture rather than the edibility of the actual plant. For example, in India, only the seed pods or drumsticks are eaten, usually in vegetable or lentil stews. In parts of Southeast Asia, only the leaves are consumed in soups or vegetable stews, or dried and deep-fried for a nutritious snack or crispy garnish.

Kidney Beans are the mature seeds of the common green bean

(see page 15). In India, where several types of kidney beans are grown, they are known as *rajmah*. Usually available dried, the beans are dark red in color when fully matured. Fresh kidney beans are sold already shelled in India and in Indonesia.

Appearance & Flavor The most common kidney bean is dark red in color, about $1/_3$ in (1 cm) in length and distinctly kidney-shaped. Some varieties are smaller and variegated pink and cream. The dark red kidney bean has a good flavor and can be used in either savory or sweet dishes. **Choosing & Storing** Look for beans which are firm and dry, without any trace of slime. Wrap in a paper towel and keep refrigerated in a plastic bag for up to 1 week. **Preparing** Wash and drain. Fresh kidney beans do not need soaking. **Culinary Uses** The fresh beans can be prepared in the same way as dried kidney beans, but the cooking time is greatly reduced and the flavor more delicious. They are frequently added to vegetable soups, or cooked in spicy sauces which often use tomato as a main ingredient. Boiled fresh or dried kidney beans are also an excellent ingredient in salads, mixed with other vegetables such as corn and celery.

Long Beans or Snake Beans are known by a greater variety of names than any

other legume—cow pea, asparagus bean, yard-long bean (somewhat of an exaggeration) and China pea are among the names for this pleasant-tasting long green bean.

Appearance & Flavor Most commonly found as a plump, pale green bean; other varieties include thinner, darker green pods, as well as very thin, long beans with a purplish black tinge and a tendency to twist. All varieties are flavorful and versatile. The fatter type softens when cooked, but compensates with a sweet flavor. Other varieties remain firm, with a more distinct taste. **Choosing & Storing** The beans should be crisp. Avoid those with developed seeds as they will be old and dry. The thinner and younger the beans, the better the flavor. Keep refrigerated in a plastic bag for 3–4 days. **Preparing** Remove the stem end and tip, then cut into bite-sized lengths before cooking. **Nutritional & Medicinal Properties** Long beans are rich in beta-carotene, vitamin C and phosphorus, and are used in traditional Chinese tonics for the kidneys and stomach. **Culinary Uses** Long beans are added to soups, salads and stir-fried dishes. Sections of very young beans are sometimes eaten raw with a dip in Southeast Asia. Dark varieties are preferred for salads, as they keep their color after blanching.

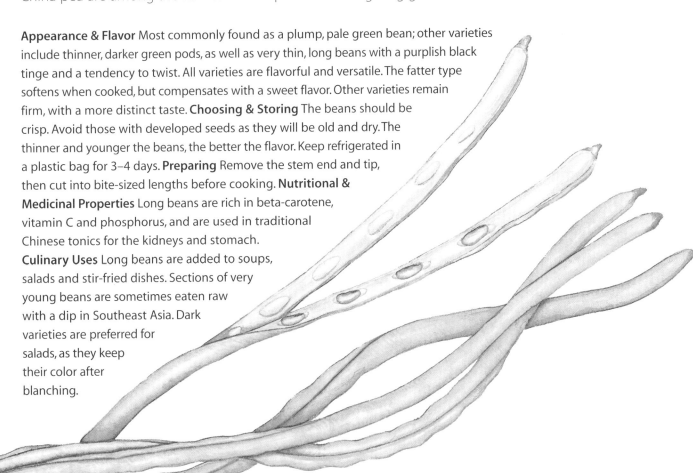

Mung Beans

Mung Beans are one of the most widely used beans in Asia. Although perhaps best known for their crisp, succulent sprouts, dried mung beans are also used both whole as well as split. Surprisingly, there are up to 2,000 varieties of mung beans, including the common green mung bean and the yellow and black mung beans.

Appearance & Flavor Mung beans are very small, hard and oblong, with the most common variety having a dark olive green color. The flavor is not particularly interesting, but their nutritional value and versatility more than make up for this. In India, split mung beans (known as *moong dal*) are available with their skins intact, as well as hulled—which makes them look like very small, yellowish orange lentils. **Nutritional & Medicinal Properties** Dried mung beans contain approximately 23% protein, and are particularly rich in carbohydrates, calcium and thiamine. They have the benefit of being low in oliosaccharides and are thus easily digested. In India, cooked mung beans are often given to invalids, while in China they are considered a highly suitable food for young children and the very elderly. **Culinary Uses** Mung beans cook fairly fast, so they do not need soaking and pre-boiling. Whole mung beans are simmered in savory stews, and are also made into a sort of sweet porridge with sugar, often with coconut milk added. Split mung beans are cooked in many savory dishes in India, usually with spices and sometimes with other added vegetables. In China, cooked green mung beans are often simmered and ground to make a sweet paste used as a filling for buns, pancakes and mooncakes, while in Korea, soaked and ground yellow mung beans are cooked with glutinous rice and sugar to make a popular cake. Mung beans are toasted and then ground to make a flour that is used in cakes and sweetmeats in several Southeast Asian countries. In addition, mung bean starch (known as *tepong hoen kwe* in Indonesia and Malaysia) is used to thicken coconut milk for cakes, or made into a type of noodle known as bean thread or cellophane noodles—or perhaps more colloquially, as *tung hoon* or glass noodles—in Malaysia and Singapore. These noodles have an intriguing jelly-like texture and are used in soups, salads and fillings in many Asian countries.

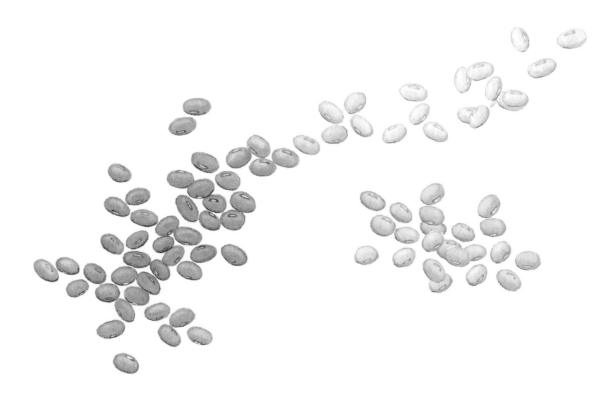

Mung Bean Sprouts

Mung Bean Sprouts are an important vegetable in much of Asia. They are grown by soaking the beans, then keeping them moist in a dark place for several days until the sprouts or shoots have emerged. There are two major types of bean sprouts, with the one most common in Asia grown from the small, oblong green mung bean, while the other is grown from soy beans.

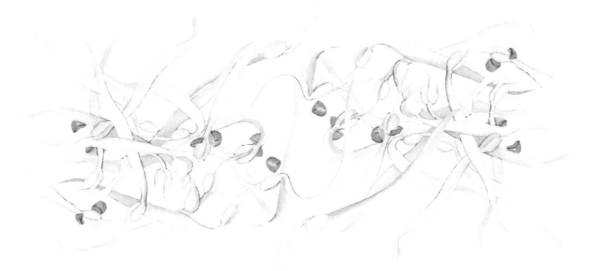

Appearance & Flavor Mung bean sprouts have small, creamy seed heads, sometimes found with the split greenish black skin clinging to them, with slender, crisp, white shoots usually finishing in a somewhat straggly tail. They are sometimes available with the seed heads and tails removed, and in this form are generally known as silver sprouts. Although they may be more aesthetic in appearance, silver sprouts are actually less nutritious than the whole sprout with the seed head intact. Fresh mung bean sprouts have a delicate flavor and, when raw or only lightly blanched, a crisp texture. **Choosing & Storing** Fresh mung bean sprouts are often stored in tubs of water in Asian markets, and lifted out when required, or they may be piled in a heap on a tray. In supermarkets, mung bean sprouts are usually packed in plastic bags and kept refrigerated. The sprouts should look crisp and bright white. Avoid any which appear limp, or which have small green leaves starting to sprout from the seed head. Refrigerate the sprouts for 4–5 days in a bowl with water to cover, changing the water daily. **Preparing** Put the sprouts in a large bowl of water and move them gently with the hand to dislodge any greenish black hulls, lift these out and discard before use and, if liked, pinch off the thin root ends. **Nutritional & Medicinal Properties** Bean sprouts are more nutritious than the dried beans from which they are sprouted, full of vitamins and natural sugars. **Culinary Uses** The crisp texture and mild flavor of mung bean sprouts is best appreciated when they are eaten raw, which is the way they are commonly served in Southeast Asia. The Chinese, however, do not like to eat raw vegetables (a precaution which lingers from the days when human waste was used as a fertilizer), so they generally blanch or stir-fry them. To blanch mung bean sprouts, put them into a colander, pour a stream of boiling water over them for about 10 seconds, then immediately plunge the sprouts into iced water to cool. Drain the sprouts well before using. Raw or blanched bean sprouts are excellent in salads and soups, and are an essential ingredient in most Vietnamese and Thai noodle soups. Care is needed when cooking mung bean sprouts as they cook very quickly. If left too long, they become limp and watery. Perhaps the best way to cook the sprouts is to wash, then drain them well, and stir-fry over maximum heat in a small amount of very hot oil for 30 seconds only.

Pea Shoots or Dou Miao

Pea Shoots or Dou Miao are a good example of Asian thrift, with none of the edible portions of the plant wasted. Pea shoots are the immature tips or shoots of the snow pea and sugar pea, and are plucked as the crop of peas keeps growing and maturing. Often sold under their Chinese name, *dou miao*, pea shoots are enjoyed as a leafy green vegetable, and fetch an even higher price than the actual peas.

Appearance & Flavor Pea shoots are often available in two sizes. The very tiny, immature shoots are picked when the leaves are about $1/3$ in (1 cm) in diameter, and the stems are so slender that they are almost hair-like. The more mature shoots, which have larger stems and more pointed leaves about $1^1/2$–2 in (4–5 cm) in length, are more commonly available. Both types of pea shoots are very delicately flavored. **Choosing & Storing** Look for pea shoots which appear fresh. Avoid any that have a yellowish tint on the leaves and show signs of wilting. The smaller variety are frequently sold in a perforated plastic bag and can be stored refrigerated in this for 2–3 days. Larger sprouts can be kept refrigerated in damp paper for up to 3 days. **Preparing** The shoots should be washed thoroughly and well drained before using. The thicker part of the stems should be discarded from the more mature pea shoots. **Culinary Uses** The smaller variety of pea shoots are good raw in salads, although they are seldom used in this way in Asia. They can also be eaten raw as a garnish, or added at the last minute to soups. The more common larger pea shoots are always cooked, with the most popular method being a quick stir-fry, with a touch of oyster sauce often added just before serving, or with minced garlic and soy sauce.

Pigeon Peas or Toor Dal are grown for their small seeds which are dried, husked and split to make one of India's most flavorful lentils, known as *toovar*, *arhar* or *paripoo dal*, depending on the region. More popular in India than anywhere else in the world, the pigeon pea is thought to be native to either Africa or India. The color of pigeon peas varies. They are sometimes known in English as red gram, however, they are most often yellow rather than red. They should not be confused with red lentils or *masoor dal*, which are slightly smaller and have a definite salmon pink color.

Appearance & Flavor Pigeon peas range in color from white through yellow to brown and even black, although those dried and split for use as lentils or *dal* have a yellowish ochre shade. With their excellent flavor, pigeon peas are arguably the tastiest of all lentils. **Nutritional & Medicinal Properties** With 20% protein and high levels of calcium, phosphorus and beta-carotene, pigeon peas are very nutritious. They are also easily digested. **Culinary Uses** Split pigeon peas do not need soaking or pre-cooking, though some Indian cooks like to soak them in tepid water for 10–15 minutes before using. They are particularly popular in southern India, where they are generally simmered with spices and water or coconut milk to make a moist lentil stew or soup. The lentils are also cooked with mixed vegetables to make the southern Indian dish known as *sambar*, usually spooned over rice or eaten as a dip with savory pancakes made from ground rice and black gram (*dosai*).

Red Lentils are known in India as *masoor dal*, and are a type of skinned split pea. In Europe, this attractive red lentil is generally associated with Egyptian and North African cuisine, which is not surprising since the plant on which it grows originated in the Middle East, and is widely used there for soups and stews. Red lentils are now widespread in India, and are popular not only for their excellent flavor but because of their digestibility and the short time required for cooking.

Appearance & Flavor This lentil is easily recognized by its beautiful salmon pink color which, rather sadly, changes to yellow after cooking. The flavor is excellent. **Nutritional & Medicinal Properties** Like all other lentils, the red lentil is nutritious, containing around 20% protein as well as carbohydrates and calcium, and is particularly rich in phosphorus and thiamine. Red lentils are also easily digested. **Culinary Uses** This is one of the quickest cooking lentils, so it does not need any soaking at all. Red lentils are widely used in soups and stews, sometimes with added vegetables. Red lentils are also cooked with rice to make the dish known as *kitchri*. This became popular with the colonial British and was taken back to Victorian India, where a modified version (usually with the addition of smoked fish) became known as kedgeree.

Red-streaked Beans or Borlotti Beans belong to the same family

as the kidney bean. Similar to pinto beans, red-streaked beans are available fresh in the summer months in Europe when they first mature. Fully matured beans are sold dried. In many parts of Asia, fresh red-streaked beans are increasingly available in supermarkets and markets although the dried variety is not used in local cooking.

Appearance & Flavor The beautiful pinkish purple-and-cream pods of this bean contain ivory-colored beans streaked with the same red color. Disappointingly however, these red streaks disappear soon after cooking. Red-streaked beans have a mild flavor and, when fresh and young, a pleasant, slightly waxy texture. **Choosing & Storing** Avoid any pods which may be starting to get a brown tinge; it is preferable to buy beans still in their pods rather than those which have been shelled, as the latter will not keep as long. To store the beans, refrigerate in a paper-lined plastic box or perforated plastic bag for 3–4 days, and peel just before using. If the beans are purchased peeled, they are best used within 24 hours. **Culinary Uses** In Asia, these beans are usually added to soups. They can also be simmered in lightly salted water and eaten as a salad vegetable, or added to other vegetables and meat to make a stewed or braised dish.

Sesbania is a small tree native to northeastern Asia, and is commonly found in many

gardens throughout Asia. It has attractive, almost lacy foliage and large, creamy white or yellow flowers, and is grown as much for its decorative qualities as for culinary purposes. The name, sesbania, is derived from its botanical name, *Sesbania grandiflora* or *Sesbania javanica*, and the plant is sometimes known as the West Indian pea tree. Producing edible leaves, pods and flowers, it is indeed a versatile plant. In Cambodia, the important Water Festival usually takes place when the sesbania flowers are blooming. According to one historian, "as people take to the water in their boats, ahead of them goes a boat in which there is a bowl of batter and a pan of hot oil. The flowers, dipped in the batter and cooked, are left on the trees so that they may be collected by those following behind."

Appearance & Flavor The curved, white or yellow flowers look like crescent moons, and are particularly prized. They taste somewhat like sweetish mushrooms. The pods are about 12 in (30 cm) in length, and very narrow, and should be eaten only when very young. The small, feathery leaves grow on either side of longish stems. **Choosing & Storing** Clusters of young leaves are sometimes sold in Asian markets. The pods are rarely available commercially. They must be very young to be edible and are normally gathered from kitchen gardens. The flowers, however, may sometimes be found in markets. **Preparing** If using the leaves, strip them from the stalks. The stamens should be pulled out of the flowers and discarded. Pods are used whole. **Nutritional & Medicinal Properties** Sesbania flowers are a good source of phosphorus, sugar and iron. **Culinary Uses** The leaves of the plant are usually added to soups and simmered briefly. The pods and leaves can be boiled or simmered in vegetable stews or curries. The flowers are eaten raw or blanched, often with a dip, and can also be dipped in Japanese tempura or Indian *pakhora* batter and deep-fried.

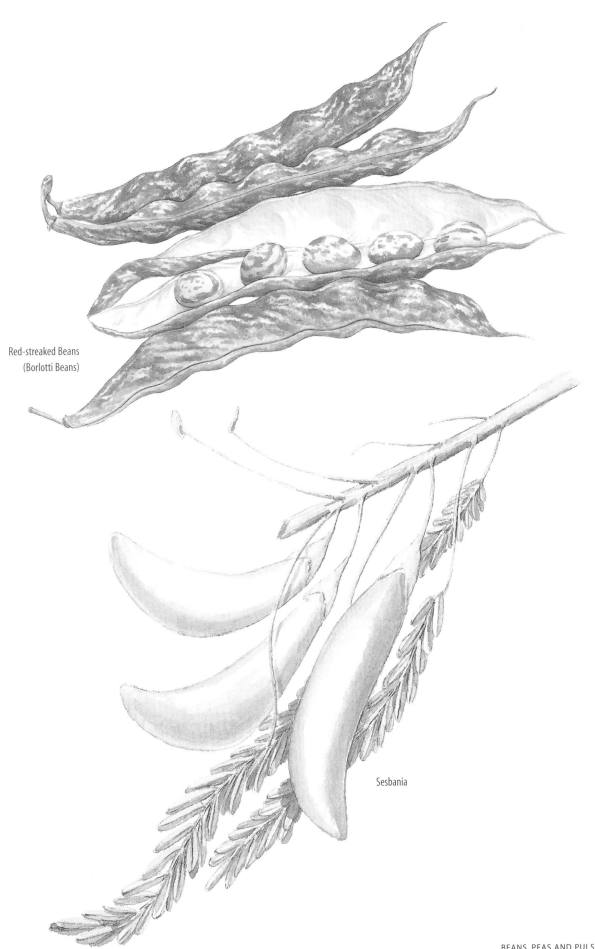

Red-streaked Beans
(Borlotti Beans)

Sesbania

Snow Peas

Snow Peas are a member of the same family as the sugar pea and are sometimes known by their French name, *mange tout*, which means "eat all." As the name implies, both the pod and immature seeds are eaten. Snow peas are grown in the cooler climate of northern Asia as well as in highland areas in the tropics. They are easier to prepare than regular green peas (they need stringing but not shelling), and have what many deem to be a better flavor.

Appearance & Flavor Snow peas look like flattened common green pea pods, with the immature seed so small that its shape is barely visible. The pods vary in size, with those found in Asia often half the size of those grown in Western countries. They have a firm texture and delicious flavor, although they are slightly less sweet than sugar peas. **Choosing & Storing** Look for firm, tender pods. If there are any with portions of the flower at the tips, choose these as they will be very young. Keep refrigerated in a perforated plastic bag for up to 1 week. **Preparing** Remove the strings by pulling from the tip of each pea and discard the stem end also. **Nutritional & Medicinal Properties** Similar to sugar peas. **Culinary Uses** Snow peas can be used as an alternative to sugar peas.

Soy Beans

Soy Beans have been appreciated by the Chinese and Japanese for centuries and are becoming increasingly known in the West where they are no longer used merely as animal feed but are promoted for human consumption as an important source of phyto-estrogens (which help balance hormonal changes) and protein. Although most soy products are made from the dried mature seed, fresh emerald-green soy bean pods are enjoyed in China, Japan (where they are known as *edamame*) and Korea between mid-June and October. They are often eaten boiled and lightly salted as a cocktail snack, together with saké or beer. Frozen pods are often available in Japanese and Korean stores as well as in supermarkets.

Appearance & Flavor Small, fresh green fuzzy pods, usually containing three seeds, are sometimes available in bundles. Their flavor is excellent and totally unlike the cooked dried soy beans or any other soy bean products. Frozen green soy bean pods can often be found in Asian stores, and although not quite as good as the fresh bean, are well worth buying. Soy beans have a taste somewhat similar to fresh young lima beans. **Choosing & Storing** Fresh pods can keep refrigerated in a plastic bag for 2–3 days. Frozen pods can be stored for up to 3 months. **Preparing** If using fresh pods, rinse well before cooking. Frozen pods should not be thawed first if the recipe calls for them to be cooked whole. **Nutritional & Medicinal Properties** Fresh soy beans contain over 12% protein and are easily digested. They are also a good source of vitamins B and C. **Culinary Uses** Fresh green soy beans are commonly boiled whole as a snack, or stir-fried and simmered. If using whole pods (either fresh or frozen), they should be added to boiling water and simmered for about 15 minutes, or until they are tender. Sprinkle with salt and serve warm or at room temperature. The seeds are sucked out and the pods discarded. The beans can also be deep-fried in tempura batter.

Soy Bean Sprouts

Soy Bean Sprouts are less common outside Asia compared to mung bean sprouts. They are very nutritious and flavorsome, and are particularly popular in Korea and among the Chinese. Unlike mung bean sprouts, they must be cooked before being eaten, but they retain an appealingly firm texture even after cooking.

Appearance & Flavor Soy beans sprouts are easily distinguished from mung bean sprouts by the large, pale yellow soy bean seed clearly visible at the top, and the thick shoots with long straggly roots. They have an excellent, almost nutty flavor, and the advantage of remaining firm after cooking. **Choosing & Storing** Soy bean sprouts are normally sold in a bundle. The sprouts should look crisp and white, with the seed heads still attached. Avoid those with any sign of green leaves sprouting at the seed end. Keep refrigerated in a bowl covered with water for 3–4 days, changing the water daily. The pale skins will normally sink. **Preparing** Keeping the sprouts tied together, cut off the straggly tails with one stroke of the knife just before cooking. Then untie, rinse and drain. Be sure not to remove the yellowish soy bean at the top of the sprout as it is the tastiest and most nutritious part. **Nutritional & Medicinal Properties** Soy bean sprouts contain high levels of protein, oil and vitamin C, and are a good meat substitute. Soy beans also have less calories per gram than any other vegetable food. **Culinary Uses** Soy bean sprouts must be cooked to remove traces of a mild toxin. They are often braised and served either hot or at room temperature, and can also be added to soups, noodle dishes, mixed salads, pickles and stir-fried vegetables, meat or poultry.

Sugar Peas

Sugar Peas are one of Asia's favorite green peas, with all of the flavor and sweetness of the common Western green pea packed inside a tender, edible skin. Although sugar peas—also known as sugar peas—look like mature snow peas with large seeds, they are actually a different cultivar.

Appearance & Flavor Sugar peas have a mild, slightly sweet taste, and look like young, common green peas. The skin remains tender after cooking. **Choosing & Storing** Look for firm, bright green pods. Keep refrigerated in a perforated plastic bag for up to a week. **Preparing** The entire pod is edible. Most sugar peas need stringing although stringless varieties may be available in some countries—test by grasping the stem end down toward the tip. The strings can be pulled off easily. **Nutritional & Medicinal Properties** Sugar peas are high in beta-carotene and phosphorus, as well as vitamin C. **Culinary Uses** Whole sugar peas are most commonly stir-fried until just cooked, thus retaining their bright green color and firm texture. They are cooked alone, often with a little oyster sauce added just before they are removed from the wok, or are stir-fried with other vegetables, meat, poultry or prawns. Their attractive color makes them a decorative element in many Chinese and Japanese dishes. Sugar peas can also be blanched in boiling water, refreshed in iced water, then used as a garnish or added to salads.

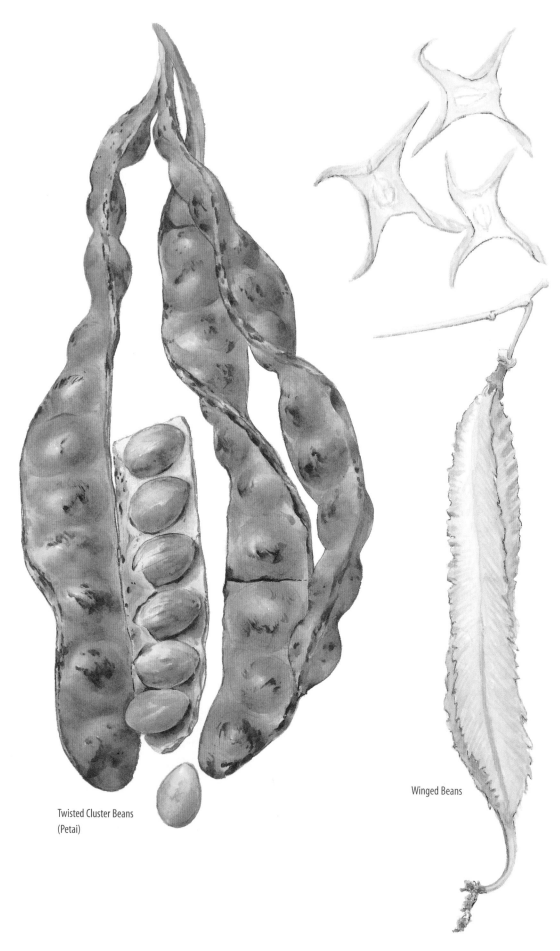

Twisted Cluster Beans
(Petai)

Winged Beans

Twisted Cluster Beans or Petai

Twisted Cluster Beans or Petai are also known as parkia beans (derived from the botanical name, *Parkia speciosa*). These pungent, slightly bitter beans are called *petai* in Malaysia, *peté* in Indonesia and *sa taw* in Thailand. The twisted pods are found on massive trees growing wild in the tropical forests, and because of their popularity, are also cultivated. Twisted cluster beans are perhaps an acquired taste, but afficionados who are unable to find the fresh beans outside tropical Asia will even resort to using the canned alternative just so they can indulge in their unique flavor.

Appearance & Flavor The pale green pods, containing around ten to 18 large green seeds, grow in twisted clusters, hence their English name. They are also somewhat impolitely referred to as stink beans, as they share with asparagus the quality of giving a very strong smell to the urine shortly after they have been consumed. Despite this, many people find the curious, pungent flavor of twisted cluster beans particularly appealing. **Choosing & Storing** Some markets sell twisted cluster beans already removed from their seed pods. However, as the beans ferment fairly quickly, check that they still smell fresh before buying shelled cluster beans. If buying whole pods, make sure they are brightly colored and firm. The beans—frequently labeled *peteh*—can been found in cans in Asian specialty stores. **Preparing** Pull off the tough strings at either side of the pod and press out the beans, then peel off the skin covering each bean. **Nutritional & Medicinal Properties** These beans are a diuretic and have a relaxing effect. **Culinary Uses** Twisted cluster beans are usually stir-fried with emphatic seasonings, including chilies, to make savory side dishes or sambal. As the flavor is quite strong, twisted cluster beans are normally eaten in small quantities.

Winged Beans

Winged Beans are also known as angled or Goa beans, and they have traditionally been cultivated in warm climates everywhere from India right across to New Guinea. Not surprisingly perhaps, the winged bean has been hailed as "the Asian miracle plant": it grows quickly, is disease-resistant and rich in protein and oils. It is now being cultivated in many parts of rural Africa. Although it is the young pod that is most commonly eaten, the shoots, leaves and flowers are also edible, and the pretty pale blue flowers are used as a natural food coloring for some rice and cake recipes.

Appearance & Flavor Winged beans are what might almost be called a "designer vegetable" because of their attractive appearance. The pods are pale green and have a frill running down all four sides. The flavor carries a slight touch of bitterness and the beans have a pleasant, crisp texture when young. **Choosing & Storing** Look for small, young beans which snap rather than bend. Young beans—those not longer than 4 in (10 cm) in length and about $1/_2$ in ($1^1/_4$ cm) in width—are sweeter and have a better texture than the more mature beans, recognizable by their greater size and the shape of the seeds clearly formed within. Winged beans can keep refrigerated in a container for 3 to 4 days. **Preparing** Before cooking, pinch the tip and pull down any strings which may have formed. **Nutritional & Medicinal Properties** Young winged beans contain complex carbohydrates and as much as 20% protein. They are rich in beta-carotene, low in sodium and contain calcium and phosphorus. **Culinary Uses** Winged beans are either eaten raw, usually with a dip, or blanched briefly in boiling water, then sliced to make salads. Combining them with naturally sweet coconut cream (as is often done in Southeast Asia) helps offset the slight bitterness. Winged beans can also be stir-fried, but should not be overcooked or they will lose their crisp texture.

Bean Sprout and Green Bean Salad

10 oz (300 g) green beans, cut
 into 1¹/₂-in (4-cm) lengths
7 oz (200 g) mung beans sprouts,
 straggly tails discarded
1 red chili, minced, or 1 teaspoon
 dried chili flakes
1 small clove garlic
¹/₂ teaspoon dried shrimp paste,
 toasted
1 cup (100 g) freshly grated or
 frozen coconut
¹/₂ teaspoon salt

1 Blanch the beans in boiling water until just cooked but still firm. Cool under running water, then drain.
2 Put bean sprouts in a sieve and pour over boiling water for 10 seconds. Plunge into ice water to cool, then drain thoroughly. Put beans and bean sprouts in a bowl.

3 Using a food processor, or a pestle and mortar, grind the chili, garlic and shrimp paste. Toss with the grated coconut and salt, mixing well. Just before serving, add the coconut mixture to the vegetables, toss well and serve at room temperature.

Korean Blanched Soy Bean Sprouts with Sesame

7–8 oz (200–250 g) soy bean sprouts
¹/₂ cup (125 ml) water
1¹/₂ tablespoons oil
1 teaspoon sesame oil
¹/₂ teaspoon salt
1 clove garlic, crushed
1 tablespoon soy sauce
1 teaspoon toasted sesame seeds,
 coarsely crushed while warm
1 tablespoon finely chopped
 spring onions

1 Keeping the sprouts still in a bundle (if they have been bought this way), cut off the straggly roots. Untie the sprouts and spread in a saucepan. Add the water, and the two types of oil, salt, garlic and soy sauce. Bring to a boil, cover, lower heat and simmer for 7 minutes.

2 Remove the pan from the heat, turn the sprouts carefully, cover the pan and let it stand for 5 minutes before transferring to a serving dish. Serve hot, or chilled, garnishing with the sesame seeds and spring onion just before serving.

Sweet Mung Beans with Coconut

1¹/₂ cups (300 g) dried mung
 beans, washed and drained
2¹/₂ cups (625 ml) water
Thin slice ginger
Pinch of salt
2 cups (500 ml) thin coconut milk
¹/₄ cup (40 g) shaved palm sugar or
 soft brown sugar
White sugar, to taste
¹/₂ cup (125 ml) coconut cream

1 Put the mung beans in a large pan with the water, ginger and salt. Bring to a boil, lower the heat, cover and simmer for 45 minutes until the liquid has been absorbed and the beans are swollen. Add the coconut milk and palm sugar, stirring over low heat until the sugar has dissolved.

2 Without covering the pan, cook the beans over low heat for about an hour, until they are very soft. Add a little water if the mixture seems too dry. Add white sugar to taste. Ladle into small bowls, and spoon some coconut cream over the porridge before serving.

Stir-fried Sugar Peas and Pumpkin

2 tablespoons oil
2–3 cloves garlic, minced
2 tablespoons fish sauce
1 teaspoon sugar
3 cups (500 g) butternut squash
 or other bright yellow pumpkin,
 peeled and cut into matchsticks
7 oz (200 g) sugar or snow peas,
 tips and strings removed

(if using large snow peas, cut
 them diagonally into halves)
2 spring onions, cut in 1¹/₂-in
 (4-cm) lengths
¹/₂ teaspoon freshly ground black
 pepper

1 Heat the oil in a wok. Stir-fry the garlic for a few seconds. Add the fish sauce and sugar, stir, then add the pumpkin and stir-fry over medium–high heat for 2 minutes.
2 Stir-fry the peas for 2 minutes, then stir-fry the spring onions for another 30 seconds. Sprinkle with pepper and transfer to a serving dish.

Spiced Indian Kidney Beans

1 lb (500 g) fresh kidney beans, shelled, 1 can (14 oz/400 g) red kidney beans or 8 oz (250 g) dried kidney beans
1/4 cup (60 ml) oil
2 cardamom pods, split and bruised, or 1/4 teaspoon cardamom powder
1 onion, minced
2 teaspoons crushed garlic
1 teaspoon grated ginger
1 teaspoon minced red chili, or 1/2 teaspoon ground red pepper
1 teaspoon ground coriander
1/2 teaspoon ground cumin
1/4 teaspoon ground turmeric
3 ripe tomatoes (about 8 oz/250 g), blanched, peeled and diced
1 large green chili, halved lengthwise, optional
2 tablespoons minced coriander leaves (cilantro)
1/4 teaspoon salt
1/2 cup (125 ml) water
1/4 teaspoon *garam masala*

1 Simmer fresh kidney beans in water to cover until tender, then drain. If using canned kidney beans, drain in a colander and then hold under running water to rinse the beans. Set aside to drain.
2 Heat the oil in a medium-sized saucepan until moderately hot. Add the cardamom and onion and stir-fry until soft and golden, about 5 minutes. Add garlic, ginger and chili and stir-fry for 3 minutes. Reduce heat, then add the ground coriander, cumin and turmeric and stir-fry for 2 minutes.
3 Add tomatoes and stir-fry for 2 minutes. Put in the green chili, 1 tablespoon of the coriander leaves, salt and water. Bring to a boil, then reduce heat and simmer uncovered for 10 minutes. Add drained kidney beans and a pinch of the *garam masala*. Simmer 8 minutes, then transfer to a serving dish. Sprinkle with the remaining coriander leaves and *garam masala*. Serve hot.

Indian Vegetable Fritters (*Pakhora*)

Oil for deep-frying
1 medium potato or sweet potato, sliced
1 slender Asian eggplant, thinly sliced
1 onion, thinly sliced, separated into rings
4 very small okra, left whole
1/2 cup (100 g) cauliflower or broccoli florets
8 spinach leaves, washed, dried and torn in half if large

Batter
1 1/2 cups (250 g) chickpea flour (*besan*)
1/2 cup (60 g) plain flour
1 teaspoon baking powder
1/2–1 teaspoon ground red pepper
1 teaspoon salt
1 egg, lightly beaten
1 tablespoon lemon juice
1 large green chili, finely chopped
Warm water to mix

1 To make the Batter, mix all the dry ingredients, then add egg, lemon juice, chili and enough warm water to make a thick paste.
2 Heat the oil in a wok and when moderately hot, dip the vegetables, one by one, into the Batter to coat. Transfer with tongs to the hot oil and deep-fry, a few pieces at a time for 3–4 minutes until the vegetable pieces are cooked and the Batter turns golden brown. Drain on a paper towel and serve hot or warm.

Indonesian Vegetable Tamarind Soup

1/4 cup (40 g) raw peanuts, boiled for 10 minutes
1/2 teaspoon dried shrimp paste, toasted until dry and crumbly
6 shallots, thinly sliced
1 clove garlic, thinly sliced
1 large red chili, deseeded and sliced
4 thin slices galangal root
2 fresh or dried *salam* leaves
3 cups (750 ml) chicken or beef stock
1 cup (250 ml) water
3 cups (200 g) sliced cabbage
1 chayote, peeled, diced
4 oz (100 g) green beans, coarsely chopped
1 teaspoon salt
1 heaped tablespoon tamarind pulp soaked in 1/4 cup (60 ml) water for 5 minutes, squeezed and strained to obtain juice
1 teaspoon palm sugar or soft brown sugar

1 Put the peanuts, shrimp paste, shallots, garlic, chili, galangal, *salam* leaves, stock and water in a saucepan. Bring to a boil, cover, reduce heat, and simmer for 5 minutes. Add the vegetables and salt. Bring back to a boil, cover, and simmer for 10–15 minutes, until the vegetables are cooked.
2 Add the tamarind juice and sugar, stirring to dissolve. Taste and add more sugar if desired. Transfer to four soup bowls and serve with steamed rice.

Indian Chickpeas in Spicy Tomato Sauce

1 cup (200 g) chickpeas
4 cups (1 liter) water
1 Indian or Ceylon teabag (optional)
$1/4$ cup ghee or butter
1 onion, minced
1 tablespoon minced garlic
1 tablespoon minced ginger
2 teaspoons ground coriander
1 teaspoon ground cumin
$1/4$–$1/2$ teaspoon ground red
  pepper
$1/4$ teaspoon ground turmeric
2 medium tomatoes, diced
$3/4$ teaspoon salt
1 tablespoon minced coriander
  leaves (cilantro), to garnish

1 Put the chickpeas in a saucepan and cover with three times their volume of water. Bring to a boil, then turn off the heat, cover the pan, and leave overnight. Drain the chickpeas and discard the water. Transfer the drained pulses back to the pan with 4 cups of water and the teabag. Bring to a boil, lower the heat, and simmer until the chickpeas are soft—this will take about 1 hour depending on the size and age of the pulses. Drain the chickpeas, reserving the liquid.
2 Melt the ghee in a medium-sized saucepan and add the onion. Stir-fry over low heat for about 2 minutes, or until the onion has softened. Add the garlic and ginger. Stir-fry for 1 minute. Add the ground coriander, cumin, pepper and turmeric. Stir-fry for another minute. Add tomatoes and salt to the saucepan. Cook the sauce for 4–5 minutes over moderate heat, stirring from time to time, until the tomatoes soften.
3 Pour in $2/3$ cup of the reserved cooking liquid to the saucepan and the drained chickpeas. Cook for 10 minutes, stirring from time to time, until the liquid has been absorbed. Transfer the chickpeas to a serving dish and garnish with the chopped coriander leaves.

Sweet Chinese Azuki Bean Pancakes

1 cup (125 g) flour
1 egg, lightly beaten
1 cup (250 ml) water
Pinch of salt
$1/4$ cup (60 ml) oil

Filling
$1/2$ cup (100 g) azuki beans
$1/4$ cup (65 g) sugar
2 teaspoons oil
$1/4$ cup (30 g) chopped walnuts
  (optional)

1 To make the Filling, put the beans in a medium-sized saucepan with water to cover. Bring to a boil, cover, turn off the heat and stand for 1 hour.

2 Drain the beans and return to the pan with fresh water to cover. Cover with the lid and simmer until soft, or for about 30–60 minutes.
3 Drain the beans, then put them in a food processor with sugar and oil. Process to a smooth paste. Transfer to a bowl and mix in the walnuts. Set aside to cool.
4 Make pancakes by putting flour in a medium-sized bowl. Make a well in the center. Add the egg, salt and $1/4$ cup of the water, stirring to blend.
5 Slowly add the remaining water to make a smooth batter. Heat a small, non-stick pan with 1 teaspoon oil. Spread batter out, using the back of a ladle in a circular motion to cover the pan. Cook over high heat for 1–2 minutes, or until golden brown. Flip and cook for another minute. Repeat until the batter is used up.
6 Put 1 tablespoon of the Filling in the center of each pancake. Fold the end closest to you, then press lightly to flatten the Filling. Tuck in sides, then roll over to enclose the Filling. Fry the pancakes 1 minute on each side in 1 tablespoon oil. Serve hot.

Pea Shoots with Black Mushrooms

8 dried black mushrooms, soaked
  in hot water to soften, halved
2 cups (500 ml) water
1 tablespoon soy sauce
1 teaspoon sugar
1 teaspoon cornstarch, mixed with
  1 tablespoon water
1 teaspoon sesame oil
2 tablespoons oil
10 oz (300 g) pea shoots
$1/4$ cup (60 ml) chicken stock
1 tablespoon rice wine or saké

1 Put soaked mushrooms, water, soy sauce and sugar in a saucepan. Bring to a boil, cover and simmer gently until the mushrooms become soft and tender.
2 Combine the cornstarch with water and add to the mushrooms, stirring constantly over low heat until the mixture thickens and clears. Sprinkle with sesame oil and keep warm.

3 Heat the oil in a wok and add the pea shoots. Stir-fry for a few seconds, then add the chicken stock and rice wine and simmer until tender.
4 Serve the pea shoots on a plate, with the mushrooms on one side.

Stir-fried Snow Peas with Mushrooms and Scallops

3 teaspoons cornstarch
$1/_2$ cup (125 ml) chicken stock
$1/_4$ cup (60 ml) oil
14 oz (400 g) fresh scallops, washed, drained and dried
1 tablespoon rice wine or saké
$1/_2$ teaspoon salt
1 tablespoon shredded fresh ginger
2 spring onions, cut in lengths
8 oz (250 g) snow peas, trimmed
3 oz (100 g) fresh button mushrooms
1 teaspoon sugar
1 tablespoon soy sauce
White pepper, to taste

1 Mix cornstarch and chicken stock in a small bowl and set aside. Put $1^1/_2$ tablespoons of oil in a wok. When very hot, add the scallops and stir-fry over high heat for 1 minute. Add the wine and salt, stir, then quickly remove the scallops from the wok with a spatula. Keep aside in a bowl.
2 Add the remaining oil to the wok and heat. When very hot, add the ginger and spring onions and stir-fry for 10 seconds. Add the snow peas and mushrooms, and stir-fry over high heat for 2 minutes. Sprinkle in the sugar, soy sauce and pepper.
3 Return the scallops to the wok, adding any juices collected in the

bowl. Stir to mix well. Give the stock mixture a stir to amalgamate the cornstarch, then add to the wok. Stir for 30 seconds or until the sauce thickens and clears, then transfer to a serving dish. Serve immediately.

Note: You can use fresh prawns instead of scallops for this recipe. Peel the prawns and discard the heads. Slice the underside of each prawn lengthwise until $3/_4$-way though and spread out with the palm of the hand or the flat of a knife to butterfly the prawn, then stir-fry the prawns for 2 minutes.

Southern Indian Dosai

1 cup (100 g) long-grain rice, soaked in water for 6 hours, then drained
$1^1/_2$ cups (375 ml) water
$1/_4$ cup (40 g) white lentils (husked black gram), soaked in water for 6 hours, then drained
$1/_2$ teaspoon salt
$1/_4$ cup (60 ml) oil
Fresh coconut chutney (optional)

1 Put the rice in a food processor or blender and process at high speed until it resembles coarse sand. Keep the processor running and slowly pour in $1/_3$ cup of the water. Process to a smooth paste, then transfer to a large bowl.
2 Put the lentils in the blender or food processor and process at high speed until fine. Keep the processor running and slowly pour in $1/_3$ cup of the water. Blend until light and frothy. Add the lentils and salt to the rice paste, stirring to mix well. Cover with plastic wrap and leave in a warm place for 4–6 hours or overnight,

until small bubbles appear. Pour in the remaining water and stir, making a light batter.
3 Pour 1 teaspoon of the oil in a non-stick frying pan or pan with a heavy base. Heat, then swirl oil to coat. When the oil is hot, pour $1/_4$ cup batter into the center of the pan. Immediately spread the batter out, using the back of a ladle, in a circular motion to cover the pan thinly. Cook over high heat until golden brown, for 1–2 minutes. Turn, cook the other side, for 1 minute. Repeat until batter is used up. Serve with the fresh coconut chutney.

Long Beans with Fermented Bean Curd

2 tablespoons oil
2 cloves garlic, minced
1 teaspoon minced ginger
2 tablespoons plain or chili-flavored fermented bean curd, mashed
1 lb (500 g) long beans, sliced into $1^1/_2$-in (4-cm) lengths
1 tablespoon rice wine or saké
$1/_2$ teaspoon sugar
$1/_4$ teaspoon salt
$1/_2$ cup (125 ml) water

1 Heat the oil in a wok. Add the garlic and ginger and stir-fry for a few seconds. Add the bean curd and stir-fry until fragrant, or for 15 seconds, then put in the long beans. Stir-fry for about 30 seconds.
2 Add the rice wine, sugar and salt and continue stir-frying until the beans are tender, adding a little water from time to time to stop the beans from sticking.

Note: Jars of fermented bean curd, either plain (white) or with chili (red), are sold in supermarkets and used as a salty, pungent seasoning. The bean curd is sometimes labeled "preserved bean curd."

CABBAGES & leafy greens

All cabbages are members of the Brassica family. They are easily hybridized and as agriculturists produce new cultivars, nature also lends a hand with spontaneous hybrids appearing. This makes identifying cabbages a challenge, and scientists have to resort to chromosonal analysis to figure out just what has been going on in the cabbage patch. Their research suggests that the common round, pale green cabbage familiar in the West—and

also grown in Asia—could perhaps be described as the "mother of all cabbages," for it is from this plant (known around the Mediterranean over 4,000 years ago) that the other cultivars developed.

Cabbages vary in nutritional value depending on the species, although most are rich in carotene and are a valuable source of calcium, vitamins A and C as well as minerals. They contain, like other cruciferous vegetables, anti-cancer properties and help in boosting the immune system.

Amaranth or Chinese Spinach,

also referred to as *xian cai* (Mandarin) or *bayam* (Malay), is a leafy green vegetable tasting fairly similar to true or English spinach, and it can be used as a substitute in any recipe requiring English spinach. Its botanical name, *Amaranthus gangeticus*, suggests an Indian origin. Widely available in both tropical and subtropical countries, amaranth grows easily in hot climates. Although grown for its leaves in Asia, amaranth is planted for its seeds in South America, where they are eaten as a grain. Although its flavor is not as sweet as true spinach, amaranth has the advantage of being less delicate and perishable when handled and stored.

Appearance & Flavor Botanists have recorded up to 50 different species of amaranth. The plant has soft leaves growing at the end of long stems. The color of the leaf can vary considerably, with the most common varieties being either pale or dark green. Some varieties are streaked with purplish red, while others have completely red leaves—these varieties are often known as red amaranth. It is sometimes possible to find bunches of short-stemmed amaranth, measuring 5–6 in (12–15 cm) long from root ends to the leaf tips. The leaves may be rounded or narrow and pointed, but all types of amaranth have the same pleasant taste, which is slightly less intense than the flavor of true or English spinach. **Choosing & Storing** Amaranth is generally sold in bunches with the roots still intact. Avoid any which look limp. Rinse briefly, drain thoroughly, then wrap in newspaper with the roots still intact. The amaranth can be refrigerated for 2–3 days. **Preparing** To prepare, pluck off the tender tips and leaves, and discard the hard portion of the central stems and the roots. Rinse the leaves thoroughly several times, then drain. **Nutritional & Medicinal Properties** Amaranth is rich in protein as well as vitamins A, B and C and, perhaps surprisingly, has twice the amount of iron as true spinach. **Culinary Uses** Amaranth leaves are very versatile and can be cooked in just about any style. In Asia, they are stir-fried, simmered, added to soups or blanched briefly and used in salads. Amaranth also makes a good substitute for the common spinach in Western and Middle Eastern recipes. Although the vegetable is not suitable for raw salads, amaranth is tasty cooked together with lentils or—in Middle Eastern style— with *burgul* (cracked steamed wheat).

Asian Lettuce

Asian Lettuce is also known as long-leaf lettuce, and is the most common type of lettuce found in Asia. Unlike the common iceberg lettuce of temperate climates, the Asian variety does not have a tight, round heart. Apart from its culinary use, this type of lettuce is traditionally eaten by the Chinese over the Lunar New Year festival, and also fed to the "lions" and "dragons" which dance in the streets during this period. This unique custom is known as *cai qing*, or "pluck the green," with the "green," or the lettuce, symbolizing fortune. The lions and dragons pluck the greens, then spit them out, and those lucky enough to be hit by the lettuce are considered to be covered by fortune for the coming year.

Appearance & Flavor Asian lettuce grows with the stems wrapped around a central core. The leaves, which have frilled edges, are relatively soft and pliable. The flavor is palatable and mild, but this type of lettuce lacks the crispness of temperate climate lettuces. **Choosing & Storing** Long-leaf lettuce is sold with its roots still intact. As the vegetables mature, they develop tough, bitter leaves and start to sprout flowers, so choose lettuce with no flowers. Bunches that have short stems and large leaves are usually the sweetest and the most tender. Avoid any with a wilted look. The lettuce can be kept refrigerated for 2–3 days, wrapped in damp paper. **Preparing** Remove the leaves from the stem, give them a thorough wash and drain before using raw or cooked. Peel the stem, wash it, then shred or chop before cooking. **Nutritional & Medicinal Properties** Asian lettuce is more nutritious than regular round or iceberg lettuce—it is very rich in beta-carotene and has appreciable amounts of vitamin C, calcium and phosphorus. **Culinary Uses** The softness of the long-leaf lettuce makes its leaves particularly useful as a wrapper for minced or barbecued meat and poultry, and for deep-fried spring rolls (it is commonly used this way in Vietnam). The lettuce is also added to salads, or shredded and added to soups or Chinese rice porridge. The stem of the lettuce can be eaten stir-fried on its own or with a variety of other vegetables. It can also be blanched and served with a dressing of soy sauce and sliced chilies.

Bok Choy

Bok Choy is referred to by botanists as white cabbage or Chinese chard, the former name referring to the bright white stems of most hybrids of this popular cabbage. These names are not commonly used, however, and the vegetable is increasingly known as *bok choy*, a variation of its Cantonese name, *pak choy*.

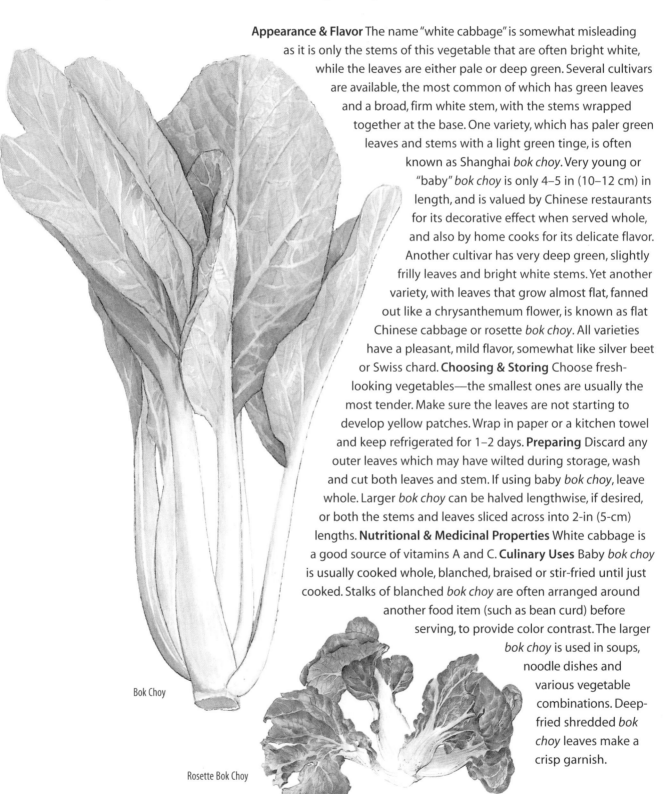

Bok Choy

Rosette Bok Choy

Appearance & Flavor The name "white cabbage" is somewhat misleading as it is only the stems of this vegetable that are often bright white, while the leaves are either pale or deep green. Several cultivars are available, the most common of which has green leaves and a broad, firm white stem, with the stems wrapped together at the base. One variety, which has paler green leaves and stems with a light green tinge, is often known as Shanghai *bok choy*. Very young or "baby" *bok choy* is only 4–5 in (10–12 cm) in length, and is valued by Chinese restaurants for its decorative effect when served whole, and also by home cooks for its delicate flavor. Another cultivar has very deep green, slightly frilly leaves and bright white stems. Yet another variety, with leaves that grow almost flat, fanned out like a chrysanthemum flower, is known as flat Chinese cabbage or rosette *bok choy*. All varieties have a pleasant, mild flavor, somewhat like silver beet or Swiss chard. **Choosing & Storing** Choose fresh-looking vegetables—the smallest ones are usually the most tender. Make sure the leaves are not starting to develop yellow patches. Wrap in paper or a kitchen towel and keep refrigerated for 1–2 days. **Preparing** Discard any outer leaves which may have wilted during storage, wash and cut both leaves and stem. If using baby *bok choy*, leave whole. Larger *bok choy* can be halved lengthwise, if desired, or both the stems and leaves sliced across into 2-in (5-cm) lengths. **Nutritional & Medicinal Properties** White cabbage is a good source of vitamins A and C. **Culinary Uses** Baby *bok choy* is usually cooked whole, blanched, braised or stir-fried until just cooked. Stalks of blanched *bok choy* are often arranged around another food item (such as bean curd) before serving, to provide color contrast. The larger *bok choy* is used in soups, noodle dishes and various vegetable combinations. Deep-fried shredded *bok choy* leaves make a crisp garnish.

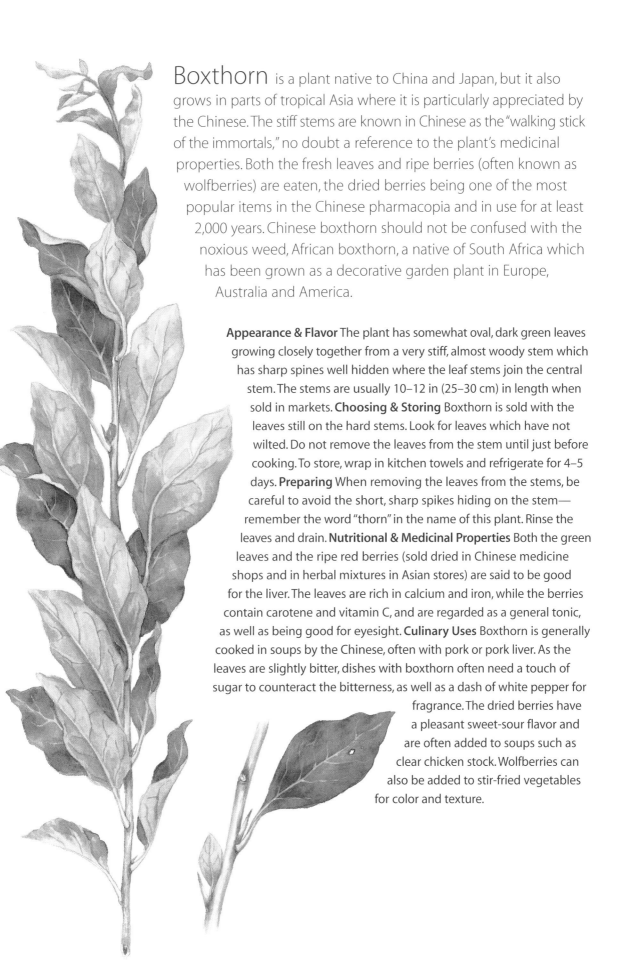

Boxthorn is a plant native to China and Japan, but it also grows in parts of tropical Asia where it is particularly appreciated by the Chinese. The stiff stems are known in Chinese as the "walking stick of the immortals," no doubt a reference to the plant's medicinal properties. Both the fresh leaves and ripe berries (often known as wolfberries) are eaten, the dried berries being one of the most popular items in the Chinese pharmacopia and in use for at least 2,000 years. Chinese boxthorn should not be confused with the noxious weed, African boxthorn, a native of South Africa which has been grown as a decorative garden plant in Europe, Australia and America.

Appearance & Flavor The plant has somewhat oval, dark green leaves growing closely together from a very stiff, almost woody stem which has sharp spines well hidden where the leaf stems join the central stem. The stems are usually 10–12 in (25–30 cm) in length when sold in markets. **Choosing & Storing** Boxthorn is sold with the leaves still on the hard stems. Look for leaves which have not wilted. Do not remove the leaves from the stem until just before cooking. To store, wrap in kitchen towels and refrigerate for 4–5 days. **Preparing** When removing the leaves from the stems, be careful to avoid the short, sharp spikes hiding on the stem—remember the word "thorn" in the name of this plant. Rinse the leaves and drain. **Nutritional & Medicinal Properties** Both the green leaves and the ripe red berries (sold dried in Chinese medicine shops and in herbal mixtures in Asian stores) are said to be good for the liver. The leaves are rich in calcium and iron, while the berries contain carotene and vitamin C, and are regarded as a general tonic, as well as being good for eyesight. **Culinary Uses** Boxthorn is generally cooked in soups by the Chinese, often with pork or pork liver. As the leaves are slightly bitter, dishes with boxthorn often need a touch of sugar to counteract the bitterness, as well as a dash of white pepper for fragrance. The dried berries have a pleasant sweet-sour flavor and are often added to soups such as clear chicken stock. Wolfberries can also be added to stir-fried vegetables for color and texture.

Broccoli is a popular vegetable in many parts of Asia and beyond. As the name implies —*brocco* is an Italian word, meaning "arm branch"—broccoli was first grown in Italy. In the early 20th century, the vegetable was cultivated in the US, then was introduced to Asia. As it can withstand more extreme climates than the closely related cauliflower, the plant has adapted to hotter, drier temperatures and can also tolerate mild winters.

Appearance & Flavor Broccoli is recognized by its green, tightly packed flower heads and thick, green central stem. It has a pronounced flavor which tastes better if the vegetable is not overcooked. **Choosing & Storing** Choose broccoli where the flowers on the head are still very tightly closed, and where the flower heads have an even, dark green color. The stems should be tender and yield when pierced with a fingernail. Avoid buying any where the flower head is starting to develop a yellowish tinge. Broccoli can keep refrigerated for 1–2 days, if it is a placed in a plastic bag and put in the vegetable drawer. **Preparing** In Asia, both the tender portion of the stem and the flowering head are eaten, whilst in other parts of the world, the latter is preferred. Wash thoroughly and cut off the flowering head where the individual stems join the main stem, separating the head into florets. The main stem is delicious and should not be thrown away. Merely trim off the very tough bottom end and peel the stem; slice thinly lengthwise and cook with the florets. **Nutritional & Medicinal Properties** Broccoli is a very rich source of vitamin C, and contains significant amounts of vitamins A and B as well as iron. The vegetable is high in fiber and low in calories, making it an ideal food. Some dieticians also believe that the plant contains properties that help combat cancer, osteoporosis, heart ailments and diabetes. **Culinary Uses** Broccoli is generally stir-fried in Asia, often with other vegetables, such as tofu, or with strong-flavored meats such as beef—some cooks think that its emphatic flavor overpowers chicken and other more delicate ingredients and foods. In Southeast Asia, a popular way of eating broccoli is to stir-fry it with a dash of oyster sauce. The vegetable can also be briefly blanched and used in salads or as a garnish. Broccoli florets are sometimes dipped in tempura or *pakhora* batter and deep-fried.

Cauliflower

Cauliflower is a temperate climate vegetable once described by American writer Mark Twain as "a cabbage with a college education." These familiar vegetables are grown in most of Asia, although in warmer countries, the plant will survive only in mountainous regions. Cauliflower is distinguished by its creamy white flower heads—which are actually immature white flower buds that were never allowed to develop chlorophyll and turn green, as the flower buds are shielded from the sun by its leaves throughout the various stages of its growth. Cauliflower is particularly popular in India and China, and in Chinese communities throughout Asia.

Appearance & Flavor Cauliflowers grown in Asia are generally much smaller and usually stronger flavored than the giants often found in temperate climates, although some cooks believe that the size of the heads does not affect its quality and taste. **Choosing & Storing** Look for heads that are bright white in color, with no traces of blackish mold. The flower buds should be firm and compact. If there are any leaves attached to the stem, these should be green and crisp. Store in a vegetable container in the refrigerator for several days. **Preparing** Wash the cauliflower, then slice off the florets around the stem core. Pull off any leaves and cut off all bruised or speckled portions. If stir-frying, the florets are generally halved in order to reduce cooking time. **Nutritional & Medicinal Properties** A good source of phosphorus, cauliflower is also rich in vitamin C, calcium and beta-carotene. **Culinary Uses** Although cauliflower is commonly used in Western dishes, it also makes a regular appearance in Asian cooking, where it is often stir-fried with garlic or added to soups and braised dishes. In India, it is simmered in a spicy sauce or dipped in batter and deep-fried. In general, do not cook the vegetable for too long—the plant acids in cauliflower form sulphurous compounds when the vegetable is heated, and the unpleasant smell of these compounds increases in intensity the longer the cooking time.

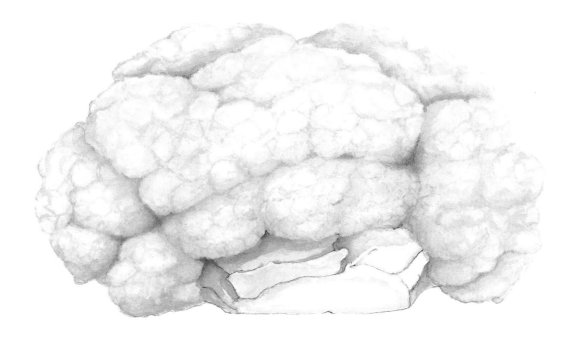

Ceylon Spinach

Ceylon Spinach is believed to have originated in India, where it is also known as *bayam* and Indian or Malabar spinach. It has been cultivated in China for centuries, and is also grown in Africa. When mature, this fast-growing, fleshy plant produces red berries which were once used by Chinese women as rouge for coloring their cheeks, and by mandarins for coloring sealing wax. Both the leaves and tender stems are edible.

Appearance & Flavor The fleshy, deep green leaves grow on either green or bright red stems. The flavor is pleasant, although the texture after cooking is somewhat sticky (the Chinese name for it translates as "mucilaginous" or "slippery vegetable"). The very young tips of Ceylon spinach are sometimes available in Asian markets, and sold as *saan choy*. **Choosing & Storing** Look for fresh, firm leaves with no sign of wilting. Ceylon spinach keeps very well, even without refrigeration, if the stems are placed in water. Wrapped in paper or kitchen towels, it will keep at least 1 week if refrigerated. **Preparing** Pull off the tender top of the stems, then remove the leaves from the harder portion of the stem. Rinse and drain. **Nutritional & Medicinal Properties** This type of spinach is rich in vitamins and minerals and also has mild laxative properties. **Culinary Uses** Ceylon spinach is added to soups and lentil dishes or blanched and used in vegetable salads. Ceylon spinach is also very good prepared Cantonese style—blanched, then tossed with oyster sauce, a touch of sugar and white pepper, and served scattered with crisp fried garlic or shallot slices.

Chinese or Napa Cabbage

Chinese or Napa Cabbage seems to have more alternative names than any other cabbage. Native to northern Asia, it is also known as long white cabbage, Tientsin or Tianjin cabbage, *wong bok* cabbage or *wong nga bok* in Cantonese. Koreans use this cabbage for the most common version of their famous pickle, *kim chee* (see page 149).

Appearance & Flavor This cabbage has crinkled, very pale green leaves at the end of long, wide, white-ribbed stalks. It grows in two main forms—a long, slender cabbage and a shorter, somewhat barrel-shaped variety. There is no difference in the flavor. Chinese cabbage is pleasantly crisp when raw, and has a slightly sweet flavor which intensifies after long, slow cooking. Chinese cabbage has the mildest taste of all Asian cabbages. **Choosing & Storing** Choose fresh-looking cabbages. Chinese cabbage is a hardy vegetable which keeps well refrigerated and at room temperature in a tropical climate, wrapped in damp newspaper and stored in an airy place for several days. In China, many cooks believe the flavor actually improves after the cabbage has been hung for a few days. **Preparing** Do not pull off any wilted outer leaves until just before cooking. Wash and drain, then separate and dry the leaves. Both the stalks and leaves are eaten, either sliced finely across or cut into larger sections, depending on the use. **Culinary Uses** This cabbage exudes a lot of moisture when cooked. It is often blanched or eaten raw in salads, shredded and added to fillings for dumplings, added to soups, or slowly braised to bring out its sweetness. It can also be stir-fried with noodles, although is not usually stir-fried on its own over high heat like most other cabbages as slower, more lengthy cooking improves its flavor.

Ceylon Spinach

Chinese Cabbage (Napa Cabbage)

Chinese Kale (Kailan)

Cucumber Shoots

Chinese Kale or Kailan is sometimes referred to as Chinese broccoli, although it is most commonly known in the West as *kailan*, a variation of its Cantonese name, *gai lan*. *Kailan* is eaten for its delicious stems rather than its leaves, which are too tough to be palatable. The crisp texture, bright dark green color and high nutritional value of this vegetable make it a favorite among the Chinese, and it is almost invariably on restaurant menus, particularly restaurants specializing in dim sum.

Appearance & Flavor *Kailan* is generally marketed when it is about 6–8 in (15–20 cm) in length, and is prized mainly for its crisp central stem as the leaves tend to be tough and bitter. It is recognizable by the thick central stem and dull, thick leaves with a bluish green tinge. The flavor is emphatic but appealing to most palates. Another form, usually referred to as "baby" *kailan*, is only 2–3 in (5–8 cm) long and is grown by crowding seedlings together and encouraging their rapid growth with liberal amounts of fertilizer. Looking rather like loosely folded brussels sprouts, these are tender and sweet, and are consequently very popular in much of Asia. **Choosing & Storing** When buying regular or mature *kailan*, look for plants with the thinnest stems, as these will be the most tender. Baby *kailan* should look fresh, with no wilted outer leaves. *Kailan* keeps for several days refrigerated in a perforated plastic bag. **Preparing** When using mature *kailan*, trim off and discard all but 1 in ($2^1/_2$ cm) of the leaves, and discard the hardest part of the stem. Peel the central stem with a sharp knife, then cut into 2–3-in (5–8-cm) lengths. If the stem is thick, slice thinly lengthwise. The tip of the root end of baby *kailan* should be cut off, and if any of the outer leaves are slightly wilted or yellowing, discard these also. Cook whole. **Nutritional & Medicinal Properties** *Kailan* is high in iron, calcium and vitamin A. **Culinary Uses** Mature *kailan* stems are often blanched in boiling water until just tender, then served with a mixture of oyster sauce, a little sugar and fried garlic or crisp fried shallots. The stems are also good in stir-fried vegetable mixtures, adding a firm texture and bright green color. Baby *kailan* is usually stir-fried briefly, with a little chicken stock or water added during the frying process to keep it from burning, then splashed with oyster sauce and sprinkled with crisp fried garlic.

Cucumber Shoots make an excellent vegetable, like the fruits of the cucumber plant itself. Throughout Asia, the leaves of many plants used as vegetables (root vegetables such as sweet potatoes and beetroots, as well as flowering vegetables such as chilies, snow peas and papayas) are not wasted. This is particularly true in rural areas, where people depend on their own vegetable crop rather than markets.

Appearance & Flavor Cucumber shoots have a pale, dull green color, and consist of approximately 6–7 in (16–18 cm) of stem with young green leaves and a few curling tendrils. They have a pleasant, mild flavor which is usually accentuated with sauces or seasonings during cooking. **Choosing & Storing** Avoid any shoots that look limp. Wrapped in kitchen paper, the shoots can keep refrigerated for 3–4 days. **Preparing** Wash and drain the shoots, and cut off any hard parts of the stem. Cut across into 2-in (5-cm) lengths. **Culinary Uses** The shoots and leaves can be eaten blanched as part of a salad or cooked. In Thailand, the shoots are often blanched and served with a sauce containing fresh crabmeat, which is a particularly pleasing combination. Cucumber shoots are also often stir-fried briefly and seasoned with oyster sauce or soy sauce, or chopped and added to soups.

Fern Tips

Fern Tips are mostly gathered in the wild rather than cultivated in Asia and as such, form an important source of nutrition for those living in isolated regions far from the nearest market. Several types of edible fern are popular in Southeast Asia, Japan and Korea. Those from northern Asia are most likely to be the fiddlehead fern (*Pteridium aquilinum*), while tropical varieties may include *Anthyrium esculentum* and *Diplazium esculentum*. Fern tips are given the generic name *pako, paku* or *pakis* in much of Southeast Asia.

Appearance & Flavor If bunches of ferns are sold in Asian markets, it is safe to assume they are edible. Some have very thin, feathery leaves which are pale reddish brown in color, while others are bright green with thicker leaves. The flavor varies depending on the type of fern, but most are highly palatable, tasting somewhat like a spinach. Fiddlehead ferns, sold while still tightly furled, have a crisp texture and an asparagus-like flavor. **Choosing & Storing** Look for young ferns, preferably with slightly coiled tips. Wrap in damp newspaper and refrigerate for 1–2 days. **Preparing** Wash well, then pluck off the tender tips and remove the leaflets from the tough, central stem. The final sprig usually has a tender stem which can be cooked together with the leaves. In some varieties, such as the fiddlehead, the coiled tips and about 3–4 in (8–10 cm) of the stems are eaten. **Nutritional & Medicinal Properties** Ferns are rich in beta-carotene, iron and phosphorus. **Culinary Uses** Fern tips are often blanched for just a minute, drained, cooled in iced water, then mixed with dressings or seasoned freshly grated coconut to make a salad. One popular Balinese recipe combines ground black pepper, aromatic ginger or *kencur*, garlic and oil. Fern tips are also popular stir-fried, often with garlic, dried prawns or dried shrimp paste and chili, and can be added to soups.

Flowering Cabbage or Choy Sum

Flowering Cabbage or Choy Sum, which is the Cantonese name for this vegetable, is also known as *cai xin* (Mandarin) and *chye sim* (Hokkien)—all of which translate as "stem vegetable." Many Chinese and Japanese regard flowering cabbage as the best of all the cabbages, and appreciate the fact that both the stems and leaves are tender and pleasantly mild in flavor. This cabbage is now increasingly available in Western countries.

Appearance & Flavor This cabbage has soft, bright green leaves with slender stems. If left to mature, small, pretty and edible yellow flowers develop on the stems (hence the name "flowering cabbage"). **Choosing & Storing** Look for fresh, unwilted leaves with tender stems. Check this by pressing the stem with your fingernail, which should go in easily. The presence of yellow flowers does not mean that the vegetable is too old. Wrap in paper or a cloth and keep refrigerated for 1–2 days. **Preparing** Wash thoroughly and drain. Both stems and leaves are used, as well as any flowers. Unless the flowering cabbage is fairly short—and thus more manageable to eat with chopsticks—the stems and leaves are generally cut in 2–3-in (5–8-cm) lengths before cooking. If there are any flowers, these can be washed and used as a garnish. **Culinary Uses** Flowering cabbage is often added to soups or blanched and served with noodles. It is also often stir-fried with a little chopped garlic, with a pinch of sugar, a little oyster sauce, and a sprinkle of sesame oil added just before serving.

Flowering Cabbage (Choy Sum)

Fern Tips

Garland Chrysanthemum is a popular vegetable among the Chinese and

Japanese. Do not mistake garland chrysanthemum for the leaves of the common flowering chrysanthemum, which may be edible but are certainly not appetizing. The type that is grown for its edible leaves is quite different to that cultivated for its familiar, showy flowers. The edible garland chrysanthemum grows in the cooler climates of north Asia, and also in the tropical highlands. There are two varieties of garland chrysanthemum: one found in China and the other in Japan. (Flowering chrysanthemum is grown in China especially for its flowers, which are used in cooling teas and in various traditional medicinal preparations.)

Appearance & Flavor The pale green, elongated leaves, similar to those of the flowering chrysanthemum, have a pungent smell and somewhat astringent flavor, and so are generally eaten in small quantities. The Chinese and Japanese cultivars vary slightly in terms of the width of the leaves, although both have the same characteristic flavor. **Choosing & Storing** The younger the vegetable, the milder the flavor. The leaves are generally sold in bunches, often with the roots still attached, and will keep refrigerated, wrapped in paper, for 1–2 days. **Preparing** Strip the leaves off the central stalk, wash well, then drain. **Nutritional & Medicinal Properties** Garland chrysanthemum is rich in vitamins A and B. The Chinese also believe it is "warming" for the body, so the leaves are often added to soups drunk during the winter months. **Culinary Uses** Garland chrysanthemum leaves are usually added to sukiyaki in Japan, and to the Chinese hotpot or fondue, also known as steamboat. To avoid a bitter aftertaste when simmering the leaves, take care not to overcook. Garland chrysanthemum leaves can also be dipped in tempura or *pakhora* batter and deep-fried, or stir-fried on their own as a vegetable, or with shredded pork or prawns and a touch of seasoning.

Kohlrabi looks as if it should be classified as a root vegetable, owing to its bulbous

appearance, but what you see is really a swollen stem of a member of the cabbage family rather than a true root. Like watercress, broccoli, cauliflower and round or iceberg lettuce, kohlrabi was introduced to Asia relatively recently. The Chinese find that it resembles the popular *kailan* or Chinese kale in texture and flavor.

Appearance & Flavor Kohlrabi looks a bit like a turnip, with a bulb-like base of purplish red or green, or sometimes a mixture of both colors. Slender stems with green leaves project from the top of this swollen base. **Choosing & Storing** The smaller the kohlrabi, the sweeter the taste and better the texture. Avoid any which have blemishes or cracks on the swollen stem or bulb. Store the kohlrabi in the vegetable drawer of a refrigerator for several days. **Preparing** Remove the stems and leaves. Peel the kohlrabi then slice, chop or shred as desired. **Nutritional & Medicinal Properties** Kohlrabi is high in vitamin C and iron, and also has appreciable amounts of calcium, phosphorus and beta-carotene. **Culinary Uses** Although not eaten raw in Asia, kohlrabi is sometimes added to salads or made into fresh pickles. It can be simmered in coconut milk or added to vegetable soups. Chinese cooks like to use kohlrabi in stir-fried vegetable combinations, and consider it particularly good stir-fried with beef and seasoned with a dash of oyster sauce, white pepper and perhaps a little Chinese rice wine.

Garland Chrysanthemum

Kohlrabi

Mizuna

Bamboo Mustard Cabbage

Mizuna

Mizuna is sometimes referred to as pot-herb mustard, although it is is more widely known by its Japanese name. This delicate member of the cabbage family is identifiable by its attractive feathery leaf, and is popularly used in Japan as an edible garnish.

Appearance & Flavor Mizuna has feathery leaves on long, slender stems, and a mild, somewhat mustardy flavor. **Choosing & Storing** Buy fresh, bright leaves, which are usually available trimmed. Make sure the leaves are thoroughly dry before refrigerating them. Store in a perforated plastic bag, or wrap in paper towels and store in a plastic bag. **Preparing** Wash and dry the mizuna before using either as a garnish or salad green. **Nutritional & Medicinal Properties** Like most members of the cabbage or Brassica family, mizuna contains carotene, calcium, vitamins A and C as well as minerals. **Culinary Uses** Because of its decorative appearance, mizuna is usually served as an edible garnish for Japanese food. It can also be added to Western-style mixed green salads.

Mustard Cabbage

Mustard Cabbage is most commonly eaten in the cooler countries of northern Asia, though it is also found in Chinese communities elsewhere in Asia. There are around ten cultivars of this particular cabbage (*Brassica juncea var. rugosa*), but only two are widely available. These are Swatow mustard cabbage (*dai gai choy* in Cantonese, also known as heart or wrapped mustard cabbage) and bamboo mustard cabbage (*jook gai choy*).

Appearance & Flavor Swatow mustard cabbage has a firmly packed, rounded head with very broad stems. It is quite bitter, so most of the crop is preserved (see page 152). Bamboo mustard cabbage has less tightly packed, longer, thinner, medium-sized green leaves and much narrower stems. It is also somewhat milder in flavor and is often eaten fresh, as well as in the form of moist pickles, or salted and dried. **Choosing & Storing** Choose only fresh, firm cabbages. Mustard cabbage keeps refrigerated for 4–5 days. **Preparing** If using Swatow mustard cabbage, separate the stems and wash the base of each well. Cut the leaves away or pluck them off and discard them. Use the thick stems as directed in the recipe. Separate the leaves of bamboo mustard cabbage and wash well before cooking. To reduce the rather strong mustardy flavor, the leaves can be briefly blanched before stir-frying, if liked. **Nutritional & Medicinal Properties** The Chinese believe that boiled Swatow mustard cabbage offsets the symptoms of flu. Fresh Swatow mustard cabbage is difficult to digest. It is also claimed to have the negative effect of diminishing male virility. **Culinary Uses** The leaves of Swatow mustard cabbage are discarded and only the stems used. They are blanched, used to hold minced pork or seafood, and then steamed. The cabbage can also be simmered in a soup. Bamboo mustard cabbage should be washed and chopped before stir-frying with minced garlic and ginger and with seasonings such as soy or oyster sauce added to balance the strong flavor.

Purslane

Purslane is a member of the *Portulacca* family, a fleshy decorative plant with small bright flowers which grows wild, from Greece right across to China. It is a very ancient plant and was known to the ancient Egyptians. Purslane can be enjoyed both raw and cooked.

Appearance & Flavor Purslane has fat, succulent stems that are often tinged with red and small, fleshy green leaves. It has small yellow flowers. The texture is somewhat sticky and chewy, like that of okra, and its flavor, sometimes described as having a sweet-sour taste, is pleasant. **Choosing & Storing** Look for bunches where the stems are firm and not wilted. Refrigerate the vegetables in a jar with the stem ends standing in 1 in (2$^1/_2$ cm) of cold water. Store for 1–2 days. Kept this way, the purslane remains fresh for 2–3 days, although the vegetable should be used as soon as possible because the plant wilts quickly. **Preparing** To prepare, cut off the root end and cut the stems together with their leaves into 2–3-in (5–8-cm) lengths. **Nutritional & Medicinal Properties** Purslane is not just one of the few plants to contain omega 3 fatty acids—which is believed to help combat high cholesterol levels—it has the highest amount of the fatty acid compared to other plants. It is also rich in beta-carotene, vitamin C and iron. In addition, it is believed to be a diuretic. **Culinary Uses** Purslane can be eaten either raw or blanched with a dip or added to soups. It is also good in stews, mixed with spices and freshly grated coconut or briefly stir-fried with garlic and lightly seasoned with soy sauce and sesame oil.

Round Cabbage,

sometimes known as white or head cabbage, is the variety most commonly eaten in the West. Since its introduction to Asia, it has become widespread and is used in both cooked and raw dishes. As this variety of cabbage will grow even in relatively warm climates, it is increasingly found in tropical Asia as well as in the cooler countries of the north. The flavor is relatively mild compared with many Asian cabbages, making it an excellent foil for a range of spices and seasonings.

Appearance & Flavor Round cabbage heads are generally smaller than those found in the West, although in other respects the vegetable is the same. One notable exception is the variety referred to as sweet cabbage in a number of Asian countries, a similar cabbage which is almost the shape of a tear-drop, with a wide base tapering to a pointed tip. As the name implies, this has a sweeter, more delicate flavor then regular round cabbage. **Choosing & Storing** Look for cabbages that are firmly packed, and without worm holes. Wrap in paper towels and keep refrigerated for up to a week. **Preparing** Discard two or three of the outer leaves, separate the fresher inner leaves, and tear into small pieces. Alternatively, quarter the cabbage, cut out the hard central core, and slice across. **Nutritional & Medicinal Properties** Round cabbage is high in beta-carotene and calcium, and also contains vitamin C. Like other crucifers, round cabbage is believed to be helpful in preventing cancer and in encouraging the immune system. **Culinary Uses** The cabbage should not be overcooked or the flavor becomes unpleasant. It is best eaten raw with a spicy dip or mixed with tangy dressings. It is particularly popular this way in Cambodia, Laos, Vietnam and Thailand. In parts of Indonesia and Malaysia, it is often blanched before being served in salads, or briefly stir-fried so that it still retains a slightly crisp texture. A number of spiced Indian dishes using this type of cabbage transform it into a remarkably tasty vegetable.

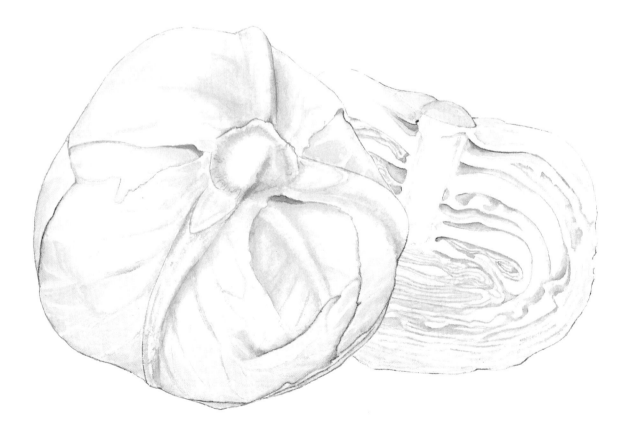

Sauropus

Stem Lettuce

Sauropus

Sauropus has no common English name. Although the plant is known botanically as *Sauropus androgynus*, it is usually called by its Malay name, *sayur manis* or "sweet vegetable," in Malaysia, Indonesia and Singapore. It grows wild in Southeast Asia, and is also cultivated for its tender tips and small, dark green leaves. When cultivated and forced to grow quickly through the liberal application of fertilizer, sauropus develops a crisp, asparagus-like stem that is highly sought after. This variety is often known as Sabah vegetable as it was first grown in this Malaysian state in the north of Borneo.

Appearance & Flavor Regular sauropus has thin, tough, inedible stems and dark green leaves growing on all sides of the stem. Sauropus has a very pleasant, almost nutty flavor. The variety that is referred to as Sabah vegetable—which has a relatively milder flavor—has tender, fleshy stems with a sprig of leaves at the top. **Choosing & Storing** The regular version of this vegetable grows on tough stems. Young Sabah vegetable is sold in bundles. In both cases, do not choose bundles with leaves that look wilted. Wrapped in paper towels and refrigerated, the vegetable can keep for 2–3 days. **Preparing** The leaves of regular sauropus should be pulled from the inedible woody stems. If using Sabah vegetable, trim off the harder end of the stems, then wash the stems and leaves. **Nutritional & Medicinal Properties** This vegetable is a good source of vitamins A and C. Traditionally the juice of the pounded leaves was used for treating infected eyes, and the pounded leaves used as a poultice. **Culinary Uses** The leaves of regular sauropus are usually added to soups. They can also be stir-fried until tender, with a beaten egg often stirred through when the leaves are cooked. The Sabah variant is usually blanched or stir-fried briefly to retain the crisp texture. Sometimes it is stir-fried with chilies and dried prawns, or splashed with oyster sauce just before serving.

Stem Lettuce

Stem Lettuce is a rather curious vegetable, better known outside of Asia as celtuce. The name "celtuce" is made up of a combination of "celery" and "lettuce," as many think its flavor resembles celery. Grown primarily in China for its edible stem, this type of lettuce has caused confusion to a number of Westerners (and others accustomed to iceberg, cos or romaine lettuce) who have purchased cans of pickled lettuce, opening them only to find sliced stems rather than the more familiar leafy green associated with the name "lettuce."

Appearance & Flavor Stem lettuce grows with a very thick stem, about 10–12 in (25–30 cm) in length, with soft green leaves at the end. The leaves are too bitter to eat except when young, but the stem has a delicious flavor, which according to some, tastes vaguely like celery, cucumber, zucchini, artichoke or a combination of these vegetables. The texture is pleasantly crisp. **Choosing & Storing** Choose those with fat stems and no trace of rot. The lettuce can be kept for 3–4 days, wrapped in a paper towel. **Preparing** Discard the leaves and peel the stem to remove the bitter skin. Slice or julienne according to taste and the recipe. **Nutritional & Medicinal Properties** Stem lettuce is said to have more phosphorus and three times the amount of vitamin C as leaf lettuce, and is relatively high in beta-carotene. **Culinary Uses** Fresh stem lettuce can be used as a salad vegetable. It can also be sliced or shredded and stir-fried, either with other vegetables or shredded pork, chicken or prawns. Most of the stem lettuce grown in China is pickled and eaten as a side dish, often mixed with sliced shallots or red chilies and a dash of soy sauce.

Watercress was once known as "the poor man's bread" in Europe—the working class often ate sandwiches stuffed with watercress, and those who had no means to buy bread would just eat the vegetable alone. Watercress is by comparison a relatively new vegetable in Asia, introduced to Hong Kong and neighboring Macau (from where it spread to southern China) by Westerners at the end of the 19th century. It is presently known as *xi yang cai* (Mandarin) or *sai yong choy* (Cantonese) in Asia. Because of its nutritional value, watercress has become very popular among the Chinese. This cold-loving plant grows only in highland areas in tropical Asia.

Appearance & Flavor Watercress is distinguished by the small, soft, bright green leaves that grow on rounded stems. The flavor when raw is peppery and the texture crisp, although most Chinese prefer to boil the vegetable to soften its flavor. **Choosing & Storing** Watercress does not keep well, so purchase watercress that looks fresh, without any yellowing leaves or limpness. Wrap in paper or a cloth and keep refrigerated for a day or two at most. **Preparing** Wash the stalks thoroughly and drain. Pick off the sprigs where the stems are tender, then strip the side stems and leaves from the central stalk.

Nutritional & Medicinal Properties Watercress is rich in vitamin C, beta-carotene, iodine, calcium and phosphorus and contains some essential oils, but may have mild laxative effects. The vegetable is generally regarded as a wonder herb—the ancient Greeks incorporated watercress in their regular diet to help maintain their wit and well-being, and the English drank watercress soup for its cleansing effect in the 18th century. The Chinese believe that watercress is "cooling" to the body—a belief that is still held by many nowadays.

Culinary Uses Sprays of watercress are an attractive edible garnish for almost any dish. Watercress is eaten raw in some Vietnamese salads, whilst the Chinese generally boil it together with pork and various medicinal ingredients such as tangerine peel and red dates to make a tonic soup drunk during the winter.

Water Spinach or Kangkung

is a member of the same family as the rampant flowering weed, morning glory or common convolvulus. Water convolvulus, swamp cabbage and morning glory are some other common names for this popular leafy green vegetable. Thought to have originated in India, where ironically it seems less popular than in other parts of Asia, water spinach is known in Cantonese as *ong choy*, while in Malaysia, Indonesia and the Philippines it is called *kangkung*. Its Mandarin name, *kong xin cai*, means "hollow stem vegetable."

Appearance & Flavor At least two varieties of this vegetable are cultivated. The more popular variety has long, narrow green leaves at the end of its crisp, hollow stems. The other has shorter, broader leaves and often grows in dryer conditions. Water spinach lacks the bitterness of many other iron-rich greens, and its inherent sweetness and soft texture contribute to its wide popularity. **Choosing & Storing** Make sure the water spinach looks fresh and has no yellowing leaves. Buy more than you think you need, as it reduces to about a quarter of its fresh volume when cooked. Do not trim, but wrap in damp newspaper and refrigerate 1–2 days only, as it deteriorates quickly. **Preparing** In the Philippines, the coarse, hollow stems are made into a pickle, but most cooks prefer to discard the stems. Pick off 3 in (8 cm) of the tender leaf end, and pull the individual leaves away from the coarse central stem just before cooking. Wash in several changes of water and drain well. **Nutritional & Medicinal Properties** Water spinach is rich in iron and vitamin A. **Culinary Uses** In Thailand, Laos and Cambodia, the young shoots are eaten raw with a dip. Elsewhere, the vegetable is normally stir-fried, often with dried prawns or dried shrimp paste and chili. It is also added to vegetable stews containing coconut milk, and can be added to soups. Steamed or blanched water spinach is often added to mixed salads in Southeast Asia, particularly in Indonesia and Thailand.

Vietnamese Shredded Chicken and Cabbage Salad

13 oz (400 g) chicken thighs
1 medium onion, halved
lengthwise, thinly sliced
across
1 teaspoon salt
1 tablespoon sugar
13 oz (400 g) Chinese or round
cabbage, washed and finely
shredded
1/3 cup coarsely chopped
polygonum (rau ram) or mint
1/3 cup coarsely chopped coriander
leaves (cilantro)

Sauce
1/4 cup (60 ml) lime or lemon juice
3 tablespoons fish sauce
2 tablespoons sugar
1 tablespoon rice vinegar
1/2 teaspoon finely minced red chili
(optional)

1 Make the Sauce by combining all ingredients, stirring until the sugar dissolves. Set aside. Put the chicken thighs in a small pan and cover with water. Bring to a boil and simmer until cooked.

2 While the chicken is cooking, put the sliced onion in a bowl, sprinkle with salt, massage, then set aside for 30 minutes. Rinse and squeeze dry, then toss with the sugar. Set aside.
3 When the chicken is cooked, leave to cool in the water, then discard the skin and shred the flesh finely by hand. Set aside.
4 Put the cabbage in a salad bowl and add the shredded chicken, onion and fresh herbs. Slowly pour the Sauce over the salad and toss to mix just before serving.

Malaysian-style Cabbage Stewed in Coconut Milk

1 tablespoon oil
4 shallots or 1 small onion, thinly
sliced
1 clove garlic, thinly sliced
1 chili, sliced
3 cups (750 ml) thin coconut milk
1/2 small head round cabbage
(1 lb/500 g), halved lengthwise
and coarsely sliced into chunks
2 tablespoons dried prawns,
soaked in warm water to soften,
ground in a blender
1/2 teaspoon salt, or more to taste

1 Heat the oil in a saucepan. Add the shallots, garlic and chili and stir-fry over low–medium heat until soft. Add the coconut milk, increase the heat and bring almost to a boil, stirring constantly. Do not let the coconut milk boil or it will separate.

2 Put in the cabbage, dried prawns and salt, stirring to mix well. Bring almost to a boil, then lower the heat. Simmer uncovered until the cabbage softens, about 15 minutes, stirring occasionally. Taste and add more salt if desired. Transfer to a serving bowl and serve hot with steamed rice.

Balinese Fern Tips with Garlic and Pepper

14 oz (400 g) young fern tips or
spinach
1/4 teaspoon black peppercorns
2–3 cloves garlic, minced
1 1/2 in (4 cm) fresh or water-packed
aromatic ginger (kencur), minced
3–4 bird's-eye chilies, minced
1 tablespoon oil
1/2 teaspoon salt

1 Blanch the fern tips in boiling water, taking care not to overcook. Drain, then plunge in iced water. Drain again thoroughly.
2 Put the peppercorns in a spice grinder and grind to a powder. Add

garlic, aromatic ginger, chilies, oil and salt and process to a paste. Just before serving, add the paste to the fern tips and toss to mix. Serve at room temperature.

Spiced Indian Cauliflower

3 tablespoons ghee or oil
$1/2$ teaspoon brown mustard seeds
$1/2$ teaspoon cumin seeds
Pinch of fenugreek seeds
2 teaspoons minced ginger
2 cloves garlic, minced
1 medium onion, thinly sliced
$1/2$ teaspoon ground turmeric
$2^1/2$ cups (500 g) cauliflower florets
1 large ripe tomato, blanched, peeled and chopped
1 green chili, sliced, or $1/4$–$1/2$ teaspoon ground red pepper
$1/2$ teaspoon salt
Freshly ground black pepper, to taste

1 Heat the ghee or oil in a saucepan and add the mustard seeds. Fry until they start to pop, then add cumin, fenugreek, ginger, garlic and onion. Stir-fry over medium heat for 3–4 minutes, until the onion slices turn golden. Sprinkle in the ground turmeric. Add the cauliflower and stir-fry for 2 minutes to coat well with the spices. Add tomato, chili, salt and pepper, and cook until the tomato softens, stirring several times.

2 Cover the pan and cook gently, stirring from time to time, until the cauliflower is cooked. Serve warm.

Sambal Kangkung (*Kangkung Tumis Belacan*)

1 lb (450 g) *kangkung* or water spinach
$3/4$ teaspoon dried shrimp paste, toasted until dry and crumbly
$1/2$ cup (125 ml) warm water
1 teaspoon rice wine
1 tablespoon oil
1 medium onion, sliced
2 cloves garlic, smashed and minced
1 red chili, sliced

1 Wash the *kangkung* in several changes of water to remove grit. Cut the stalks and leaves into 2-in (5-cm) lengths. Discard the tough lower portion of the stalks. Drain and set aside.
2 Place the shrimp paste in a bowl and mash with the back of a spoon. Add water and rice wine and stir until the shrimp paste dissolves.

3 Heat the oil in a wok for 30 seconds until moderately hot. Stir-fry the onion, garlic and chili for 2 minutes. Add the *kangkung* and stir-fry for 1 minute, mixing thoroughly.
4 Add the shrimp paste mixture to the wok. Cook, stirring frequently, until the *kangkung* is tender, for about 3 minutes. Serve hot.

Stir-fried Kailan or Choy Sum with Oyster Sauce

1 lb (500 g) *kailan* or *choy sum*
2 teaspoons oil
1 clove garlic, minced
3 tablespoons chicken stock or water
1 tablespoon oyster sauce
1 teaspoon sesame oil
$1/2$ teaspoon sugar
White pepper, to taste

1 Trim off all but the base of the leaves and cut the *kailan* stems into 3-in (8-cm) lengths. If *choy sum* is used, chop the leaves and tender stems into 2-in (5-cm) lengths and blanch for about 1 minute. Cook the stems in boiling water until just tender but still firm, for about 2 minutes. Drain and transfer to a serving dish.

2 Heat the oil in a small pan and add the garlic. Stir-fry for a few seconds until it turns golden brown, then add the stock, oyster sauce, sesame oil and sugar. Bring to a boil, stirring constantly. Simmer for a few seconds, then pour over the *kailan*. Sprinkle with pepper and serve immediately.

Chinese Spinach with Tangy Soy and Sesame Dressing

1 teaspoon salt
1¹/₂ lbs (700 g) Chinese or English spinach, roots and stems discarded, leaves washed and drained

Soy and Sesame Dressing
2 cloves garlic, minced
¹/₂ teaspoon salt
2 tablespoons soy sauce
1 tablespoon white vinegar
2–3 teaspoons Korean fermented chili paste (*gochu jang*) or regular crushed chili paste
2 teaspoons sesame oil
2 teaspoons toasted sesame seeds, lightly crushed while warm
2 teaspoons soft brown sugar

1 To make the Soy and Sesame Dressing, crush garlic and salt together in a small bowl, using the back of a spoon. Transfer garlic and salt to a large bowl and stir in soy sauce, vinegar, chili paste, sesame oil, sesame seeds and sugar, mixing well.
2 Bring a saucepan of water to a boil. Add salt and stir to dissolve, then add spinach leaves and blanch 1 minute, turning a couple of times with a wooden spoon. Drain the spinach, rinse with cold water, and drain again, pressing to expel all the moisture. Chop coarsely.
3 Add spinach leaves and toss by hand or with two wooden spoons, mixing thoroughly. Serve at room temperature with steamed white rice and other dishes.

Cucumber Shoots in Crabmeat Sauce

¹/₂ cup (125 ml) chicken stock
1 tablespoon cornstarch
1 bunch (about 10 oz/300 g) cucumber shoots or pea shoots
2 tablespoons oil
3 cloves garlic, minced
7 oz (200 g) canned or freshly cooked crabmeat
1 tablespoon fish sauce
White pepper, to taste

1 Combine chicken stock and cornstarch and set aside. Wash and drain the cucumber or pea shoots. Cut off the hard ends of the shoots, then blanch in boiling water for 1 minute. Drain, cool in iced water, then cut across in 3-in (8-cm) lengths. Do not blanch if using pea shoots.
2 Heat the oil in a wok and add the garlic. Stir-fry over medium heat until softened then add the cucumber shoots and stir-fry for 1–2 minutes, or until cooked. Add the crabmeat, fish sauce, and the cornstarch mixture. Cook for about 30 seconds, stirring until the sauce thickens and clears. Sprinkle with pepper and serve with rice and other dishes.

Mustard Cabbage Stir-fried with Ginger

14 oz (400 g) bamboo mustard cabbage
1 tablespoon oil
2 tablespoons finely shredded ginger
1 teaspoon salt
3 tablespoons chicken stock or water

1 Separate the leaves and wash well, trimming off the hard ends. Slice the stems thinly on the diagonal, and cut the leaves in thin slices.
2 Heat the oil in a wok and add the ginger and salt. Stir-fry over high heat for a few seconds, then add the leaves and stems.
3 Stir-fry for 3–4 minutes, or until the stems are starting to soften, then add the chicken stock and stir-fry for another 3–4 minutes, or until the cabbage is cooked but not soft.

Blanched Water Spinach and Tofu with Spicy Peanut Sauce

1 cake pressed bean curd (8 oz/ 250 g) or cooked chicken breast, shredded

Oil for deep-frying

1 lb (500 g) water spinach, thick stems discarded, washed and drained

1 tablespoon oil

2 cloves garlic, minced

1 tablespoon Thai red curry paste

$1/2$ cup (125 ml) thick coconut milk

1 tablespoon fish sauce

1 teaspoon finely shaved palm sugar or brown sugar

3 tablespoons coarsely ground dry-roasted peanuts or chunky peanut butter

Salt, to taste

1 If using bean curd, pat dry then deep-fry in hot oil until golden brown on both sides and cooked through. This should take 3–4 minutes. Drain and slice thinly.

2 Blanch the water spinach in a saucepan of boiling water for 2 minutes. Drain, cool under running water and drain again. Arrange the water spinach on a plate, then scatter the bean curd or chicken shreds on top.

3 Heat 1 tablespoon oil in a saucepan or a small pan and add the garlic. Stir-fry until fragrant, then add the curry paste and stir-fry for another 30 seconds. Pour in the coconut milk and bring almost to a boil. Season with fish sauce and sugar, then stir in peanuts. Add salt to taste, then pour the sauce over the top of the bean curd.

Lettuce with Bean Curd and Mushroom

$1/4$ cup (60 ml) oil

1 lb (500 g) Asian lettuce, torn into 2–3 in (5–8 cm) lengths

2 cakes pressed bean curd (8 oz/250 g each)

4 dried black mushrooms soaked in 1 cup (250 ml) hot water to soften, soaking water reserved

1 tablespoon ginger, sliced into thin shreds

1 tablespoon oyster sauce

1 teaspoon cornstarch

1 tablespoon water

$1/2$ teaspoon sesame oil

White pepper, to taste

1 Heat 2 teaspoons of the oil in a wok and add lettuce. Stir-fry over high heat until just cooked, about 1 minute, then transfer to a plate. Wipe the wok, add remaining oil and fry the bean curd for about 4 minutes, turning when golden brown and cooked. Remove bean curd, drain, and cut into thick slices. Remove all but 1 tablespoon of oil from the wok.

2 Slice the mushroom caps, then add together with ginger and stir-fry 1 minute. Return the bean curd to the wok and add reserved soaking liquid. Sprinkle with oyster sauce, cover, and cook over medium heat for 3 minutes. Combine cornstarch and water and add to the wok. Stir until the sauce thickens and clears, then put the bean curd mixture on top of the lettuce. Sprinkle with sesame oil and pepper. Serve hot.

FRUITING vegetables

Fruiting vegetables are a group of vegetables which are technically the fruit of a plant. These include the big family of gourds (see Gourds & Melons, page 80) and various other fruiting vegetables such as okra, eggplant, bell pepper and tomato, as well as tropical varieties such as breadfruit, plantain, jackfruit and papaya, all of which are used as vegetables in their immature state.

Fruiting vegetables are very diverse in flavor, and can be prepared in a wide variety of ways. Many fruiting vegetables native to Central and South America were introduced to Asia only after the arrival of Portuguese and Spanish colonists. Some of these have become such an essential part of local cuisine that it is surprising to learn that they are not native to Asia. The hot chili, indispensable in most Asian cuisines, is undoubtedly the most striking example of this.

Asian Chilies

Asian Chilies have become an essential culinary item in almost every Asian country. This American native was brought back to Europe by Columbus in 1493, and just 50 years later had become established in India by the Portuguese, who called it "pepper of Calicut." Although black pepper was the original hot spice in Asian cuisine, perhaps the only Asian country where black pepper is preferred to chili today is Cambodia.

Appearance & Flavor The varieties of chilies found in the Asian region differ from those of Mexico and Central America. They range in color from green (unripe) to red (ripe), with some yellow and almost white varieties also available. Generally speaking, the smaller the chili, the greater the amount of capsaicin, which is the active ingredient in the seeds and membranes which gives the chili its heat. The flavor of fresh chilies differs slightly depending on the variety and state of maturity. Dried red chilies are often preferred in curries in some parts of Asia for the deep red color they give to a dish and their lack of smell.
Choosing & Storing Look for bright, plump chilies, with neither sign of wrinkling nor dampness. Wrap in a paper towel and store in a plastic bag for about 1 week. Chilies can also be deep-frozen whole for several months, and chopped while still in the frozen state. This is a good idea if a regular supply is not available.
Preparing Take care when handling chilies as the juice can burn the skin. Wash your hands with soap after cutting, and never rub your eyes or nose with chili juice on your hands. Chilies are often sliced across or shredded lengthwise, although they are sometimes halved lengthwise and added to food, seeds and all. Fresh chilies are frequently ground to a paste together with other seasoning ingredients such as ginger, garlic and shallots. The chilies should be chopped before adding to a spice grinder or small blender. To ensure a ready supply of crushed red chilies—a common ingredient in Asian cuisine—chop large, fresh red chilies coarsely, then process with a large pinch of salt in a spice grinder to make a smooth paste. Deep-freeze in an ice-cube tray for small portions. When frozen, transfer these to a plastic bag and deep-freeze for up to 6 months. **Nutritional & Medicinal Properties** Chilies are excellent in encouraging circulation. They make the blood rush to the surface of the skin and thus facilitate perspiration, the body's way of cooling down in a hot climate. They are rich in vitamin C, and are a good cure for a head cold—a spicy hot curry will help clear blocked nasal passages.
Culinary Uses Fresh chilies are used in literally thousands of dishes across Asia. Even in Japan, where the cuisine is mild, dried chilies are mixed with other tangy peppers to make a popular sprinkle for grilled chicken and other dishes. Chilies appear in sauces, curries, condiments, stir-fried dishes and pickles. They are also often stuffed and steamed in southern China, while in southern India, green chilies are soaked in yoghurt and salt, sun-dried, then deep-fried to make a tangy accompaniment to vegetarian meals.

Baby Corn

is a hybrid of maize, one of the many vegetables which first originated in Central America and have now spread throughout the world, including most Asian countries. The miniature corn is harvested from immature, regular-sized corn. Although many varieties of corn are grown for animal feed, several types of hybrid sweet corn are popular for human consumption as a vegetable and an ingredient in cakes or desserts—although baby corn is almost never used in desserts. In parts of China and in Southeast Asia, finger-length baby corn is even more popular than the mature sweet corn cobs.

Appearance & Flavor Regular sweet corn has bright yellow kernels, although some hybrid varieties which are starchier have almost white kernels. Baby corn, with their cream-colored kernels, is one of the latter varieties. Baby corn is harvested when about 3–4 in (8–10 cm) long and $1/2$ in ($1^1/_4$ cm) in diameter and has a very good flavor. **Choosing & Storing** Baby corn is often sold in Asia with part of the husk cut back. In Western countries, baby corn is most commonly sold peeled and packed on small trays. If buying peeled corn, check that the corn is not withered or turning brown. If buying fresh corn still wrapped in its green husks, ensure that the kernels inside are firm and not sunken or wrinkled. Make sure also that there is no worm infestation. Baby corn should be refrigerated in loose plastic or its original wrapping. Stored this way, the corn keeps 2–3 days, although immediate consumption is recommended for maximum sweetness. The corn is also available in cans, jars and in tubs in supermarkets. **Preparing** Peel back the husk and silk and trim off the stem end of the kernel. Regular corn is generally cooked whole, while baby corn may be left whole or cut on the diagonal in 1-in ($2^1/_2$-cm) lengths for stir-frying. **Nutritional & Medicinal Properties** Baby corn, like all varieties of corn, is a good source of carbohydrates. It contains less phosphorus than regular corn, but has considerably more vitamin C than mature sweet corn. Baby corn also contains moderate amounts of protein and some calcium and vitamin A. **Culinary Uses** Baby corn is a popular ingredient in Thai and Chinese dishes. It is most commonly used in stir-fried vegetable combinations, and in soups and braised dishes. It can also be eaten raw with dips, or used as a salad vegetable. The corn can also be pickled in vinegar, water, salt, dill and other spices, then eaten as a snack or as a side dish.

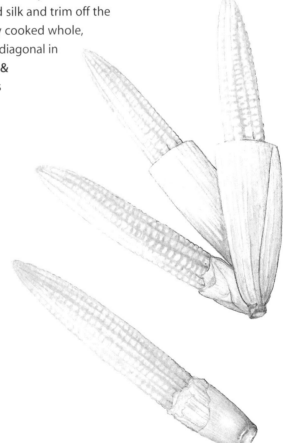

Banana Flower

is a popular vegetable throughout tropical Asia, and is a good example of the philosophy that no edible part of a plant should be wasted. The unopened male flowers of the banana—a purple-red inflorescence tinged with yellow at the base which hangs at the tip of a clump of developing bananas—can often be found in specialty stores outside Asia, particularly those stocking Vietnamese and Thai ingredients. The hearts or "buds" of all varieties of edible banana can be eaten.

Appearance & Flavor The banana flower looks like a fat teardrop, about 8–10 in (20–25 cm) in length, with overlapping petals that cover rows of tiny yellow stamens attached to the central core of the bud. The flavor of the cooked banana flower is surprisingly similar to that of the globe artichoke. **Choosing & Storing** If you happen to have bananas growing in your own garden, cut off the banana flower with an oiled knife while the bananas (which grow above the heart) are still very small. If buying banana flowers, check that the outer leaves are not wilted. Keep the banana flower in a loosely packed plastic bag and refrigerate it in a vegetable drawer for up to 1 week. **Preparing** To prepare, pull off the outer petals and the long, narrow yellow blossoms until the pinkish white inner heart is revealed. Quarter the heart lengthwise with an oiled knife, to avoid the sticky sap clinging to it. Do not leave the cut bud exposed to the air as it will start to brown, but put it in cold water if not cooking immediately. To cook, simmer in plenty of lightly salted water until tender, for about 15–20 minutes. Drain, cool then slice across using the top of a knife or use the fingers to pull out the hard filaments inside each cluster of yellow stamens. Although this may seem too painstaking a job, the stringy filaments must be discarded as they have an unpleasant texture. **Nutritional & Medicinal Properties** Banana flower has appreciable amounts of beta-carotene. **Culinary Uses** Cooked banana flower is often made into a salad, sometimes with a little shredded chicken or cooked prawns for flavor and textural contrast. Simmered banana bud is also used as an edible garnish in some Southeast Asia cuisines, particularly in Vietnam. It can also be finely shredded lengthwise, blanched briefly in water, then added to soups, or simmered in seasoned coconut milk. You could also try cooked banana flower with a Western salad dressing, such as vinaigrette or a light mayonnaise.

Bilimbi or Belimbing

is a small, very acidic tropical fruit. It gets its name from the botanical *Averrhoa bilimbi*, and is closely related to the large, sweet starfruit *Averrhoa carambola*. Unlike the starfruit, *bilimbi* is considered too sour to be eaten as a fruit (except by children). The *bilimbi* tree, with its small, soft leaves and fruit growing directly from the tree trunk, is a common sight in kitchen gardens throughout Southeast Asia, although because of the relative fragility of the fruit, it is not always easy to find in local markets.

Appearance & Flavor *Bilimbi* fruits resemble tiny cucumbers growing in clusters directly from the trunk and branches of a small tree. They have a thin, delicate skin and bruise easily. *Bilimbi* is very acidic, but has a fruitiness and adds a distinctive sourness to food. **Choosing & Storing** Make sure the fruits are still firm and unblemished, and not starting to soften or ferment. They deteriorate relatively quickly at room temperature in the tropics, so keep refrigerated for 2–3 days only. **Preparing** Wash and use either whole, halved lengthwise, or sliced as directed by the recipe. **Nutritional & Medicinal Properties** *Bilimbi* has appreciable amounts of both vitamin C and beta-carotene. **Culinary Uses** *Bilimbi* is frequently added to give a sour, fruity tang to curries, particularly those containing fish. They are also made into a pickle in several Southeast Asian countries, or used as a sambal or condiment.

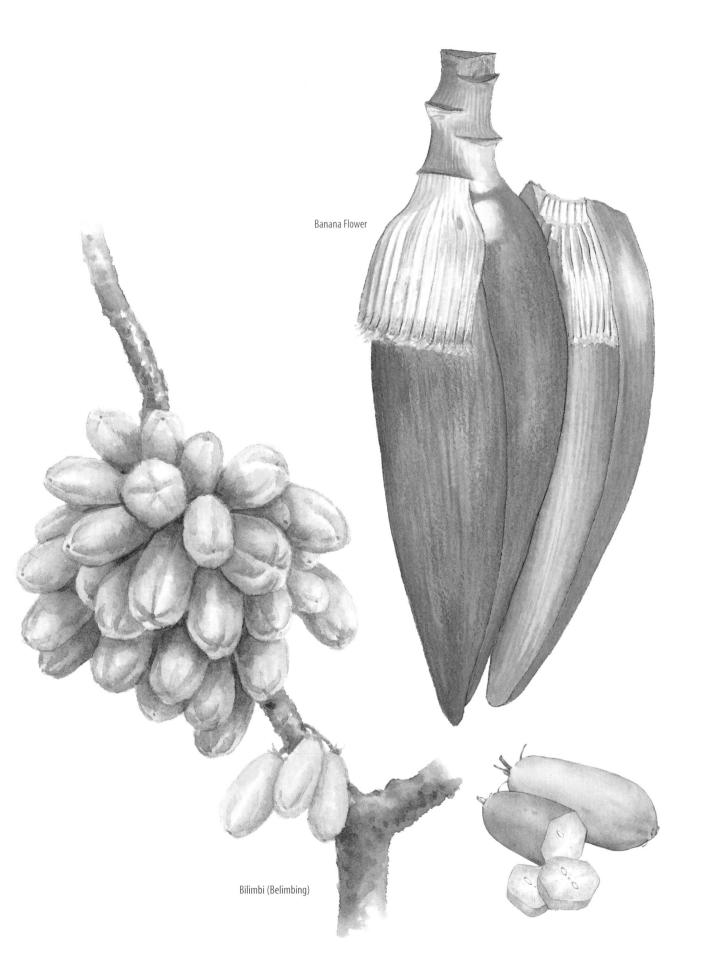

Banana Flower

Bilimbi (Belimbing)

Breadfruit

Breadnut

Breadfruit

could be described as the fruit which launched a mutiny—sailors on the *HMS Bounty*, whilst gathering breadfruit in the Pacific for replanting in the French Caribbean, mutinied against their commander, Captain Bligh. Although the breadfruit has an appealing aroma and pleasant flavor when left to ripen on the tree, it is almost always picked while green and immature and treated as a vegetable in Asia.

Appearance & Flavor Breadfruit are large and round, with a green, rather bumpy skin, which changes to yellowish brown as the fruit ripens. Small fruits can weigh as little as 2 lbs (1 kg), but they more commonly weigh in at around 7–9 lbs (3–4 kg). The flavor is mild and starchy—hence the name breadfruit. **Choosing & Storing** Breadfruit are often sold pre-cut in chunks or slices, and should be cooked as soon as possible. The whole fruit can, however, be kept for a couple of days at room temperature—but be aware that it continues to ripen after picking. If stored refrigerated, the whole, unripe fruit can keep for up to a week. **Preparing** To avoid the sticky sap in breadfruit, oil the knife and cutting board, and put your hand in a plastic bag before cutting off the thick skin. The flesh can then be cut across into chunks, or thinly sliced. Unless the breadfruit is being thinly sliced and deep-fried, the pieces are usually simmered in lightly salted water for about 10 minutes before further cooking with other ingredients. To ensure a pleasant color, add a little ground turmeric to the simmering water. **Nutritional & Medicinal Properties** Breadfruit is relatively high in carbohydrates and has reasonable levels of phosphorus and vitamin C. **Culinary Uses** Breadfruit is versatile and because of its mild flavor, lends itself well to cooking with a variety of seasonings. Blanched breadfruit is often simmered in spiced coconut milk, or simply boiled in water until soft, and served with a spicy condiment or sambal. Breadfruit is sometimes also used as a substitute for potatoes. It is also excellent cut in thin slices and deep-fried to make crisps. Whole breadfruit can be oven-baked and served with butter, a method of cooking common in the Pacific.

Breadnut

is very closely related to the breadfruit. It is found in tropical Asia as well as in the Pacific and New Guinea. Breadnut is often eaten in the immature form as a vegetable, although in many areas it is left to ripen, after which the highly nutritious seeds are extracted, cooked and eaten like chestnuts.

Appearance & Flavor The breadnut is an oval green fruit covered with soft spines, and is slightly smaller than its close cousin, the breadfruit. Breadnuts are often sold halved lengthwise, revealing their well-formed seeds. The flesh is creamy white and the flavor similar to breadfruit. The nuts of the mature fruit have a delicious chestnut-like taste. **Choosing & Storing** If serving as a vegetable, look for a breadnut where the seeds are not large and hard. When you are purchasing the nuts for cooking, choose a mature fruit where the seeds or nuts are well formed. They keep well refrigerated for 1–2 days. **Preparing** If using young breadnut, prepare as for breadfruit. Do not discard the edible young seeds. If the seeds are mature, remove them with a knife and discard the fibrous flesh of the fruit. **Nutritional & Medicinal Properties** Immature breadnut fruit contains calcium, phosphorus and vitamin C, and is low in carbohydrates. The mature nuts are high in calories and contain around 15% protein, as well as high levels of phosphorus, thiamin, riboflavin and beta-carotene. **Culinary Uses** Breadnut with immature seeds can be cooked in any recipe using breadfruit. If cooking the nuts alone, boil them in lightly salted water, or roast them as for peanuts. The raw nuts can be added to coconut milk, and cooked together with other ingredients such as cabbage or gourd, or added to curries.

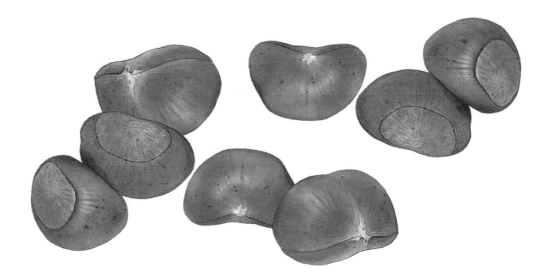

Chestnuts

Chestnuts roasting at a street stall have an irresistible aroma and are an integral part of the autumn and winter scene in China, Japan and Taiwan, as well as in Southeast Asian cities where they are eagerly snapped up by local Chinese. Fresh, raw chestnuts are usually available in the markets for 3–4 months from late September, while at other times of the year, dried chestnuts are sold in Asian stores.

Appearance & Flavor Raw chestnuts are covered with a reddish brown shell. Dried chestnuts, which are available all year round, have had both the outer shell and skin removed. With their sweet flavor and floury texture, chestnuts are treated as a vegetable and also used in sweet dishes. Dried chestnuts are best used only in savory dishes. **Choosing & Storing** Press each chestnut to make sure it is firm, discarding any with soft spots or blemishes, or which smell musty. Refrigerated in a perforated plastic bag, the chestnuts can keep for up to a month. They can also be deep-frozen in the shell for several months. **Preparing** Cut a shallow cross in the wide, rounded end of each chestnut, then cook in boiling water for 20 minutes. Drain, and as soon as they are cool enough to handle, pull off the brown skin. Remove the wrinkled, slightly furry inner skin using a small knife. If the skin is difficult to remove, drop the shelled chestnuts in boiling water for 1–2 minutes. For dried chestnuts, leave them in boiling water for 30 minutes, drain, place them in more boiling water, then leave them for another 30 minutes. **Nutritional & Medicinal Properties** Chestnuts contain sugars and starch, and are low in oil. **Culinary Uses** Peeled chestnuts are sometimes added to braised dishes—particularly those with pork or chicken—or are made into a sweet soup by the Chinese. In Japan, they are used in a wide variety of sweets, and are also grilled, baked, steamed and cooked with rice. The Koreans enjoy chestnuts cooked with rice, mushrooms or meat. They also make a sweetmeat out of them by mashing the cooked flesh with sesame seeds and honey, shaping it into balls, and rolling these in crushed pine nuts.

Jackfruit has been cultivated in India for so long that it is mentioned in ancient Sanskrit literature. Also spelt "jak fruit," it is widely grown in tropical Asia, where it is often known as *nangka*. The fruit can grow into a real monster weighing up to almost 100 lbs (45 kg) when ripe. The immature fruit, which is often picked when around 8–10 in (20–25 cm) in length, is popular as a vegetable throughout the warmer countries of Asia.

Appearance & Flavor Young jackfruits are oval in shape and have pale green skin (which turns yellowish brown as the fruit ripens) with hard bumps. Although the flesh is bright egg-yellow or lemon-colored when ripe, the immature fruit is creamy white in color. The flavor of the young fruit is pleasant and slightly sweet, with a good texture. The immature seeds, which are often visible although not well-formed, are delicious cooked with the flesh, while mature seeds can be boiled in salted water and taste somewhat like chestnuts. Slices of young jackfruit are often sold in plastic bags in Asian markets, as a whole fruit is normally too much for one family. **Choosing & Storing** If buying sliced jackfruit, make sure the flesh is not turning brown. Refrigerate in a plastic bag for 1–2 days. **Preparing** Whole fruit should be peeled with an oiled knife, cut in 1-in (2^1/$_2$-cm) thick slices, leaving the immature seeds intact, then cut into wedges. These are usually simmered in lightly salted water until slightly soft, for about 15 minutes, then cooked together with seasonings. **Nutritional & Medicinal Properties** Young jackfruit is a good source of vitamin C, phosphorus and calcium. **Culinary Uses** Immature jackfruit is simmered in seasoned liquid or coconut milk.

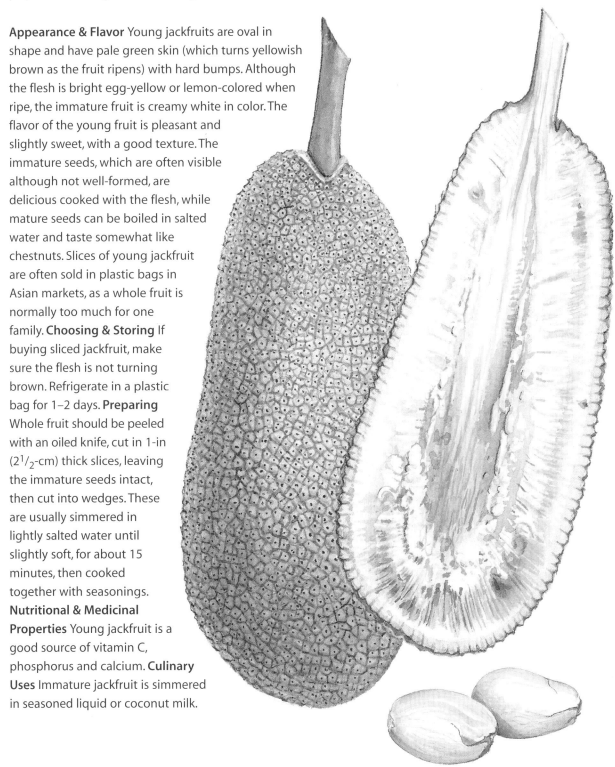

Mangoes have a succulence and flavor that make them one of the finest of all tropical fruits. Huge mango trees are a common sight in the warmer countries of Asia, and usually bear such a prolific amount of fruit that much of it is picked before it ripens, and is enjoyed while in its immature green state, perhaps relished even more than the sweet ripe fruit. Green mangoes are eaten raw in salads or enjoyed with pungent dips. The unripe fruit can also be cooked as a vegetable, or transformed into fresh pickles. It is particularly popular for store-cupboard chutneys, especially in India and Sri Lanka.

Appearance & Flavor Unripe mangoes have pale green skins. Many different varieties are found throughout Asia, and all cultivated varieties can be eaten young. The taste is somewhat fruity and pleasantly sour. **Choosing & Storing** Make sure that there are no tiny black holes, as these would indicate the presence of worms or weevils. The mangoes should be firm. Refrigerated in a vegetable drawer, the mangoes can keep for up to 2 weeks. **Preparing** Peel, then cut the flesh away from the stone, taking care not to get the sap on your hands if you have sensitive skin, as some people are allergic to this. The flesh can be sliced or diced for use in cooking or making into pickles. Mangoes are usually salted, to help draw out the moisture, and then sun-dried before being cooked with spices, vinegar and sugar to make pickles and chutneys. Fresh green mango flesh is generally sprinkled with salt, left to stand for approximately 15 minutes, then rinsed and squeezed dry to reduce the sourness before being used in salads or stir-fried dishes. **Nutritional & Medicinal Properties** Mangoes are rich in vitamin C and contain some vitamin B6 and E. It is not known how the unripe variety compares to the ripe, yellow mango—the latter probably contains more beta-carotene. **Culinary Uses** Fresh green mango flesh is served in wedges, for dipping into a hot, spicy sauce. It is also stir-fried, often with pork or prawns, and shredded and made into salads, especially in Southeast Asia. As a salad, green mango slices are often mixed with chili-based dressings.

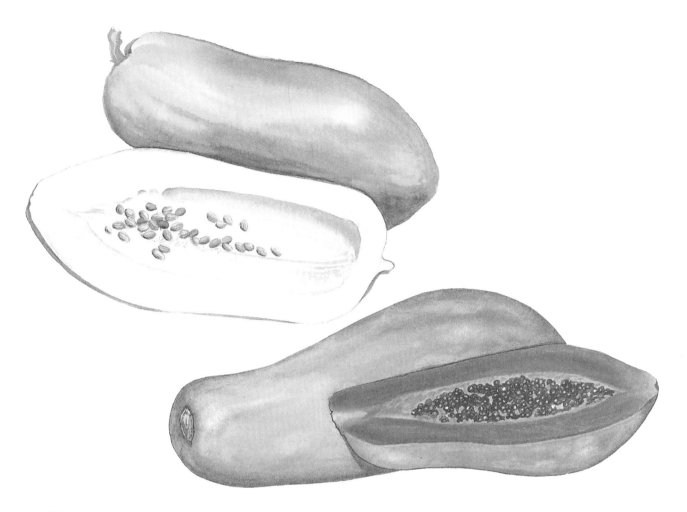

Papayas are tropical fruits, which like mangoes, are widely enjoyed as a vegetable when still hard and green. Although immature papayas lack the high vitamin A and C content of the ripe fruit, they make an excellent vegetable both raw and cooked, and one commonly eaten in rural areas of tropical Asia where almost every garden has a few papaya trees. The somewhat bitter flowers of the male papaya tree are used as a vegetable (added to soups, particularly in the Manado region of Indonesia). The enzyme contained in the sap of young papayas, papain, is used as a meat tenderizer.

Appearance & Flavor Green papayas are usually quite small, averaging 6–8 in (15–20 cm) in length. They have a mild flavor and a firm texture when raw. **Choosing & Storing** Asian stores, especially those that specialize in Thai and Vietnamese ingredients, often sell green papayas. They are also usually available in fresh food markets in Asia itself. Make sure the papaya is still very hard and green, with no trace of yellow which would indicate that the papaya is beginning to ripen. Keep refrigerated in a vegetable drawer, and use within 3–4 days. **Preparing** Peel off the skin and remove any pith and immature seeds from the center before shredding, slicing or dicing. **Nutritional & Medicinal Properties** Young papaya leaves are rich in beta-carotene, while papaya seeds are renowned for their ability to get rid of intestinal worms. They are also believed to cause abortion. In some places, the sap or papain is used to remove skin blemishes and warts, and to relieve the pain of burns. **Culinary Uses** Green papaya is used raw to make salads, garnishes and pickles, and a Thai green papaya salad (often sold by itinerant hawkers in Thailand) is almost a must on any Thai menu in restaurants abroad. Diced or sliced green papaya is added to soups and simmered vegetable dishes. The leaves of the papaya tree are boiled in lightly salted water until tender, then eaten as a vegetable.

Peanuts

Peanuts are often known as groundnuts in Asia, perhaps a more accurate name for the nut as they are actually nodules which form on the roots of a bushy leguminous plant. Peanuts are often sold in their immature state while still in their pods, just shortly after they are harvested. More commonly, however, peanuts are sold raw, after they have been dried and extracted from their shells.

Appearance & Flavor Raw peanuts are sometimes sold in their fibrous shell, and are also available shelled, still covered by their light brown skin. Shelled and skinned peanuts are creamy white in color. The flavor and texture of peanuts are widely enjoyed in Asia. **Choosing & Storing** In humid conditions, peanuts may develop a toxic mold, so do check the nuts for any with traces of this before buying. If the immature, pre-shelled peanuts are available, make sure they smell fresh, not musty. Keep peanuts in a dry, airy place. **Nutritional & Medicinal Properties** Peanuts have a high oil content, and are also rich sources of calcium, thiamine, carbohydrates, phosphorus and niacin. **Culinary Uses** Immature fresh peanuts are usually left in their shells, which should be washed well to remove any traces of dirt, then are usually either steamed or boiled in salty water until tender, and eaten as a snack. Dry-roasted peanuts are crushed to make sauces, such as gravy for satay and *gado gado*—an Indonesian salad—or sprinkled over many dishes. Raw pea-nuts are added to vegetable soups, or mixed with a savory batter and made into crisp, deep-fried wafers known as *rempeyek* in Indonesia. Cooked peanuts crushed to a fine powder are used to make a very special light and flaky peanut cake in China, and as a filling for pancakes in other parts of Southeast Asia, while in India toasted peanuts are often added to savory mixtures known as *bhaja* mix or *murruku*.

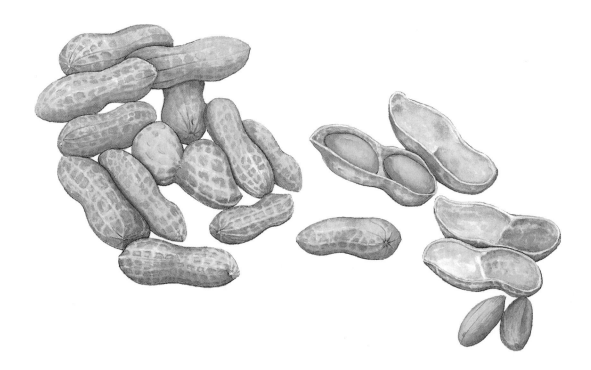

Plantains are a type of banana, known botanically as *Musa paradisica*, which is used only for cooking. Left to mature, this banana does not develop a sweet flavor so it is not eaten as a conventional fruit. Most other varieties of banana can likewise be cooked as a vegetable in their unripe green state, although strictly speaking they are not plantains. Plantains are particularly popular with vegetarians in South India, and are also frequently encountered in Sri Lankan curries with a coconut-milk base.

Appearance & Flavor The true plantain has a thick, green skin and a rather angular shape with either three or four flat surfaces. The interior of the fruit is very starchy and the taste is rather unpalatable if eaten raw, but is transformed into a mild, pleasant taste after cooking. **Choosing & Storing** Plantains can sometimes be found in Asian stores and are also sold in markets specializing in Latin American as well as Polynesian ingredients. Any large green and totally unripe bananas can be used as a substitute. Store the plantains at room temperature for 2–3 days, but use immediately if the skin starts to turn yellow. **Preparing** Plantains contain a slightly sticky sap, so oil the hands and a cutting knife lightly before cutting off the skin with a knife just before using (plantains do not peel easily like ripe bananas). Slice thinly if using for crisps, or cut across in bite-sized pieces for simmering. **Nutritional & Medicinal Properties** Like the other members of the banana family, plantains are a rich source of energy, potassium and magnesium. They also contain relatively high levels of vitamin C. **Culinary Uses** In most of tropical Asia, plantains are generally peeled and simmered, often in a curry-like sauce, although sometimes Indians and Sri Lankans cook them with the skins intact. Plantains can be peeled, sliced very thinly, and seasoned with salt, chili and ground turmeric, and then deep-fried to make very tasty crisps. The Filipinos, who have a very sweet palate, like to fry plantains in oil, then douse them with sugar and continue cooking until the sugar caramelizes.

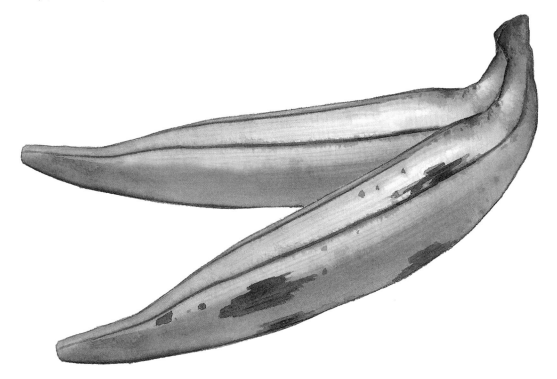

Claypot Rice with Chestnuts and Chicken

10 oz (300 g) boneless chicken thighs, cut in bite-sized pieces
2 tablespoons oil
2 cups (200 g) uncooked rice, washed and drained
1 in (2 1/2 cm) ginger, sliced into thin shreds
12 fresh or dried chestnuts, boiled until just soft, cut in half
2 dried Chinese sausages (*lap cheong*) sliced diagonally
Crisp fried shallots, to garnish
2 tablespoons minced spring onions, to garnish

Marinade
1 tablespoon black soy sauce
1 tablespoon oyster sauce
1 tablespoon rice wine or saké
1 teaspoon sugar
1 tablespoon sesame oil
1/2 teaspoon cornstarch

1 Put the chicken pieces in a bowl and stir in all Marinade ingredients. Set aside to marinate for 20 minutes.
2 Heat the oil in a large claypot. Add the rice and stir over medium heat for about 1 minute, until the rice is well coated. Add sufficient water to cover the rice by about 3/4 in (2 cm). Bring to a boil over high heat, then cook with the pot uncovered for about 5 minutes, or until the water is absorbed and "craters" appear in the surface of the rice.
3 Add the ginger, chestnuts and marinated chicken pieces, pushing them well into the rice. Lay the sliced *lap cheong* on top, cover and cook over low heat for 20 minutes. Do not remove the lid.

4 Stir the rice with a chopstick or fork, then cover and cook over very low heat until the chicken is done and the rice is dry. This should take about 15 minutes. Garnish with the crisp fried shallots and spring onions before serving. If desired, serve with a soup and vegetable dish, with sliced red chilies and soy sauce on the side.

Young Jackfruit and Prawns in Coconut Milk

1 1/2–2 lbs (750 g–1 kg) unripe jackfruit
1 teaspoon coriander seeds, lightly dry-roasted in a pan
1 tablespoon freshly grated coconut, or soaked desiccated coconut
4–5 shallots
2–3 red chilies
Thin slice of fresh turmeric root, or 1/2 teaspoon ground turmeric
3 tablespoons oil
1 kaffir lime leaf, torn
1 stem lemongrass, thick bottom third only, bruised
3 cups (750 ml) coconut milk
7 oz (200 g) fresh prawns, peeled and deveined
Salt, to taste

1 Oil a knife blade and cut away the coarse skin of the jackfruit. Cut the flesh into bite-sized chunks and discard the skin, seeds and sheaths. Cook in a large pan of boiling water until just tender. Drain and set aside.
2 Put the coriander seeds in a blender and grind to a powder. Add the coconut and grind until smooth, then add the shallots, chilies and turmeric and grind to a paste, adding a little oil if needed to keep the mixture turning.

3 Heat the oil in a pan and add the ground mixture. Stir-fry over low to medium heat for 4–5 minutes, or until fragrant. Add the kaffir lime leaf, lemongrass and coconut milk and bring to a boil. Keep stirring frequently. Add the prawns, salt and reserved jackfruit, and simmer the mixture uncovered for 10 minutes. Serve hot with steamed rice and other dishes.

Green Chili Lassi

2 1/2 cups (625 ml) chilled plain yoghurt
1/2 teaspoon salt
2 green chilies, sliced
1/2 cup (125 ml) iced water
4–8 ice cubes

1 Put 1/2 cup of the yoghurt, salt and chilies in a blender and process until smooth, adding a little more yoghurt if necessary to keep the mixture turning. Pour through a fine sieve, pressing down gently with the back of a spoon. Discard any residue.

2 Return the yoghurt mixture to the blender, add the remaining yoghurt, water and ice cubes and process for a few seconds. Divide the yoghurt mixture among four glasses.

Sri Lankan Breadfruit Curry

1¼ lbs (600 g) unripe breadfruit, cut in bite-sized pieces
1 medium onion, halved lengthwise, thinly sliced
1 clove garlic, minced
1 teaspoon finely grated ginger
2 pieces pandanus leaf, each about 5 in (12 cm) long, raked with a fork
1 sprig curry leaves
2 green chilies, halved lengthwise
2-in (5-cm) stick cinnamon
2 cups (500 ml) coconut cream
¼ teaspoon ground turmeric
¼ cup (60 ml) coconut cream
Salt, to taste

1 Simmer the breadfruit in a pan of lightly salted water for 10 minutes. Drain and set aside.
2 Put all the remaining ingredients, except the coconut cream, in a saucepan and bring slowly to a boil, stirring frequently.
3 Simmer gently with the pan uncovered for 10 minutes, then add the breadfruit and simmer until the breadfruit is soft. Stir in the coconut cream and taste, adding salt as desired. Serve hot with rice and other dishes.

Sour Fish Curry with Bilimbi

8 shallots
1-in (2½-cm) turmeric root, or 1 teaspoon ground turmeric
4 thin slices galangal
1 stem lemongrass, thick bottom third only, bruised
1–1½ teaspoons Sambal Belacan (see below)
2 cups (500 ml) water
1 teaspoon salt
4 firm fish steaks or fillets
8–10 bilimbi, halved lengthwise

1 Using a blender, food processor or a mortar and pestle, grind the shallots, turmeric and galangal to a smooth paste, adding a little water if needed to keep the mixture turning.
Put the paste mixture, lemongrass, Sambal Belacan, water and salt into a saucepan.
2 Bring to a boil, cover, lower heat and simmer for 30 minutes. Remove the lemongrass, then add the fish and bilimbi. Cook gently until the fish is done. Serve hot with rice.

Thai Hot Sour Green Papaya Salad

2 cloves garlic
3–4 bird's-eye chilies
2 tablespoons dried prawns, soaked in warm water for 10 minutes to soften, drained well
2 cups (200 g) grated green papaya
2 long beans, cut in lengths
1 medium tomato, cut in wedges
2 tablespoons lime or lemon juice
1 tablespoon fish sauce
1 tablespoon sugar

1 Pound the garlic using a pestle in a large mortar, then add the chilies and the prawns and pound until coarsely ground. Add the papaya and pound lightly, stirring several times with a spoon to ensure all the papaya is bruised. Add the beans and pound lightly just to bruise.
2 Do the same for the tomato, then stir in the lime juice, fish sauce and sugar. Transfer to a serving bowl. Stir well before serving.

Sambal Belacan

1 teaspoon dried shrimp paste
4–6 red chilies, sliced
Pinch of salt
Round green musk limes (kasturi/kalamansi) or 1 large lime, halved

1 Wrap the shrimp paste loosely in a piece of foil and flatten so that the paste is very thin. Place in a small frying pan and cook for about 3–4 minutes on each side, until the paste is dry and crumbly and fragrant.
2 Using a blender, food processor or mortar and pestle, pound or process the shrimp paste, chilies and salt until finely ground. Transfer to small sauce bowls and serve each with a halved lime.

Stir-fried Rice Vermicelli with Baby Corn

2 teaspoons cornstarch
$3/4$ cup (185 ml) water
2 teaspoons white vinegar
2 tablespoons oil
2 cloves garlic, minced
4 dried black mushrooms, soaked to soften, stalks discarded and caps thinly sliced
2 tablespoons fish sauce
1 tablespoon soy sauce
1 tablespoon black bean sauce
1 teaspoon sugar
2 cups (250 g) broccoli, cut into small florets
8–10 baby corn, sliced diagonally in small pieces
1 red chili, minced
12 oz (375 g) dried rice vermicelli (*bee hoon* or *mifen*), soaked in warm water to soften, drained and cut into lengths
$1/4$ cup (40 g) coarsely crushed, dry-roasted unsalted peanuts (optional)
$1/4$ teaspoon white pepper

1 Combine the cornstarch, $1/2$ cup of the water and vinegar in a bowl, stirring to dissolve the cornstarch. Set aside.
2 Heat oil in a wok. When very hot, stir-fry the garlic and mushrooms for 10 seconds.
3 Stir in the fish sauce, soy sauce, black bean sauce and sugar. Add the broccoli, baby corn and chili and stir-fry over high heat. Add the rest of the water slowly, until the vegetables are just cooked, or for about 3 minutes.
4 Add the noodles and stir-fry for about 1 minute, until well mixed and heated through. Stir the cornstarch mixture, then add to the wok. Cook and toss for 30 seconds. Sprinkle with crushed peanuts and pepper. Serve immediately.

Plantains in Coconut Milk

1 lb (500 g) plantains, peeled and cut into long, thin slices
1 teaspoon salt
1 teaspoon ground turmeric
Oil for deep-frying
$1/4$ teaspoon fenugreek seeds
12–14 curry leaves
1 onion, diced
1–2 green chilies, halved lengthwise
2 cups (500 ml) thin coconut milk
$1/4$ cup (60 ml) thick coconut milk
Salt, to taste

1 Put the sliced plantains in a bowl, sprinkle with the salt and ground turmeric and toss. Set the plantains aside for 10 minutes, then deep-fry the slices, a few at a time, just until golden brown. Remove the slices with a slotted spoon, chopsticks or a spatula and drain on paper towels.
2 Heat 1 tablespoon of the oil in a wok and add the fenugreek seeds and curry leaves. Fry for 2 minutes, then add onion, chili and the thin coconut milk. Bring to a boil while stirring constantly, then let the mixture simmer uncovered for 10 minutes. Add the plantain slices and simmer until they are soft. Add thick coconut milk and heat through. Taste and add salt if desired.

Banana Flower Salad with Coconut Cream

$1/2$ cup (125 ml) coconut cream
1 tablespoon Sambal Belacan (see page 75)
1 tablespoon lime or lemon juice
1 teaspoon salt
2 teaspoons sugar
1 large banana flower, pinkish white inner heart sliced with
an oiled knife, soaked in lightly salted water for 15–20 minutes until tender
1 medium onion, halved and very thinly sliced
7 oz (200 g) cooked prawns, peeled and deveined, halved if large

1 Combine the coconut cream, Sambal Belacan, lime juice, salt and sugar in a small bowl, stirring until the sugar has dissolved.
2 Put sliced cooked banana heart, onion and prawns in a large bowl and add the coconut cream mixture. Toss to mix well, then serve.

Chestnuts with Chinese Cabbage

12 fresh chestnuts (about 7 oz/
  200 g) in the shell, or 5 oz (150 g)
  dried chestnuts
1/2 head of Chinese cabbage
  (about 1 1/2 lbs/675 g)
1 tablespoon oil
2 tablespoons soy sauce
1 tablespoon sugar
1 teaspoon salt
1/2 teaspoon sesame oil
1 tablespoon cornstarch
3/4 cup (185 ml) water

1 If using fresh chestnuts in the shell, boil 2 cups (500 ml) water in a small saucepan, cut a shallow cross in the rounded end of each chestnut, then cook them in the boiling water for 20 minutes.

Drain, cool and peel off the outer skin. If the skins are difficult to peel, soak the shelled chestnuts in boiling water for 1–2 minutes. If using dried chestnuts, cook them in boiling water for 30 minutes, drain and peel.
2 Reserve three outer leaves of the cabbage and tear in half. Separate the remaining leaves and slice into 2-in (5-cm) sections. Heat the oil in a wok until the oil is moderately hot. Add the cabbage and stir-fry over low–moderate heat until the cabbage starts to wilt. This should take about 3 minutes—take care not to let the cabbage brown. Add the peeled chestnuts, soy sauce, sugar, salt and sesame oil, and stir-fry briefly to mix well.

3 Transfer the contents of the wok to a heatproof bowl with a lid. Mix the cornstarch and water, pour over the chestnuts, then cover with the reserved cabbage leaves. Cover the bowl and put it on a rack set over boiling water in a wok. Cover with a wok lid and steam over boiling water for an hour, adding boiling water to the wok every 10–15 minutes. Alternatively, bake the cabbage in a low to moderately hot oven, preheated at about 160 °C (320 °F), for 1 hour.

Thai Mango and Cashew Salad

2 tablespoons raw cashew nuts
2 sour green mangoes (about 10 oz/
  300 g), peeled and cut into thin
  shreds
1 teaspoon sugar
1 tablespoon fish sauce
1 clove garlic, minced
2–3 shallots, thinly sliced
2–3 bird's-eye chilies, minced
1 tablespoon minced coriander
  leaves (cilantro)

1 Put the cashew nuts in a cold wok and heat gently. Stir-fry over low heat until the nuts are crisp and golden. Set aside to cool.

2 Place the shredded mangoes in a bowl and add sugar then add the fish sauce, minced garlic, shallots, chilies, coriander leaves and cashews. Toss to mix well and serve.

Spiced Breadnut Slices

1 small breadnut, peeled and thinly
  sliced
1 teaspoon ground turmeric
1 teaspoon salt
Oil for deep-frying
Dried chili flakes or ground red
  pepper, to taste

1 Put the breadnut slices, ground turmeric and salt in a saucepan and add water to just cover. Bring to a boil, lower heat, and simmer for 5 minutes. Drain the slices well, then pat dry with paper towels and set aside to cool.

2 Heat oil in a wok, then deep-fry the breadnut slices, a few at a time, until golden brown. Drain them on a paper towel and sprinkle lightly with chili to taste. Serve hot.

GOURDS & melons

Gourds are all members of the Curcubitaceae family, and are a widely used vegetable in almost every Asian country. The gourd family includes the pumpkin, cucumber, winter melon and many different types of tropical gourd (such as snake gourd, angled gourd and bitter gourd). Gourds and melons are, strictly speaking, fruiting vegetables, since they are the fruit of a plant. However, they are normally treated as a savory ingredient, just like other vegetables,

although in some Asian countries, pumpkin is used in cakes and desserts (as It Is In America, with the famous pumpkin pie). Many of them are relatively neutral in flavor, so they lend themselves well to cooking in curries or soups, and are also delicious when paired with plain yoghurt and freshly grated coconut.

Angled Gourd is closely related to the loofah or sponge gourd, and indeed it is
sometimes called angled loofah. It is particularly appreciated in India (especially among
vegetarians), a country which probably consumes more gourds than anywhere else in
Asia. Angled gourd is also enjoyed in Southeast Asia, as well as in the hotter, more humid
southern regions of China. It is known as *ketola* in Malaysia, while the Filipinos call it *patola*.

Appearance & Flavor It is easy to recognize this gourd, which has a tough, pale green skin with ten firm,
angular ridges running from the stem end to the tip of the fruit. Angled gourd is eaten only when young,
as the flesh becomes tough and fibrous as it matures. The flavor of the young angled gourd is pleasantly
mild, almost sweet, making it, like the sponge gourd, one of the best of this family. **Choosing & Storing**
Select the smallest and youngest gourds available, preferably less than 8 in (20 cm) in length, and keep
refrigerated for a few days. **Preparing** Use a sharp knife to trim off the hard ridges and then peel off the
rest of the bitter skin only if the vegetable is starting to mature. Young or immature gourds need only
the ridges trimmed off—the remaining strips of dark green skin give the gourd a decorative appearance
and a contrasting texture to the pale, spongy flesh. Slice across. Do not remove the pithy center with the
immature seeds. **Nutritional & Medicinal Properties** Angled loofah is rich in beta-carotene and contains
moderate amounts of phosphorus. **Culinary Uses** This gourd is often added to soups or stir-fried dishes.
The Chinese like to add other ingredients with contrasting textures and flavors—such as crunchy wood
ear fungus and sliced pork—when stir-frying angled gourd. In India, the angled gourd, like most others,
is popular simmered until tender, then mixed with yoghurt, freshly grated coconut and spices.

Bitter Gourd is eaten in most parts of Asia, where there is a widespread belief that
anything that is bitter must have medicinal value. To reduce excessive bitterness, however,
the gourd is always salted. It is also thought by the Japanese to be helpful in counteracting
summer heat and humidity.

Appearance & Flavor The thin, corrugated skin of this gourd, which can be anything from 7 to 12 in (18 to
30 cm) in length, has wart-like bumps and is indeed very bitter. **Choosing & Storing** The younger, thinner,
shorter and brighter green in color, the less bitter the taste. Avoid any gourds which are slightly yellow, as
they are too old. Refrigerate in a plastic bag for up to 2 days. **Preparing** As the skin is very thin and tender,
do not peel. Wash, then slice the bitter gourd thinly, sprinkle liberally with salt and set aside for about 30
minutes to draw out some of the bitterness. Squeeze, rinse, squeeze again and pat dry before using. To
remove even more bitterness, the sliced and salted gourd can be blanched in boiling water until it turns
brighter in color. Plunge in ice water, then drain before further cooking. **Nutritional & Medicinal
Properties** It is rich in vitamins A and C and contains quinine—its anti-malarial properties, once a folk
belief, are now upheld by some in the medical profession. It is also believed to be good for low blood
pressure and for removing toxins from the body, or so the Chinese think. **Culinary Uses** Some Asians eat
thinly sliced gourd raw—after the initial salting—mixed with onions and perhaps a little chili, but
unaccustomed palates would almost certainly prefer it cooked. In India and Sri Lanka, bitter gourd slices
are seasoned with salt, turmeric and a little chili and deep-fried, while in China it is often left whole, the
central pith removed, and the gourd stuffed with seasoned minced pork or fish paste. It is then sliced and
steamed. The Chinese also stir-fry sliced bitter gourd, often adding an egg to the wok at the last minute.

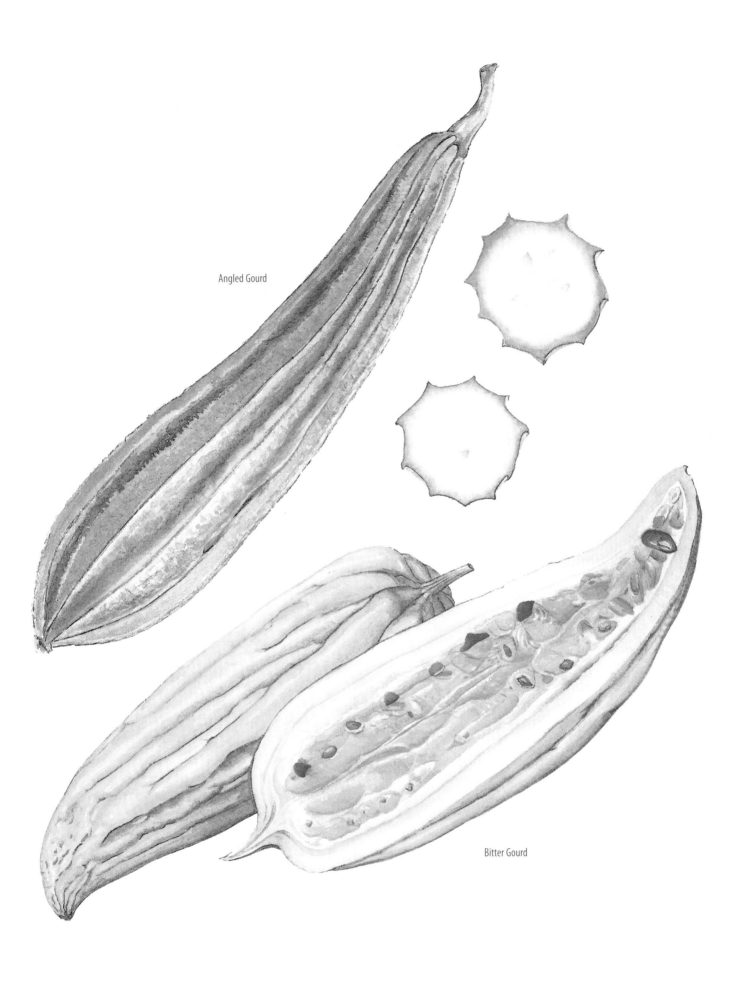

Angled Gourd

Bitter Gourd

Bottle Gourd has been cultivated in Africa and Central America for thousands of years, and is also found in most tropical and subtropical Asian countries. These gourds, left to mature and dry until the skin is tough and woody, resemble bottles—until recently, they were used as a common and inexpensive container in parts of rural Asia, especially those without a tradition of making pottery. Quite apart from its practical uses, the bottle gourd is appreciated throughout Asia as a vegetable. In Japan, strips of bottle gourd are dried (and known as *kanpyo*) and used to tie sushi or other foods.

Appearance & Flavor Two main varieties of bottle gourds are found—one is slim and relatively straight, and the other which has a bulbous base with a nipped "waist" before another slight bulge at the top or stem end. Both have the same mild flavor and fine-grained, soft texture. **Choosing & Storing** Choose the youngest, smallest bottle gourds available. Older gourds will be fibrous and contain tough seeds. Keep refrigerated in a vegetable drawer for 2–3 days. **Preparing** Peel the gourd and slice across. There is no need to discard the pith and immature seeds. **Nutritional & Medicinal Properties** Bottle gourds contain small amounts of phosphorus, calcium and vitamin C. **Culinary Uses** Throughout most of Asia, bottle gourds are stir-fried with onions, meat, prawns or vegetables. They can also be simmered in seasoned liquid or coconut milk. Bottle gourds are often diced and added to soups, especially in Chinese cuisine.

Chayote is an easily grown gourd which tends to run riot once the plant has taken root. It is not widespread in tropical Asia, although is very popular in the Philippines. A native of Central America, chayote is known by a long list of alternative names including custard marrow, choko, christophene and vegetable pear—a name which perhaps describes the size and shape of chayote perfectly. Its Chinese name *fuo shou gua* translates as "Buddha's hands." In Indonesia, it is called *labu siam*, *labu jepang* and *walu jepang*.

Appearance & Flavor This is a pale green, pear-shaped vegetable, covered with slightly prickly hairs. It has a delicate flavor and, when young and raw, a pleasant, crisp texture. **Choosing & Storing** Avoid buying any chayote which are starting to send out shoots, as these will be older. Choose young chayote, which are firm and lack well-developed hairs, and keep refrigerated for a few days. The skin of the chayote wrinkles when stored in a dry environment. **Preparing** It is difficult to completely remove all of the wrinkled skin with a vegetable peeler, and a small knife may be needed to get into the grooves. The chayote can be halved, sliced or diced as required. **Nutritional & Medicinal Properties** Chayote is rich in vitamin C, but the gourd is otherwise relatively low in nutrient content. **Culinary Uses** Finely sliced raw chayote can be used as a substitute for celery in salads. It can be simmered or halved lengthwise and steamed or baked with a savory filling. Do not discard the seed, which has a delicious flavor when boiled. Chayote can even be used as a substitute for cooked apple in countries where these are difficult to obtain or expensive. If using it in place of cooking apples, simmer the gourd until soft with traditional apple pie spices such as cinnamon, nutmeg and cloves, together with a little citric acid and brown sugar—chayote prepared this way tastes surprisingly like applesauce.

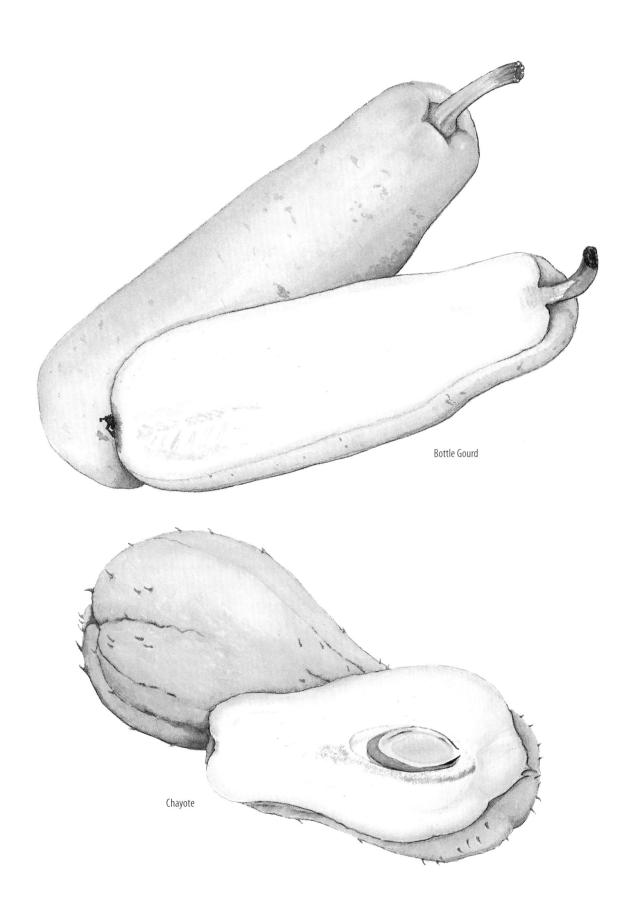

Bottle Gourd

Chayote

Eggplants are native to India, where they are commonly referred to as *brinjal*, while outside of Asia, they are sometimes known by their French name, aubergine. Other perhaps less common names for the plant include *melanzana*, garden egg and *partlican*. Eggplants are a member of the potato family. A wide variety of eggplants found in Asia, all of them considerably smaller and less bitter than the large, somewhat bulbous vegetable that is common in the West. The mild flavor of eggplants makes them a very versatile vegetable, and one which is enjoyed all the way from the cooler regions of northern Asia right through Southeast Asia to India.

Appearance & Flavor Eggplants come in a wide variety of shapes, sizes and colors in Asia. Their sizes range from the tiny, hard pea-sized vegetables to egg-shaped vegetables and long, slender eggplants. The pea-sized variety, known as *makhua puang* in Thailand, is generally pounded raw and mixed with seasonings to make a spicy dip, or used whole in Thai green curries. The color of eggplant ranges from white through bright orange to pale green, pale purple and deep purple and even green and purple varieties with bright white streaks. Apart from the bitter, pea-sized eggplant and a round, tough-skinned orange variety which is very sour, most eggplants have the same mild flavor, which lends itself well to all types of seasoning. **Choosing & Storing** Make sure the eggplants have no soft, spongy spots or tiny worm holes, and that their flesh is firm. Gently press a finger on the eggplant. If your finger leaves an indentation, the eggplant is probably too old. Conversely, unripe eggplants are hard. Gently tap your knuckles on the eggplant. If it sounds hollow, the flesh is probably too dry. The stems should be firm, as shriveled stems indicate the vegetables are too old—eggplants tend to turn bitter with age. Refrigerate the vegetable for a maximum of 3–4 days in a plastic bag, although eggplants are perhaps best consumed on the day of purchase. Many specialty stores outside Asia sell slender Asian eggplants, which are sometimes referred to as Japanese eggplants. **Preparing** Unless you are using the vegetable for pickling, Asian eggplants do not need salting—unlike their larger, more bitter Western counterparts—and their tender skin is edible. **Nutritional & Medicinal Properties** Eggplant has traces of phosphorus and beta-carotene and moderate levels of thiamin. The flesh contains about 6% carbohydrates and 1% protein. Some people believe ripe eggplant can be used as an expectorant, and can help prevent the onset of diabetes. **Culinary Uses** Eggplants are very versatile, and are cooked in countless ways from India through Southeast Asia and up to Japan, Korea and China. They are covered in batter and deep-fried in India and Japan; cooked and then spread with miso paste in Japan; deep-fried then braised in China; grilled and mashed with spicy seasonings and yoghurt (in India) or fish sauce (in Thailand, Cambodia, Laos and Vietnam); used whole; pan-fried with spicy sambals and dried prawns in Malaysia and Indonesia. In India, eggplants are sometimes pickled, or thinly sliced and dried for crisp frying at a later date, and added to curries or lentil stews.

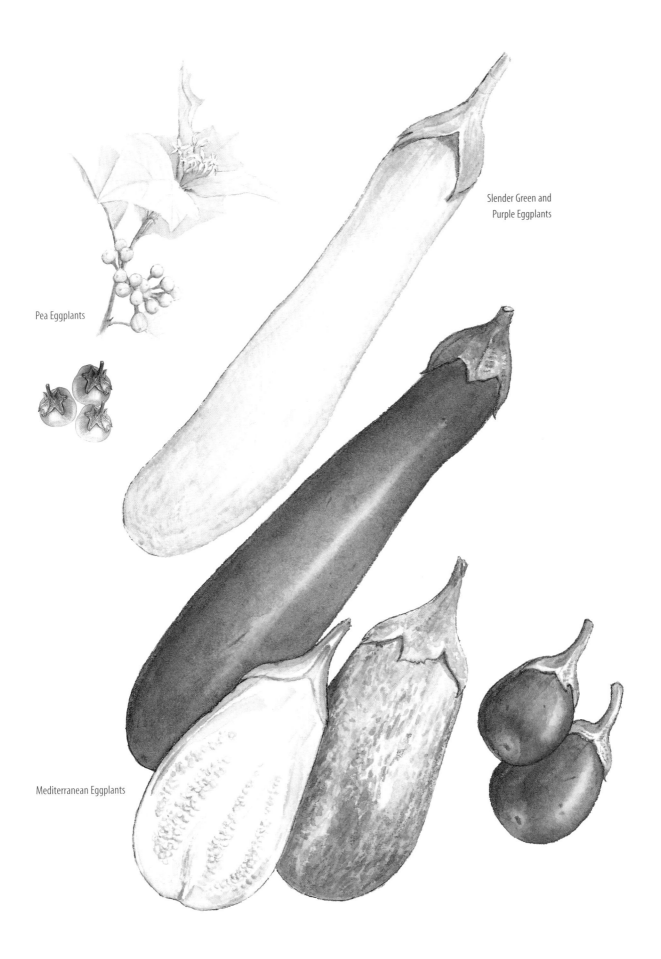

Slender Green and
Purple Eggplants

Pea Eggplants

Mediterranean Eggplants

Fuzzy Melons

Fuzzy Melons are related to the huge, round winter melons. Sometimes known as hairy melons, these small, elongated, fuzzy gourds are thought to have originated in Japan. They are popular in most of Asia for their pleasant flavor and fine texture.

Appearance & Flavor This gourd is fairly short, about 6–8 in (15–20 cm) in length, and looks somewhat like a zucchini or courgette, although it is slightly fatter in relation to its length. Fuzzy melons have rather blotchy, bright green skin covered with fine, soft hairs—hence their name. The vegetable has a pleasant, mild flavor and fine texture. **Choosing & Storing** Look for young gourds, which are bright green in color, the smaller the better in terms of texture after cooking. Keep refrigerated for a few days. **Preparing** Fuzzy melon is usually peeled and sliced or cubed for cooking, although its flesh can also be thinly sliced and eaten raw. Because of its convenient size, fuzzy melons are often halved lengthwise, the central pith removed, and then stuffed. **Nutritional & Medicinal Properties** This vegetable is easily digested, and does not contain significant amounts of vitamins or minerals. **Culinary Uses** Halved fuzzy melon is often filled with flavored minced pork and steamed. Slices or cubes can be stir-fried or are used in soups, stews and curries. Its relatively bland taste benefits from the addition of tasty seasonings such as ginger, spring onion, dried prawns and spices. If stir-frying, add other vegetables with contrasting colors and textures, such as black mushrooms, whole sugar peas, snow peas or water chestnuts and fried cashews.

Green Cucumbers

Green Cucumbers are thought to have originated in northern India and have spread throughout the world. In Asia, not only the fruit of the plant is eaten as a vegetable but the young shoots and leaves of the cucumber are also enjoyed. A range of different varieties are found in Asia, including the yellow-skinned cucumbers which are treated like a gourd and the small, thin Japanese cucumbers, as well as the most widespread variety, which has green skin and is medium in size.

Appearance & Flavor A number of varieties are found in Asia. In Southeast Asia, large oval cucumbers, with either green or yellowish skins, tend to have developed seeds and rather watery, bland flesh. The better varieties are slender, medium-sized green fruits, often with lighter green streaks, and average about 7 in (18 cm) in length. The slender, small, dark green-skinned variety popular in Japan and Korea (known in some other countries as Armenian, Japanese or Kirby cucumbers) has the best flavor of all, the thinnest skin and the finest texture. **Choosing & Storing** Choose firm cucumbers with no signs of yellowing. Keep refrigerated in the vegetable cooler for 4–5 days. **Preparing** Most Asian varieties do not need peeling, although the skin is often raked with a fork, and salt rubbed into the skin, left for a couple of minutes, and then rinsed off before slicing. This adds a very slight saltiness and gives the cucumber a decorative appearance when sliced. If the cucumber is young, there is no need to remove the seeds. Sliced or diced cucumber is frequently sprinkled with salt and left to stand for 15 minutes, squeezed and rinsed to draw out excess moisture. This is particularly the case if it is being mixed with yoghurt to make an Indian *raita*. **Nutritional & Medicinal Properties** Cucumber contains traces of calcium and phosphorus and moderate amounts of beta-carotene. Cooked immature cucumbers are a traditional cure for dysentery in children in Vietnam, Cambodia and Laos. **Culinary Uses** Although normally eaten raw, the Chinese pickle or stir-fry diced cucumber or cook it in soups.

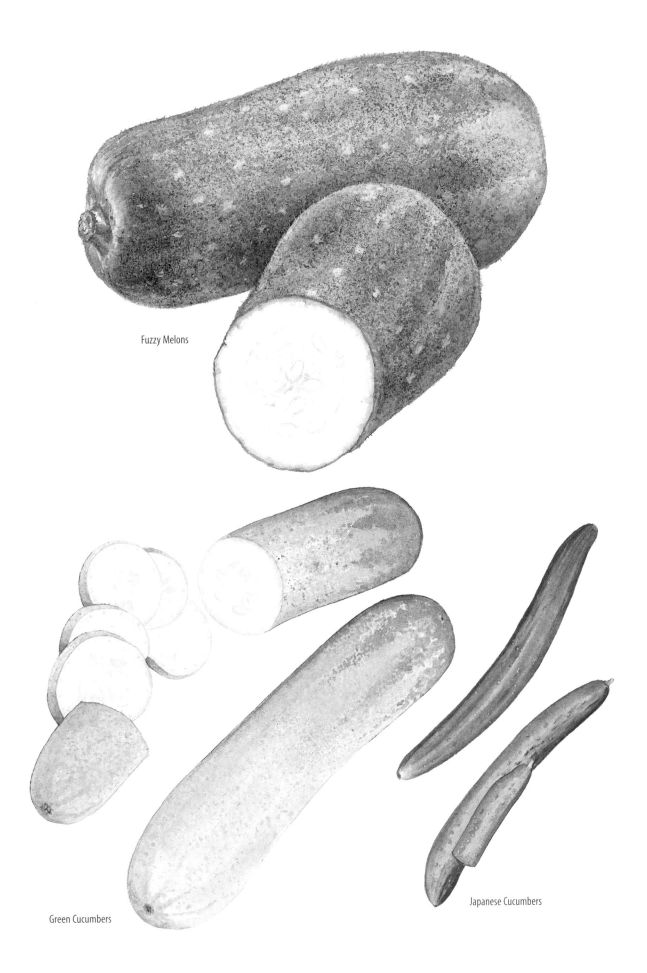

Fuzzy Melons

Green Cucumbers

Japanese Cucumbers

Loofah is closely related to the angled gourd (see page 80). The dried, mature form of this vegetable may be familiar to many who have never eaten it, for it is used to make the common loofah or coarse "sponge" found in bathrooms across the world. Because of this usage, the loofah is sometimes referred to as the sponge gourd or the "dishrag gourd" in Asia.

Appearance & Flavor These gourds are rather like large, slender cucumbers, with faint stripes running down the length of their rough skins. Young loofahs have a sweet flavor and soft texture. **Choosing & Storing** Look for the smallest, most slender gourds, preferably no longer than approximately 8 in (20 cm) in length, as older gourds are tough and fibrous, and better left to mature and become bathroom sponges. If still very young, loofahs often have the remnants of the flower still attached—generally, these flowers drop off after pollination and as the plant matures. Keep loofahs refrigerated in a vegetable drawer for 4–5 days. **Preparing** Wash the loofah well, then peel off the thin skin and slice the loofah across, leaving the soft central pith intact. **Nutritional & Medicinal Properties** Loofah contains traces of phosphorus and vitamin C and good levels of beta-carotene, and is classified as a "cooling" food in Chinese cuisine. **Culinary Uses** Think of this vegetable as a rather moist summer squash, zucchini or courgette. In Southeast Asia, it is often stir-fried with garlic and onion, with seasonings such as dried prawns or sauces such as soy sauce added to enhance the mild taste. Some cooks add a beaten egg at the last minute. Chinese cooks usually add this gourd to soups, such as pork rib soup or soups with tangy, preserved mustard cabbage for a flavor contrast. Loofah exudes quite a lot of moisture and cooks quickly.

Snake Gourd originated in India and enjoys popularity among Indian communities throughout Asia. Because of its tendency to twist while growing, the end of the gourd is often weighted with a stone on a piece of string to encourage it to grow straight.

Appearance & Flavor The snake gourd is a pale green vegetable, with an overlay of waxy white, revealing some darker green streaks beneath. The gourds generally grow with a slight twist at the end. Although they can measure up to 40 in (1 meter) or more, they are generally sold when they are in the region of 14–20 in (35–50 cm). The flavor of the snake gourd is slightly bitter, and its nutritional content somewhat higher than that of most other gourds. **Choosing & Storing** Choose the youngest, smallest snake gourds you can find, for as they mature the bitterness increases. Keep snake gourds refrigerated for 2–3 days. **Preparing** Sprinkle the skin with coarse salt and rub with a cloth to remove the waxy white coating, then cut it into thick slices. **Nutritional & Medicinal Properties** Snake gourds are very rich in beta-carotene and they also have reasonable levels of phosphorous. They are regarded as a general tonic, mainly because of the association of bitterness with health-giving properties in most of Asia. Some believe that the gourd is beneficial for treating jaundice, diabetes and coughs. In some parts of Asia, the fruit is dried and used as a substitute for soap. **Culinary Uses** Snake gourd is often used in vegetable stews and curries. It can also be simmered in water flavored with a little salt and turmeric, and when tender, tossed with freshly grated coconut pounded with onion, brown mustard seeds and chili.

Loofah

Snake Gourd

Winter Melons

Winter Melons are a favorite among Chinese chefs, who carve dragons or other auspicious symbols into the skin and use the melons as giant soup bowls at restaurant banquets. Closely related to the smaller fuzzy melon, the huge winter melon is sometimes known as wax gourd because of the waxy white coating on the skin. The flesh of this vegetable is excellent in soups. The Chinese also dry and crystalize diced winter melon.

Appearance & Flavor Winter melons are generally oval in shape and have a green skin covered with a waxy coating. Some are relatively small in size, weighing in the region of 2–4 lbs (1–2 kg). Others are positive giants, weighing up to 22 lbs (10 kg). The flesh is finely textured, and the flavor delicate, with no trace of bitterness. As the vegetable is 96% moisture, it is much appreciated for the juiciness of its flesh, especially in hot climates. **Choosing & Storing** Unless you want to try copying a Chinese chef, look for chunks or slices of winter melon in Asian stores. Make sure they smell fresh, and that the flesh is crisp. Keep refrigerated in a covered container for no longer than 1–2 days, as the flesh deteriorates once it has been cut. **Preparing** Remove the pith and seeds, and slice off the skin before dicing. **Nutritional & Medicinal Properties** Winter melons have moderate amounts of vitamin C and a high quantity of sodium, which is lost during perspiration. The Chinese believe that winter melon soup is helpful in cleansing the kidneys and encouraging urination. **Culinary Uses** Winter melon is almost exclusively used in soups in China, although it can also be stir-fried. Because of its mild flavor, it is generally simmered in chicken or pork stock, with flavorful ingredients such as shredded ham, dried prawns, preserved mustard cabbage and mushrooms. It can also be simmered with barley (believed to be cooling by the Chinese), azuki beans, mung beans or soy bean sprouts or, as in India, mixed with yoghurt, spices and freshly grated coconut.

Yellow Cucumber

Yellow Cucumber should not be confused with the common green cucumber or the crisp little Japanese cucumber, for this variety is not normally eaten raw. Found in China and also sometimes seen in markets in Southeast Asia (where it is popular mainly among the Chinese), this vegetable is treated much the same as any other gourd.

Appearance & Flavor Given its common name, it's not surprising that this oval vegetable (ranging from about 10–14 in/25–35 cm in length) has a coarse, yellowish brown skin that bears an appearance similar to that of cantaloupe. The texture and flavor are similar to the common cucumber, although the seeds are well developed by the time the vegetable reaches the market. The mature vegetable can weigh as much as 2 lbs (1 kg). **Choosing & Storing** Choose firm, fresh-looking cucumbers and keep refrigerated for 3–4 days. **Preparing** As this cucumber is normally cooked in pieces, leave the skin on to help prevent the slices or chunks from disintegrating. Wash the skin thoroughly, then halve lengthwise and remove the seeds—this is not essential and some cooks prefer to leave them intact. Cut the skin and flesh into slices or small chunks. **Nutritional & Medicinal Properties** The Chinese believe that this vegetable helps moisturize the lungs and prevent coughs, making it popular during hot, dry weather. **Culinary Uses** Yellow cucumber is normally cut into chunks, with the skin, pith and seeds left intact, and commonly added to Chinese soups made with chicken or pork stock. It is also made into a sweet pickle, which is often used in soups, piquant sauces or steamed fish.

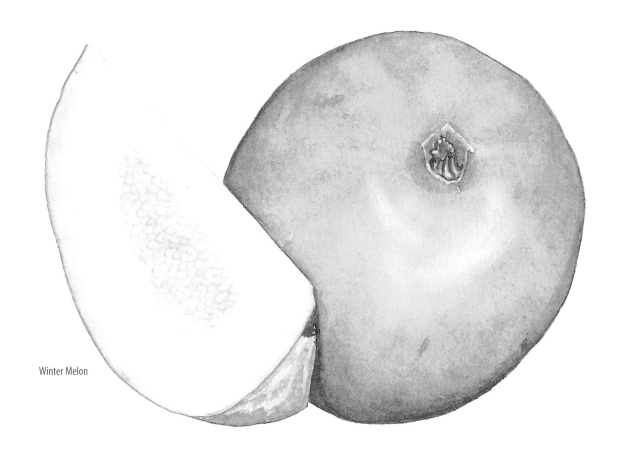

Winter Melon

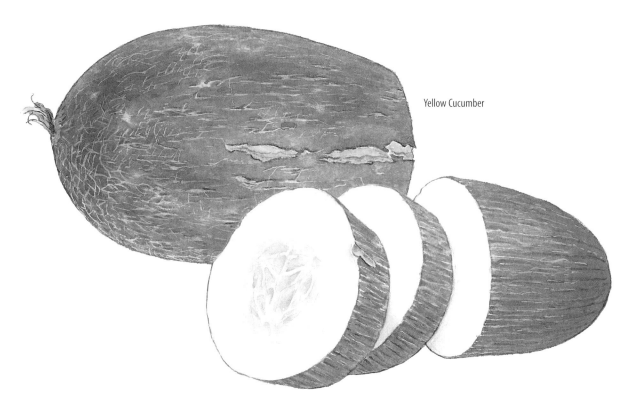

Yellow Cucumber

Eggplant Tamarind Curry

4 teaspoons *sambar* powder
1 teaspoon salt
4 cups (1 lb/500 g) eggplant
  chunks
5 tablespoons oil
1 teaspoon brown mustard seeds
1 teaspoon cumin seeds
1 onion, sliced
2 sprigs curry leaves
2 tomatoes, diced
1/2 cup (80 g) tamarind pulp mixed
  with 2 cups (500 ml) water, stirred
  and strained to obtain juice
1/2 teaspoon salt
1 2/3 cups (170 g) grated fresh
  coconut ground in a blender
  or food processor with 1/2 cup
  (125 ml) water until smooth

1 Mix 2 teaspoons of the *sambar* powder with the salt and coat all surfaces of the eggplants. Heat 3 tablespoons oil in a wok or a large frying pan, and toss the eggplants quickly to brown and soften slightly. Set aside.
2 Heat the remaining 2 tablespoons of oil in a large saucepan, add the mustard and cumin seeds and fry until aromatic. Add the sliced onion and curry leaves and stir-fry for 5 minutes, or until golden brown. Add the tomatoes and the rest of the *sambar* powder and fry for 1 minute. Reduce heat and stir-fry for about 5 minutes, until the oil separates.

3 Add the tamarind juice and salt and bring to a boil, then simmer for about 3 minutes. Add the fried eggplant and cook until soft, then add in the ground coconut and simmer for a further 2 minutes.

Note: *Sambar* powder can be bought in shops specializing in Indian ingredients.

Indian Mixed Vegetables with Coconut and Yoghurt

1 1/2 lbs (750 g) mixed vegetables
  such as bottle gourd, angled
  gourd, loofah, chayote, okra,
  round cabbage, green beans
  or parboiled potatoes
3–4 green chilies, halved lengthwise
1 teaspoon salt
1/2 teaspoon ground turmeric
1/4 teaspoon ground cumin
4–6 shallots, minced
1 cup (100 g) freshly grated or
  moistened desiccated coconut
1/2 cup (125 ml) plain yoghurt

1 Peel and prepare the vegetables, cutting into bite-sized pieces. Put in a saucepan and add chilies, salt, turmeric and ground cumin. Stir well and add just enough water to prevent the vegetables from drying out. Cover, then cook over low–medium heat until the vegetables are done. Remove the lid and continue cooking to evaporate all the liquid.

2 Pound the coconut and shallots together coarsely, then add to the yoghurt. Pour the yoghurt mixture to the cooked vegetables, and stir to mix well, then serve with rice and other dishes.

Eggplant Stir-fried with Basil

4 small, slender Asian eggplants,
  thinly sliced on the diagonal
Oil for deep-frying
4 cloves garlic, minced
1 teaspoon grated ginger
1 spring onion, thinly sliced
2 tablespoons soy sauce
2 teaspoons sugar
1/2 teaspoon sesame oil
2 tablespoons Thai *horapa* basil
  leaves, sweet basil or coriander
  leaves (cilantro)

1 Rinse the eggplant in salted water, drain and pat completely dry with paper towels.
2 Heat the oil in a wok over high heat for 30 seconds. When very hot, add the eggplant pieces and deep-fry for 1 minute. Remove and drain on paper towels.
3 Remove all but 2 teaspoons of the oil from the wok. Heat the oil and stir-fry the garlic, ginger and spring onion for 15 seconds. Add the

eggplant, soy sauce, sugar and sesame oil and stir-fry until the eggplant is tender. Sprinkle with basil or coriander leaves, stir to mix well then transfer to a serving dish.

Cucumber and Pineapple Salad

1 cucumber (about 1 lb/500 g)
1 teaspoon salt
2 slices fresh pineapple (10 oz/ 300 g) peeled, cored and diced
2 tablespoons thinly sliced torch ginger bud (optional)

Dressing
4 tablespoons dried prawns, dry-roasted in a work for 4–5 minutes
1–2 red chilies, sliced
1 teaspoon dried shrimp paste, toasted
1–2 tablespoons lime juice, depending on sweetness of the pineapple
2 tablespoons water
1 teaspoon sugar
1 teaspoon salt

1 To make the Dressing, put all the ingredients in a spice grinder or blender and grind to a paste.
2 Rake the skin of the cucumber with a fork and then rub it all over with the salt. Rinse under running water, squeeze the cucumber, then dice and place in a bowl with the pineapple and ginger bud (if using).

3 Add the Dressing to the diced cucumber and pineapple, toss and serve immediately.

Poached Eggplant Salad

3 slender Asian eggplants
Sprigs of coriander leaves (cilantro), to garnish

Dressing
6 cloves garlic, minced
1 teaspoon soy sauce
2 teaspoons white rice vinegar
$1/2$ teaspoon salt
1 teaspoon sugar
1 teaspoon black pepper
1 tablespoon sesame oil

1 In a small bowl, stir together all the Dressing ingredients, except the sesame oil. Then, using a whisk or fork, add in the sesame oil while beating continuously until the Dressing is well blended.
2 Bring a large pot of water to a full boil, then add the eggplants whole. Let the water return to the boil, then lower the heat and simmer until the eggplants change color and begin to wilt. This will take about 8 minutes.

Remove the eggplants from the water and set in a colander to drain.
3 Halve the eggplants lengthwise, then cut each half into 2-in (5-cm) pieces, and place in a mixing bowl.
4 Pour the Dressing evenly over the eggplants and toss to coat. Transfer to a smaller serving dish and serve.

Angled Gourd Soup

1 tablespoon oil
1 small onion, thinly sliced
1–2 cloves garlic, minced
4 oz (125 g) minced lean pork, (optional)
3 cups (750 ml) chicken stock
1 medium angled gourd, peeled and cut into thin slices
3 oz (100 g) glass noodles (*tung hoon*), soaked in warm water until soft

Salt, to taste
White pepper, to taste

1 Heat the oil in a saucepan and add the onion and garlic. Stir-fry until the onion becomes transparent, then add the pork and stir-fry until it changes color. Add the chicken stock and bring to a boil. Add the gourd and cook, with the pan covered, until the gourd is tender.

2 Add the noodles and salt to taste. Simmer for 1 minute, then transfer to soup bowls. Sprinkle with pepper and serve hot with rice together with other dishes.

Chinese Winter Melon Soup

5 cups (1$^1/_4$ liters) homemade
  chicken stock
2 dried black mushrooms, soaked
  in hot water to soften, stems
  discarded, caps thinly sliced
2 thin slices ginger, bruised
14 oz (400 g) winter melon or
  fuzzy melon, peeled, deseeded
  and cut into chunks
4 oz (125 g) pork fillet or loin, cut
  in very thin strips
White pepper, to taste

1 Put the chicken stock, mushrooms and ginger in a large saucepan and bring to a boil. Cover, lower heat and simmer for 5 minutes. Add winter melon and bring the mixture back to a boil. Partially cover the pan and simmer over low–medium heat for about 3 minutes.

2 Add the sliced pork, stir gently, and bring to a boil. Lower heat and simmer uncovered for 2 minutes. Using a ladle, transfer to a large soup bowl, sprinkle with pepper, and serve hot with rice and other dishes.

Indian Fried Eggplant with Yoghurt Sauce

$^1/_2$ cup (125 ml) oil
1$^1/_4$ lbs (600 g) eggplant, preferably
  slender Asian eggplant, cut in
  thin slices
1 clove garlic, minced
$^1/_2$ teaspoon salt
1 cup (250 ml) plain yoghurt
$^1/_2$ teaspoon ground cumin
$^1/_4$ teaspoon freshly ground
  black pepper
$^1/_4$ cup crisp fried shallots

1 Heat 1 tablespoon of the oil in a large skillet. Fry as many eggplant slices as possible over medium heat for 3–4 minutes, until golden brown. Turn the eggplant slices and pour 1 tablespoon oil around the sides of the pan. Fry until the eggplant is cooked, which should take another 3 minutes, then drain on paper towels. Repeat until all the eggplant has been cooked.

2 Place the garlic in a small bowl and add the salt. Crush as finely as possible with the back of a spoon. Stir in the yoghurt, ground cumin and pepper, mixing well. Serve the eggplant immediately or chill in the refrigerator. Just before serving, transfer the eggplant slices to a serving dish. Spoon the yoghurt sauce over the eggplant. Scatter with crisp fried shallots and serve as part of an Indian meal.

Indian Cucumber Raita

1 medium green cucumber
2 teaspoons salt
1 cup (250 ml) thick, plain yoghurt
2 shallots, very thinly sliced
2 tablespoons coarsely chopped
  coriander leaves (cilantro) or mint
  leaves
$^1/_2$ teaspoon ground cumin

1 Rake the skin of the cucumber lengthwise with a fork, then quarter the cucumber and remove any seeds. Dice the cucumber, then put in a bowl. Add salt, toss and refrigerate for 15 minutes.
2 After 15 minutes, rinse under running water, then squeeze the cucumber gently to remove liquid and place in a bowl.

3 Add the yoghurt, shallots and herbs, mixing well. Taste and add more salt if desired. Chill for about 1 hour.
4 Sprinkle the cucumber mixture with the cumin (preferably freshly ground from lightly toasted cumin seeds) and serve hot with rice and other dishes such as curries.

Stir-fried Loofah with Oyster Sauce

1 tablespoon oil
2 cloves garlic, minced
1$^1/_4$ lbs (600 g) loofah, peeled and
  thinly sliced
1 tablespoon oyster sauce
White pepper, to taste

1 Heat the oil in a wok or wide saucepan and add the garlic. Stir-fry over low–moderate heat for a few seconds, then add the loofah and stir-fry for 1 minute.

2 Cover the wok and cook for about 5 minutes or until the loofah slices are tender and the liquid has come out. Stir in the oyster sauce, sprinkle with pepper, then serve.

Fuzzy Melon with Black Mushrooms

2 tablespoons oil
1 tablespoon dried prawns, soaked to soften
1 medium onion, thinly sliced
2 dried black mushrooms, soaked to soften, caps thinly sliced
1 small fuzzy melon, peeled and cut into thick slices
1 in (2$^1/_2$ cm) ginger sliced into thin shreds
$^1/_2$ teaspoon salt
3 tablespoons water
White pepper, to taste

1 Heat the oil in a wok and add the dried prawns, onion and mushrooms. Stir-fry until the onion softens, then add the shredded melon, ginger and salt. Stir-fry for another 1 minute, then pour in the water, cover the wok and cook until the melon is tender. Sprinkle with pepper and serve.

Burmese Stir-fried Chayote

4 oz (125 g) lean pork, very thinly sliced
2 teaspoons rice wine or saké
$^1/_2$ teaspoon salt
White pepper, to taste
1 tablespoon oil
1 tablespoon garlic, minced
1 tablespoon fish sauce
2 small or 1 large chayote (about 14 oz/400 g), peeled, stone discarded, flesh sliced into thin shreds
$^1/_3$ cup (85 ml) water

1 Put pork in a bowl and sprinkle with wine, salt and pepper. Massage so that the wine is absorbed, and set aside to marinate for 15 minutes. Heat the oil in a wok and add the garlic. Stir-fry for a few seconds, then add the pork and stir-fry over high heat for 2 minutes. Splash with the fish sauce, stir for a few seconds, then add the chayote. Stir-fry for 1 minute, then add the water and continue frying for another 5 minutes, or until the vegetable slices are tender. Add a little water if the mixture threatens to burn. Serve hot with rice.

South Indian-style Snake Gourd

1 large onion, chopped
2–3 cloves garlic
2–3 green chilies, sliced
1$^1/_2$ lbs (600 g) snake gourd, skin salted, then rubbed with a cloth to remove the waxy white coating, and cut into thick slices
1 teaspoon ground cumin
1 teaspoon salt
$^1/_2$ cup (50 g) freshly grated or moistened desiccated coconut
Lime juice, to taste

Final Seasoning
2 teaspoons oil
1 teaspoon white lentils (husked black gram or *urad dal*)
1 teaspoon brown mustard seeds
12–16 fresh, frozen or dried curry leaves

1 To prepare the Final Seasoning, heat the oil in a small saucepan. Add the lentils, mustard seeds and curry leaves and stir-fry until the mustard seeds start to pop.
2 Coarsely grind the onion, garlic and chilies in a blender or food processor. Put in a saucepan and add the snake gourd, cumin and salt. Pour in sufficient water to just cover the gourd slices, then bring to a boil and simmer until tender. Pour the Seasoning into the snake gourd mix and add lime juice to taste.

HERBS

Herbs are an essential part of most Asian cuisines, and nowhere more so than in the tropical countries of Southeast Asia. While spring onions (see page 140) are perhaps the most important herb in Chinese cuisine, with fresh coriander leaves or cilantro also being popular, cool-climate Japan has a wider range of herbs, many of which are now available outside Asia.

Both India and Sri Lanka favor a limited range of herbs, generally preferring dried spices to give flavor to food. However, when it comes to Southeast Asia, a huge number of cultivated and wild herbs are used with almost gay abandon. They are added to cooked food (often at the last minute to retain maximum aroma), as a garnish, and frequently served raw as part of a platter of fresh herbs and vegetables that often includes bean sprouts, lettuce and other leafy vegetables.

Asian Basils

Asian Basils come in three different varieties in the warmer countries of Asia. The most common variety has an intense aroma, and is generally known abroad as Asian or Thai basil and as *horapa* and *daun kemangi* in Malaysia and Indonesia. Lemon-scented basil (*manglak* in Thai) is usually cooked rather than eaten raw. Hot basil or holy basil, known as *kaprow* in Thai, is so called because it is sacred to the Hindus and planted around temples. *Kaprow* has a strong aroma and is used in only a few dishes.

Appearance & Flavor Thai basil has medium to dark green leaves with a purple tinge to the upper stems, purplish flower heads and an intense aniseed aroma. Lemon-scented basil has smaller, soft pale green leaves and a distinct lemony fragrance which is intensified after brief cooking. Holy basil has small, dark green leaves and a strong flavor. **Choosing & Storing** Choose brightly colored, fresh-looking basil without any hint of wilting. Wrap leaves (still on the stems) in paper towels and keep refrigerated in a covered container or sealed plastic bag for 2–3 days. **Preparing** Wash and dry well. Tender sprigs can be used, but separate the leaves from the harder stems. **Nutritional & Medicinal Properties** Asian basil contains an appreciable amount of vitamin C. The leaves are also thought to help digestion. **Culinary Uses** Asian or Thai basil can be eaten raw, added to soups and salad platters, and also added at the last minute to stir-fried or simmered dishes. Lemon-scented basil is usually cooked to help intensify its flavor; in addition, the seeds are soaked until they swell and develop a jelly-like coating and are used in a number of desserts. Holy basil is cooked with some beef, chicken and noodle dishes.

Thai Basil (Horopa)

Lemon Basil (Manglak)

Holy Basil (Kaprow)

Asian Pennywort

Asian Pennywort is a powerful little leaf, full of medicinal value, which grows wild throughout tropical and subtropical regions. It is one of the most popular folk medicines in Asia, its medicinal value confirmed by Western research. The herb is sometimes known by its Sinhalese name, *gotu kala*, or the Vietnamese *nuoc rau ma*.

Appearance & Flavor Asian pennywort grows in clumps of long, thin stems with rounded, penny-sized leaves from long runners which, if planted in the vegetable garden, soon take over. When sold in markets or Asian stores, the stems and leaves are usually tied together to form a bundle. The flavor is slightly bitter, but this is often offset by combining Asian pennywort with sweet ingredients such as freshly grated coconut, or by making them into a sugared drink (a Vietnamese favorite). **Choosing & Storing** Buy leaves which look fresh and firm. Wash well, wrap in kitchen paper, and keep refrigerated for 2–3 days. **Preparing** Pull the leaves off the stems, wash, drain, then blanch or use raw. Most Asians believe Asian pennywort has more medicinal value when used raw. The leaves should be sliced finely just before eating. **Nutritional & Medicinal Properties** Asian pennywort is rich in vitamin A. The plant has been shown to have anti-inflammatory properties, and is recommended for the relief of arthritic or rheumatic pains. It is thought by many Southeast Asians to be good in purifying the blood and medical research does indicate that it helps thin the blood, and in large doses, it helps lower blood sugar levels. In India, Asian pennywort is regarded as a cure for dysentery, and is also seen as good for fevers, asthma and bronchitis and for boosting memory and concentration. **Culinary Uses** Because of its slight bitterness, Asian pennywort is often mixed with freshly grated coconut and spices, and served as a side dish with rice at meals. Asian pennywort can also be made into the popular Vietnamese drink, named *rau ma* after the herb, by blending a handful of leaves with water and a little sugar syrup.

Chinese Celery

Chinese Celery is thought to be native to northern Asia and the Asian variety bears very little resemblance to the broad-ribbed, blanched celery grown in the West. Chinese celery, which has been cultivated for around 2,500 years, is a much smaller plant, and is considerably more pungent in flavor than the Western variety. This being the case, it is used as a seasoning herb rather than as a vegetable.

Appearance & Flavor Usually the whole plant, about 7–8$^1/_2$ in (18–22 cm) in length, is sold with the roots still intact. Chinese celery has thin, light green stems and leaves like those of Western celery. The flavor is very strong, so this type of celery is used as a flavoring vegetable or herb rather than as a main vegetable. Take care not to confuse this plant with fresh coriander plants, which are somewhat similar in size and shape. **Choosing & Storing** Look for plants with firm stems and leaves which are not wilting. Keep refrigerated for up to 1 week with the roots in a jar containing a little water, covering the entire plant and jar with a large plastic bag. **Preparing** Wash well and chop the stems, if using. The leaves are either sliced as a garnish, or used whole in soups, often attached to their stems. **Nutritional & Medicinal Properties** Both celery stems and seeds have medicinal qualities, acting as a diuretic and urinary antiseptic and helping to lower blood pressure. Chinese celery is also nutritious, rich in both vitamins and minerals. **Culinary Uses** The stems and leaves are used sparingly, generally as a flavoring vegetable rather than eaten alone. The stems make a pleasant addition to stir-fried dishes, especially noodles and rice, while the leaves are used either raw as a garnish, or stir-fried in vegetable or noodle dishes. A sprig of stems and leaves is frequently added to meaty soups, especially those using beef. Chinese celery is so popular for flavoring soups in Malaysia that it is known as *daun sop*, literally "soup leaf."

Coriander Leaves or Cilantro

are found in most Asian cuisines as well as in the Middle East, Greece, Mexico, Central and South America. The coriander plant is ancient —coriander seeds have been found in Egyptian tombs dating back some 3,000 years. The plant reached China about 1,000 years ago. Today, the coriander leaf is used throughout Asia, although the root is an important seasoning only in Thailand.

Appearance & Flavor The coriander plant has delicate, feathery leaves growing on long, slender stems, with a creamy white root about $1^1/_2$–2 in (4–5 cm) in length and a few hair-like straggly rootlets. The plant is normally sold whole, the presence of the root helping it keep better. The leaves have a distinctive aroma, which is quite unique and delicious, although it reminds some of those who do not care for it of squashed insects (the English name comes from the Greek word *koris* for "bug"). **Choosing & Storing** Look for plants where the stems and leaves are still firm and bright and not starting to wilt. Stand the plant with the roots still intact in a jar containing about 1 in ($2^1/_2$ cm) of water. Cover the entire plant and jar with a roomy plastic bag and keep refrigerated for up to a week. If condensation forms inside the bag after 2–3 days, wipe it off with a towel. When the leaves have been used, wash and slice the roots finely and deep-freeze in a small container for use in Thai cooking. **Preparing** Wash and dry the coriander leaves and use either whole or chopped, according to the recipe.

Nutritional & Medicinal Properties Coriander leaves are very rich in beta-carotene, calcium, phosphorus and vitamin C. They are believed to be a mild stimulant and are a traditional ingredient in cough mixtures and herbal brews given after childbirth in some Asian countries. **Culinary Uses** Coriander leaves (and often the stems) are pounded or processed and added to curry pastes in Thailand, Laos and Cambodia. Fresh coriander chutney is very popular in India. Chopped coriander leaves are added to many salads and fillings throughout Asia, and served as part of a platter of fresh green vegetables and herbs in Southeast Asia. They are used as an edible garnish in many dishes and added to soups and noodle dishes. The root is pounded with black peppercorns and garlic to make a seasoning in Thailand.

Curry Leaves give a distinctive flavor to many dishes in South India, Sri Lanka and Burma. In Singapore and Malaysia, they are used not only by cooks of Indian origin but by those of other ethnic backgrounds. They are often available deep-frozen or dried in Asian stores, especially those specializing in Indian ingredients.

Appearance & Flavor Curry leaves grow on a small–medium tree found in the wild but often cultivated in kitchen gardens. In markets, curry leaves are generally sold in sprigs consisting of 12–16 small, slightly pointed, dull green leaves. The flavor is faintly spicy and the leaves very aromatic. **Choosing & Storing** The fresh leaves are generally sold on the stems. They should look fresh; wrap in paper towels and refrigerate in a covered container for up to 2 weeks. Curry leaves keep well if deep-frozen; pull the leaves off the stems and store them in a loose, tightly sealed plastic bag. You can also dry the leaves gently over low heat in an oven and store them in an airtight container. **Preparing** Wash and dry, then pull the leaves off the stem before using. **Nutritional & Medicinal Properties** The exact nutritional content of the leaves is not known. Some believe the leaves are good for the stomach, but may be a mild laxative. **Culinary Uses** Curry leaves release their flavor only after cooking. They are generally fried in a little oil, sometimes together with mustard seed and black gram lentils, before being added at the last minute to lentil, vegetable and rice dishes. Do note, however, that some cooks recommend that you always stir-fry the curry leaves first before adding any other ingredients. Stand back from the fire when frying fresh curry leaves as they cause much splattering and hissing when added to hot oil—dried curry leaves do not splatter as much, but they burn rapidly and lack the intensity of the fresh leaves. Curry leaves are also often added to fish curries, fried together with other seasonings before the fish and liquid are added.

Kaffir Lime Leaves have an intense and inimitable citrus fragrance which is indispensible in many dishes throughout Southeast Asia. The lime trees are often available in specialist nurseries and grow well in temperate and tropical climates. Fresh or frozen kaffir lime leaves are increasingly found in Asian stores. Dried leaves are a poor substitute.

Appearance & Flavor The kaffir lime leaf is recognizable by its double-leaf structure resembling a figure "8." The leaves have an intense citrus aroma and flavor. **Choosing & Storing** Fresh kaffir lime leaves are available in most grocery stores and markets in Asia. Alternatively, you may use dried or frozen leaves, or even grow your own kaffir lime tree—nurseries in many parts of the world have begun selling the plant. Kaffir lime trees grow well in both tropical and temperate climates. Freeze fresh leaves in a bag. Chop or tear the edges slightly before adding to simmered dishes while still frozen. **Preparing** To shred, fold the leaf in half lengthwise and cut out the tough central rib. Roll up the leaves from the tip to stem, like a cigar, then lay on a board and cut into hair-like shreds with a sharp knife. **Nutritional & Medicinal Properties** The leaves are said to contain some essential oils. **Culinary Uses** Whole leaves are frequently added to soups or curries, often at the last minute to preserve their aroma. Tender and young fresh leaves can be sliced into hair-like strips—discard the tough mid-rib—and used raw in salads. As a last resort, you may substitute kaffir lime leaves with the young leaves of lemon, lime or grapefruit. The rind of the kaffir lime is also a common seasoning in Southeast Asia.

Curry Leaves

Kaffir Lime Leaves

Kinome is the Japanese name for the young sprigs of the prickly ash, a tree which develops pods that are ground to make a type of pepper known as *sansho* in Japan; the pods are very similar to the Sichuan pepper used in Chinese cuisine. Fresh sprigs of *kinome* are sometimes found in Japanese stores during the springtime.

Appearance & Flavor The bright green sprays of small, fragrant young leaves have a pleasant delicate flavor somewhat like mint, and a tender texture. **Choosing & Storing** *Kinome* is seasonal; it is found only in spring. Sprays of the leaf are usually sold in plastic containers kept in the cold section of Japanese stores. The leaves are best used as soon as possible after purchase, although they can be kept refrigerated in a plastic bag in the vegetable drawer for 3–4 days. **Preparing** Wash the leaves and dry them. **Culinary Uses** Sprigs of *kinome* make a beautiful edible garnish for soups, bean curd dishes, grilled and simmered food.

Lemongrass is one of the most important herbs in Southeast Asia, and is widely enjoyed for its distinctive lemony flavor and fragrance. Packets of thinly sliced, deep-frozen lemongrass are often available in Asian stores abroad and are a good substitute for the fresh product. Only the inner part of the thick lower third of the stem is edible—the edible portion of a single stalk is equivalent to 2 tablespoons of frozen lemongrass slices. If you live in a moderately warm climate and would like to grow lemongrass, keep the cut stems of fresh lemongrass in water until they start to send out roots. Transfer to a large pot and place in a sunny spot in the garden (gloves are advised when handling the plant as the edges of the leaves are very sharp) and keep watering the shoot regularly. The lemongrass should multiply during the summer.

Appearance & Flavor Lemongrass grows in clumps up to about 32 in (80 cm) in height. The lower portion (about 8 in/20 cm) of each plant is a tightly packed bulb, a little like a miniature leek, while the top part of the lemongrass has coarse, broad leaves which are not used in cooking. Lemongrass has a strong citrus flavor and aroma. **Choosing & Storing** Look for firm stems which show no signs of wilting and are not starting to dry out. Trim off the leaves and keep about 5–6 in (12–14 cm) of the stem. Stand the stem in a glass, with the end in a small amount of water and keep in a warm place for up to about 2 weeks before using it as required. Alternatively, trim the lemongrass and store in the refrigerator for 2–3 weeks, or slice finely and place in a sealed plastic bag in the freezer. Kept this way, lemongrass can be stored for several months. **Preparing** Usually, only the tender inner part of the bottom one-third or 3 in (8 cm) is used for slicing and pounding; peel off two or three of the tough outer leaves to get to the inner portion. As even the inner stem is fibrous, it must be sliced as finely as possible before being used pounded or processed. If using the stem whole, bruise by pounding with a pestle before adding to the pan to release the fragrance. **Nutritional & Medicinal Properties** Tea made from simmered lemongrass is used to treat fever, diarrhea and headaches. The leaves are added to a bath to help improve circulation, to perfume the body as well as to reduce swelling. The essential oil extracted from lemongrass is a very common ingredient in aromatherapy, contains antiseptic properties and is also thought to help circulation. **Culinary Uses** Very finely sliced lemongrass is used raw in many salads; the inner part of the stem is often ground and used as part of a seasoning paste, while bruised lengths of stem are added to soups and curries. Lemongrass stems can also be used as an aromatic skewer.

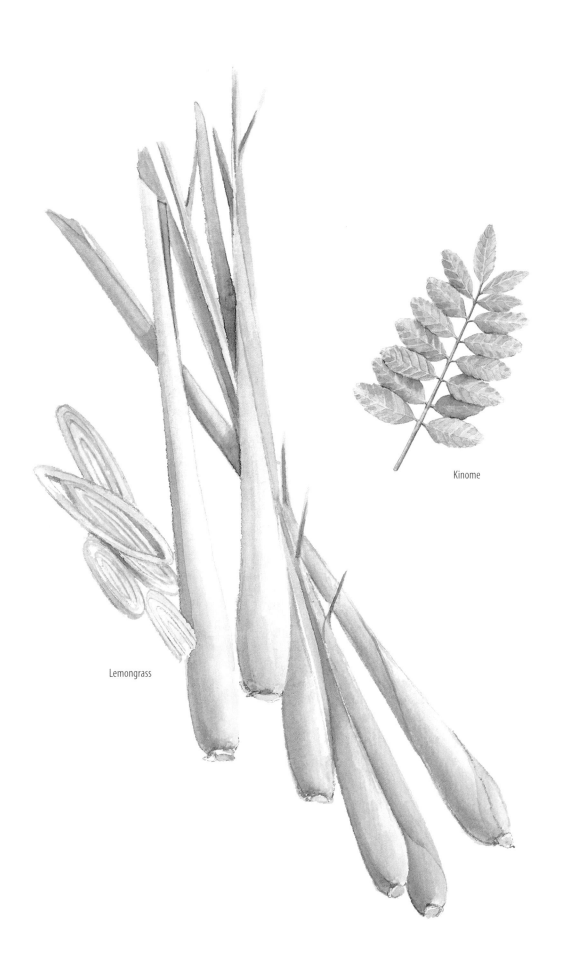

Kinome

Lemongrass

Mitsuba is the Japanese name for what is also known as Japanese parsley or trefoil, meaning "three leaves." In Japan, stalks of *mitsuba* are tied into a knot and added to a dish on important occasions—the knot is regarded as an auspicious symbol. *Mitsuba* grows readily in a temperate climate and is often sold packaged in plastic bags in the refrigerated section of Japanese or other Asian stores.

Appearance & Flavor This decorative vegetable has three small leaves growing from a narrow stem. The flavor is somewhat reminiscent of parsley mixed with fresh coriander leaves. **Choosing & Storing** Look for fresh-looking, young leaves and keep refrigerated in a paper-lined plastic container for 2–3 days. **Preparing** Rinse and drain before using raw or adding to cooked dishes. **Nutritional & Medicinal Properties** Mitsuba is believed to be rich in vitamin C and carotene although its nutritional properties are largely unknown. **Culinary Uses** Mitsuba is added whole to salads or used as a garnish. It can also be shredded and added to soups or steamed Japanese custard. Several stalks can be tied together and the whole lot dipped in tempura batter and deep-fried. Do not overcook or it loses its delicate fragrance.

Pandanus Leaves come from a variety of pandanus plant and are sometimes called fragrant screwpine or pandan. Fragrant pandanus leaves grow easily in tropical climates and are used widely in both savory and sweet dishes. Pandan essence, sold in small bottles, is sometimes used as a substitute in cakes and desserts.

Appearance & Flavor The blade-like leaves grow up to about 20 in (50 cm) in length, but are often sold trimmed. They have a strong but very pleasant, almost woody perfume. **Choosing & Storing** Whereas the leaves are widely available in Asian countries—both in the markets and in the garden—pandanus leaves are sold either in powdered form or frozen in other parts of the world. The fresh pandanus leaves are often cut into more manageable lengths, then sealed in plastic packs, which can be kept refrigerated for several days; any left over can be deep-frozen. **Preparing** Rake the leaves with a fork to help release the juice, and tie into a knot if using long leaves. If making pandanus juice for cakes, slice finely and process. Add 2–3 tablespoons water while processing, then strain. **Nutritional & Medicinal Properties** Pandanus leaves are thought by Asians to have a "cooling" effect on the body and believed to be good for treating bleeding gums, internal inflammation, colds and coughs. The leaves have another interesting application —they are commonly used as insect repellents in Singapore and other parts of Southeast Asia: pandanus leaves seem to release some chemicals that keep cockroaches at bay. **Culinary Uses** To the Asian chef, the pandanus leaf is perhaps what vanilla essence is to his or her Western counterpart. Cooks often add pandanus leaves to the pot when cooking rice for their subtle, sweet fragrance—rice cooked this way tastes like it has been newly harvested. Pandanus leaves are also used in some curries. The leaves are often chopped and processed for the bright green fragrant liquid used to make pancakes or desserts. Thai cooks also use the leaves as a wrapper for various sweetmeats, desserts and jellies, and for pieces of marinated chicken which are deep-fried in the leaves.

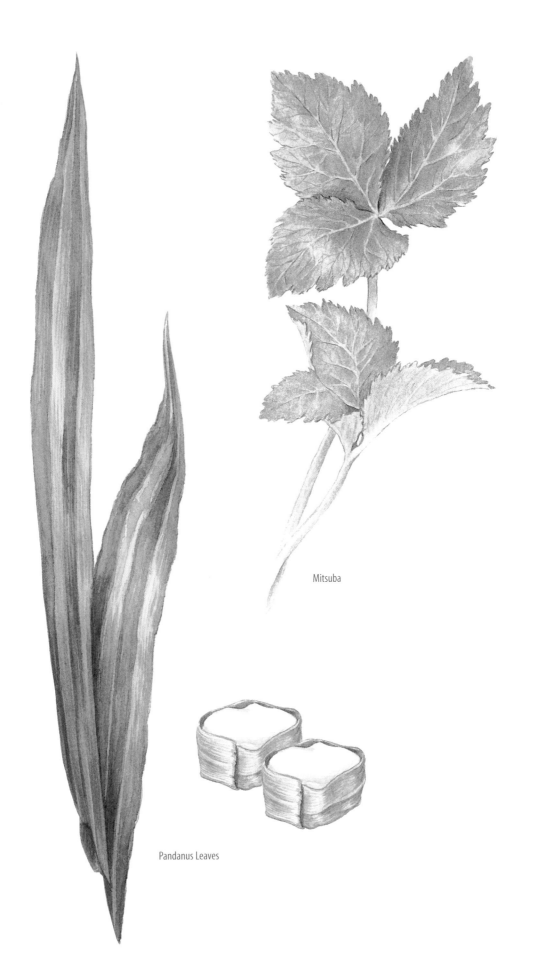

Mitsuba

Pandanus Leaves

Peperomia is a tropical American native, although it grows wild in much of Southeast Asia. Botanists have discovered more than a thousand species of the herb. The delicate, heart-shaped leaf of peperomia makes it easily recognizable in the stores. The herb is particularly popular in Thailand and Vietnam, where it is eaten raw or blanched. It can often be found in Asian, particularly Vietnamese, stores in the West. The Vietnamese name is *cang cua*, while the Thais refer to it as *phak krasang*.

Appearance & Flavor Small, heart-shaped leaves grow on short stems from a central stem; because of its decorative appearance, peperomia is sometimes grown for ornamental purposes. Peperomia belongs to the Piperaceae family and like many of its other members, the vegetable has a fairly pronounced taste and smell—some think the herb has an almost fishy smell. **Choosing & Storing** The plant is usually sold in bunches, with leaves growing from succulent stems. They should look plump and fresh. Wrap in paper and keep refrigerated for 2–3 days. **Preparing** Strip the stems and tender stalks from the central stem before using. **Nutritional & Medicinal Properties** The leaves of peperomia are a good source of beta-carotene, iron and calcium and also contain appreciable amounts of phosphorus. The crushed leaves are used for curing headaches and fever in Indonesia, while the juice squeezed from the leaves is taken as a medicine for stomach pains. **Culinary Uses** Sprigs of peperomia are usually eaten raw or lightly blanched with a dip, or added to mixed salads.

Polygonum or Laksa Leaf is known by a number of other names including hot mint, Vietnamese mint (*rau ram*) and long-stemmed mint. It is used in Malaysia, Thailand, Vietnam, Cambodia and Laos. The plant is often sold in Asian stores overseas. Alternatively, you can grow your own polygonum if you live in a relatively warm climate. Stand a few stems in water in a glass set in a sunny spot (the window sill, perhaps); as soon as you see white roots appearing, plant it in soil in a sunny position and water frequently. Perhaps an easier way to ensure a ready supply of fresh leaves would be to visit a nursery selling Asian plants and see if you can find polygonum.

Appearance & Flavor Polygonum leaves grow on thin stems. They are narrow and dark green in color, sometimes with small pinkish purple flowers growing at the tip. The herb has an intense peppery flavor and despite what some of its names suggest, is not really similar to mint. **Choosing & Storing** Look for fresh stems. Stand in a jar with about 1 in (2$\frac{1}{2}$ cm) of water, cover with a plastic bag and refrigerate for a few days. **Preparing** Wash, dry and chop coarsely or use whole as directed by the recipe. **Culinary Uses** This distinctively flavored herb is frequently part of a platter of fresh herbs served with noodle soups, spring rolls and other foods in Laos, Cambodia and Vietnam. It is an essential ingredient in Singapore's famous laksa noodle soup, hence one of its common names.

Peperomia

Polygonum (Laksa Leaves)

Rice Paddy Herb

is known as *ngo om* in Vietnam and *ma om* in Cambodia. This distinctive herb is one of several similar species that grow wild in rice paddies and ponds. In Vietnam, because of its popularity, rice paddy herb is cultivated in flooded rice fields. It can be grown in any warm, humid environment.

Appearance & Flavor The plant has a fleshy pale stem with narrow, light green leaves. The trumpet-like flowers grow at the tip of the stem and are pale purple with a white heart. The flavor of rice paddy herb is unique, somewhat lemony, with perhaps a hint of cumin. **Choosing & Storing** Choose fresh-looking plants and stand them in a glass or jar containing a small amount of water. Put in the plants and cover the jar entirely with a plastic bag to retain moisture. Keep refrigerated for 3–4 days. **Preparing** Wash and use the leaves whole. **Nutritional & Medicinal Properties** The plant is used in Asia for almost everything, from the treatment of wounds to indigestion, fever and dysentery. The leaves of the rice paddy herb contain a small amount of essential oils. **Culinary Uses** Rice paddy herb is often eaten raw, served as part of a herb platter or eaten with dips. It seems to have an affinity for fish, and is added to fish soups, fish stews and steamed fish, as well as to mild chicken curry in Vietnam.

Salam Leaves

grow on a large tree that is a member of the *Cassia* family. The leaf, either fresh or dried, adds a distinctive note to many Indonesian dishes, particularly in Java and Sumatra. There is no substitute for *salam* leaves.

Appearance & Flavor *Salam* leaves are large and green in color, and are rather stiff and dry. When fully dried, they lose most of their green color, turning light brown. The flavor of *salam* leaves is unique but hard to describe. It is, however, quite different to the Western bay leaf which is sometimes wrongly suggested as a substitute. **Choosing & Storing** If you can obtain fresh *salam* leaves, keep them in a bag in the freezer; otherwise, keep dried leaves in an airtight container in the freezer for lengthy storage. **Preparing** Add the whole leaf as required. **Culinary Uses** *Salam* leaves are used in soups, curries and dishes which require simmering in Indonesian cuisine.

Sawtooth Herb

is often referred to as sawtooth coriander, owing to its strong resemblance in flavor to that popular herb. Sawtooth herb is also known in Cambodia as *chi bonla* or *chi barang*, *prik chee farang* in Thailand and *ngo gai* in Vietnam. In Western countries, it is sometimes referred to by its botanical name, eryngo.

Appearance & Flavor The flat, broad leaves of this plant have distinctly serrated leaves, hence the name "sawtooth." The mature plant, which grows easily in warm areas, spreads quickly. It develops a long central spike containing green, star-like flower heads, which make an attractive (though non-edible) garnish. The flavor resembles a cross between coriander, mint and basil. **Choosing & Storing** Sometimes the entire plant is sold, or the leaves may be packed loose in a plastic bag. Wrap in paper towels and keep refrigerated in a covered container. **Preparing** Wash, dry and serve the leaves either whole, torn or coarsely chopped. **Culinary Uses** Sawtooth herb is frequently added to soups and are sometimes served as part of a platter of herbs with Vietnamese food. Coriander leaves are its best substitute.

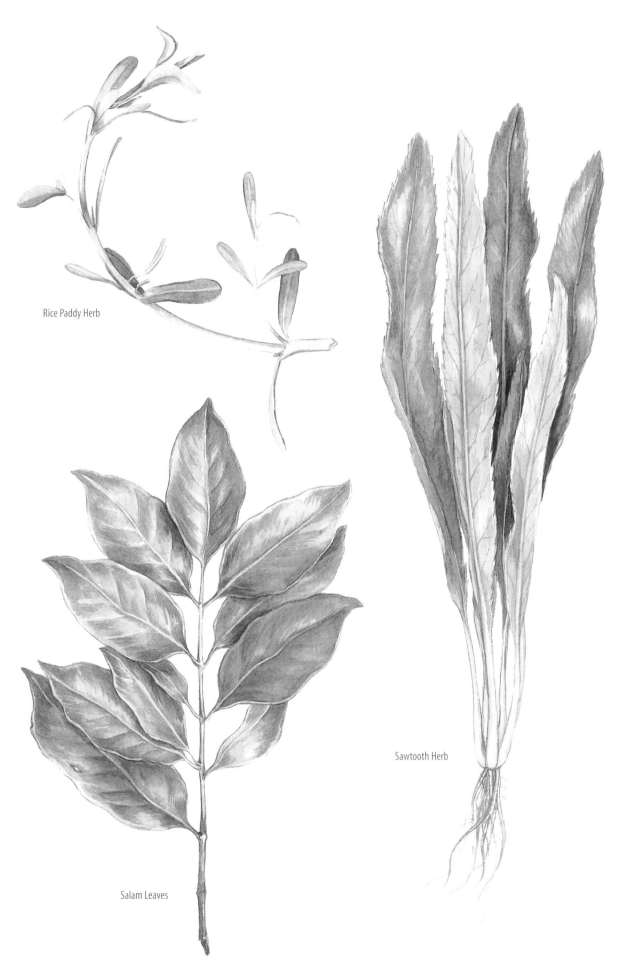

Rice Paddy Herb

Salam Leaves

Sawtooth Herb

Shiso or Perilla

is an aromatic plant popular in Vietnam and Japan as well as in the neighboring countries of Laos and Cambodia. Although it is rarely used in contemporary Chinese cuisine, *shiso* was once a common vegetable and a source of cooking oil in ancient China. The spicy leaf is sometimes referred to as beefsteak plant. Both the leaves and the delicate flower sprigs can be used, with the latter being a popular edible garnish in Japan.

Appearance & Flavor Two varieties of *shiso* are available. One has flat, green leaves yielding a more intense spicy taste than the other, which is somewhat crinkly and purplish red in color. The red variety is often known as beefsteak plant probably because of its red, beef-colored leaves. The herb has a flavor that is a combination of basil and mint, but with the intensity of anise. **Choosing & Storing** *Shiso* is sometimes sold in plastic packs in Japanese stores. Keep the leaves refrigerated for 2–3 days—do not remove the plastic packaging or the leaves may dry out. **Preparing** Wash, dry and use the leaves whole. If there are any flower sprays, wash, dry and use fresh. **Nutritional & Medicinal Properties** *Shiso* is believed to have antibiotic properties and is used by Asian herbalists to prevent influenza, treat coughs, lung ailments and seafood poisoning. **Culinary Uses** *Shiso* is used extensively in Japanese cooking. Whole leaves can be used as an edible garnish, dipped in tempura batter and deep-fried, or used to wrap sushi. Southeast Asian cooks sometimes use *shiso* as a substitute for common basil in western dishes, and also add *shiso* to a platter of fresh herbs served with barbecued and grilled foods and fried spring rolls. In Japanese or Korean cooking, the leaves—either fresh or pickled—are used as a seasoning for fish, rice, vegetables and soups. The red variety is also used to make a pink dye used to color vinegar and rice.

Wild Pepper Leaves

are frequently but incorrectly referred to as betel leaves. Wild pepper leaves are botanically known as *Piper sarmentosum*, while the leaf used to wrap sliced areca nut to form what is known as a betel nut chew is actually *Piper betel*. Used mainly as a wrapper and a flavoring herb, wild pepper leaves are known as *daun kaduk* in Malaysia, *cha plu* in Thailand and *bo la lot* in Vietnam.

Appearance & Flavor Wild pepper leaves are soft and heart-shaped, with prominent veins radiating out from a central rib—they are distinguished from betel leaves by their brighter green and softer texture. The leaves have a mildly peppery flavor. **Choosing & Storing** Look for fresh, unwilted leaves. Wrap in paper or a cloth and keep refrigerated for 1–2 days. **Preparing** Wash thoroughly, drain and dry. If adding to a rice salad such as the Malay *nasi ulam*, shred finely. Otherwise, trim off the stem and use the leaves whole. **Nutritional & Medicinal Properties** The plant can be processed and taken as an expectorant. In Thailand, wild pepper leaves are made into a tea used to lower blood sugar. **Culinary Uses** Wild pepper leaves are a popular choice of wrapping for morsels of food in parts of Southeast Asia. In Thailand, they are used to enfold a selection of finely diced savory items to make the popular snack known as *miang kum*, which is dipped into a spicy sauce before being eaten. In Vietnam, the leaves are wrapped around pieces of beef which are then briefly grilled, or used to wrap grilled meat or barbequed minced pork balls. The leaves can also be finely shredded and added to salads.

Shiso (Perilla)

Wild Pepper Leaves

Malay Rice Salad with Herbs and Salted Fish

3 cups (500 g) cold cooked rice
1/2 cup (100 g) thinly sliced salted fish or 1 1/4 cups (250 g) shredded smoked fish
1 cup (100 g) cucumber, finely diced
1 cup (100 g) young long beans or green beans, very thinly sliced
1 tablespoon Sambal Belacan (see page 75)
1 tablespoon lime juice
4 shallots, thinly sliced
4 spring onions, thinly sliced
2 stems lemongrass, tender inner part of bottom third only, thinly sliced

2 kaffir limes leaves, cut into hair-like shreds
1 1/2 cups finely chopped mixed herbs, such as polygonum (*rau ram*), coriander leaves (cilantro), Asian basil, Asian pennywort, mint and turmeric leaves
1 teaspoon salt, to taste

1 Place the rice in a large bowl and stir with a fork to ensure all the grains are separated.
2 If using salted fish, deep-fry in oil until golden brown and crisp. Cool, then crumble coarsely. If using smoked fish, flake it with a fork.

3 Add fish, cucumber and long beans to the rice. Combine Sambal Belacan and lime juice in a small bowl, then add to the rice. Add the shallots, spring onions, lemongrass, lime leaves and chopped herbs. Toss well to mix thoroughly, then season with salt to taste. Serve immediately at room temperature.

Chinese Celery, Cashews and Barbecued Pork

5 oz (150 g) dried, sweetened barbecued pork slices (*chu yuk kan* or *bah kwa*), cut into narrow strips
1 cup (150 g) raw cashews, dry-roasted in a wok over low heat until golden brown and crisp
2–3 shallots, thinly sliced
1 stem lemongrass, tender inner part of bottom third only, very thinly sliced

1–2 stalks of Chinese celery, stems only, coarsely chopped to make 1/3 cup
1/3 cup coriander leaves (cilantro), coarsely chopped
1/3 cup mint leaves, coarsely chopped
1 spring onion, thinly sliced
1 tablespoon lime juice
1 tablespoon fish sauce
1/2–1 teaspoon dried chili flakes

1 Buy dried, sweet sheets of barbecued pork (not fresh red roasted pork or *char siew*) from any vendor in the nearest Chinatown area. Put all ingredients in a wide bowl. Toss to mix thoroughly, then serve immediately.

Fresh Coriander Leaf and Coconut Chutney

1 tablespoon tamarind pulp
1/4 cup (60 ml) water
1 cup (40 g) coriander leaves (cilantro)
8 shallots or 1 medium onion
1–2 green chilies
1/2 in (1 cm) ginger root
1 tablespoon grated fresh or desiccated coconut
1 teaspoon salt
1 teaspoon sugar

1 Soak the tamarind in water until soft, then squeeze and strain through a fine sieve to obtain tamarind juice. Put all the other ingredients in a blender or food processor and grind until fine.

2 Add the tamarind juice and continue blending until well mixed. Refrigerate in a covered container. The herb chutney makes a good accompaniment to *tandoori* chicken, grilled lamb and samosas.

Thai Wild Pepper Leaf Parcels

1¹/₂ cups (8 oz/250 g) cooked chicken breast, diced

²/₃ cup (60 g) freshly grated or desiccated coconut, dry-roasted in a wok until golden brown

6 shallots, minced

4 in (10 cm) ginger, diced

¹/₂ cup (75 g) raw peanuts, dry-roasted in a wok, coarsely crushed

¹/₄ cup (25 g) dried prawns, soaked in water to soften, then chopped

2 tablespoons crisp fried garlic

1 lime or lemon, washed and dried, skin and flesh diced, deseeded

4 bird's-eye chilies, deseeded and minced

36 wild pepper leaves or small butter lettuce leaves

Sauce
2 teaspoons dried shrimp paste, toasted

3 shallots, sliced

1 in (2¹/₂ cm) galangal root

2 tablespoons raw peanuts, dry-roasted in a wok until golden brown

2 tablespoons freshly grated or desiccated coconut, dry-roasted in a wok until golden brown

1 tablespoon dried prawns, soaked in water to soften

Thin slice ginger

1¹/₄ cups (300 ml) water

¹/₃ cup (60 g) shaved palm sugar or soft brown sugar

¹/₂ teaspoon salt

1 Prepare the Sauce first. Process the shrimp paste, shallots, galangal, peanuts, coconut, dried prawns and ginger in a blender, adding a small amount of water if needed to keep the mixture turning.

2 Transfer the ground mixture to a small saucepan and add the water, palm sugar and salt. Bring to a boil, stirring constantly. Lower the heat and simmer uncovered for about 10 minutes, until reduced to ³/₄ cup. Set aside to cool, then transfer the Sauce to four individual bowls.

3 Arrange the chicken, coconut, shallots, ginger, peanuts, dried prawns, garlic, lime and chilies in separate piles on a large serving dish. Arrange wild pepper leaves on a separate plate and serve. To eat, place a small amount of the filling in the middle of the leaf, fold into a parcel and dip it in the sauce.

Vietnamese Peperomia Salad

1 clove garlic, minced

1 red chili, minced

2 tablespoons caster sugar

2 tablespoons lime juice

¹/₄ cup (60 ml) rice vinegar

¹/₄ cup (60 ml) fish sauce

¹/₄ cup (60 ml) water

2–3 cups (80–120 g) peperomia sprigs

1 medium tomato, diced

2–3 shallots, thinly sliced

1 In a mortar and pestle, crush the garlic and chili together with a little of the sugar until it is well blended. Add the remaining sugar, lime juice, vinegar, fish sauce and water. Mix until the sugar dissolves.

2 Put the peperomia sprigs, tomato and shallots in a bowl and pour the dressing over the vegetables. Toss to mix, and serve immediately.

Stir-fried Thai Minced Beef and Basil

1 tablespoon minced garlic

1 teaspoon minced ginger

1 tablespoon oyster sauce

2 teaspoons fish sauce

¹/₂ teaspoon freshly ground black pepper

1 lb (500 g) lean ground beef

3 tablespoons oil

3–4 bird's-eye chilies, minced

1 cup (40 g) Asian basil (*horapa*) leaves

1 Combine the garlic, ginger, oyster sauce, fish sauce and pepper in a medium-sized bowl, stirring to mix well. Add the beef and mix well with the seasonings. Set the beef aside to marinate for 5 minutes.

2 Heat the oil in a wok and when very hot, add the beef and chilies and stir-fry until all the moisture dries up and the beef starts to brown (this will take 4–5 minutes). Add half the basil and stir-fry for about 30 seconds. Transfer the beef to a serving dish and scatter with the remaining basil leaves. Serve hot with steamed white rice.

Chicken Pot Roast with Lemongrass

1 fresh chicken, about 3 lbs
  (1$^1/_2$ kg)
3 tablespoons oyster sauce
2 teaspoons Chinese rice wine
  (preferably Shao Hsing)
1 teaspoon salt
12 lemongrass stems
$^1/_3$ cup (85 ml) oil

Dip
1 tablespoon freshly ground black
  pepper
2 teaspoons salt
1 lime or lemon, quartered

1 To make the Dip, combine the pepper and salt in a small bowl. Transfer to four sauce bowls and put a lime or lemon piece on each bowl. Set aside.
2 Dry the chicken inside and out with paper towels. Mix the oyster sauce, rice wine and salt, then smear about a tablespoon of this inside the stomach cavity. Rub the outside of the chicken with the remaining sauce and put the chicken in a bowl to marinate for 30 minutes.
3 Trim the lemongrass so that the stems will fit inside a casserole or heavy saucepan just large enough to contain the chicken. Place the coarse leaves of the lemongrass in a layer at the bottom of the casserole, then slit the lower part of each lemongrass stem and bruise with a cleaver or pestle so it will release its fragrance during cooking. Cut 1 lemongrass stem into 2–3 pieces and tuck it inside the chicken.
4 Arrange the remainder of the bruised stems on top of the leaves already on the bottom of the casserole, then drizzle the oil evenly over the top. Put the casserole over moderate heat, and when the oil starts to sizzle, drain the chicken of excess oyster sauce and lay on top. Cover the casserole with a tight-fitting lid and cook over low to medium heat, turning the chicken each 15 minutes, until the chicken is cooked, about 1$^1/_4$ hours. Cut the chicken into pieces and serve with the Dip.

Fish and Vietnamese Mint Parcels

10–14 oz (300–400 g) very fresh
  white fish filets, skinned and
  boned
1 cup (250 ml) rice vinegar
1 large onion, very thinly sliced
1 tablespoon sugar
1 teaspoon salt
1 heaped tablespoon finely
  chopped mint
1 heaped tablespoon finely
  chopped Vietnamese mint
1 red chili, deseeded and finely
  chopped
2 tablespoons crushed, dry-roasted
  unsalted peanuts
1 heaped tablespoon crisp fried
  shallots
12 lettuce leaves, preferably long-
  leaf or cos lettuce

1 Cut the fish fillets into sashimi-thin slices and place in a wide bowl. Pour the vinegar over and stir. Set aside to marinate at room temperature.
2 After the fish has been marinating for 30 minutes, place the onion in a separate bowl and sprinkle with sugar and salt, massaging with your fingers to mix well. Marinate for another 30 minutes.
3 When the fish has marinated for a total of 1 hour, transfer to a colander. Discard the vinegar then rinse fish briefly under running water. Drain thoroughly, pat dry with paper towels and place in a bowl.
4 Squeeze the onion to remove any liquid, then combine with the fish, mint, Vietnamese mint, chili, peanuts and shallots. Fill each lettuce leaf with a few slices of fish and herb mixture and roll up before serving.

Stir-fried Chicken with Lemongrass

1 lb (500 g) chicken thigh fillets, cut
  in bite-sized pieces
1$^1/_2$ tablespoons fish sauce
2 tablespoons sugar
2–3 teaspoons crushed chili
$^1/_4$ teaspoon freshly ground black
  pepper
1 stem lemongrass, tender inner
  part of bottom third only, very
  thinly sliced
3 cloves garlic, smashed and
  minced
2 tablespoons oil
$^1/_2$ cup (125 ml) chicken stock
1 tablespoon tamarind pulp,
  soaked in $^1/_4$ cup (60 ml) warm
  water, squeezed and strained to
  obtain juice
Salt, to taste
Sprigs of coriander leaf, to garnish

1 Place the chicken pieces in a bowl and add 1 tablespoon fish sauce, 1 tablespoon sugar, chili, pepper, lemongrass and half of the garlic, stirring to mix well. Cover the chicken and set aside to marinate for 30 minutes.
2 Heat the oil in a wok then add the remaining garlic and stir-fry for a few seconds. Add the chicken and stir-fry over high heat until it has turned brown, about 2 minutes. Reduce the heat, then add the remaining 1 tablespoon of sugar, the chicken stock and tamarind juice. Simmer until the chicken is tender, about 3 minutes, stirring frequently. Taste, adding salt if desired. Transfer to a serving dish and garnish with the coriander.

Chicken Deep-fried in Pandanus Leaves

1/2 teaspoon black peppercorns
2 shallots, chopped
1 in (2 1/2 cm) ginger, chopped
1 clove garlic, chopped
1 teaspoon finely chopped
  coriander root
1 stem lemongrass, tender inner
  part of bottom third only, sliced
2 teaspoons finely shaved palm
  sugar
1/2 teaspoon salt
1/2 cup (125 ml) coconut milk
3 teaspoons thick black soy sauce
1 lb (500 g) chicken thigh fillets or
  breast, cut in 1 1/2-in (4-cm) cubes
30 pieces pandanus leaf, cut into

12-in (30-cm) lengths
2–3 cups (500–750 ml) oil for deep
  frying
1 cup (250 ml) sweet chili sauce, for
  dipping

1 Put the peppercorns in a spice grinder and process until coarsely ground. Add shallots, ginger, garlic, coriander root, lemongrass, palm sugar and salt. Process to a smooth paste, adding a little of the coconut milk if needed to keep the mixture turning. Transfer to a large bowl. Stir in the coconut milk and soy sauce, then add chicken. Marinate 1 hour.

2 Remove the chicken from the marinade. Place the chicken on one end of a pandanus leaf and twist the leaf over and around the chicken, rolling up to hold firmly. Tuck the loose end of the leaf through the folded part and leave the end free.
3 Heat the oil in a wok. When very hot, deep-fry the wrapped chicken, a few pieces at a time, for 3–4 minutes. Drain on paper towels and serve with sweet chilli sauce.

Indonesian Sambal Bajak

2 tablespoons oil
4 red chilies, sliced
6 shallots, chopped
3 cloves garlic, chopped
1 tablespoon finely chopped
  galangal
1 stem lemongrass, bottom third
  only, thinly sliced
6 candlenuts, chopped
1 teaspoon dried shrimp paste
2 kaffir lime leaves
2 *salam* leaves, optional
3 tablespoons finely shaved
  palm sugar

3/4 teaspoon salt
2 tablespoons tamarind pulp,
  soaked in 3/4 cup (185 ml) warm
  water, squeezed and strained to
  obtain juice

1 Heat the oil in a wok or small saucepan and add the chilies, shallots, garlic, galangal, lemongrass, candlenuts and shrimp paste. Cook over low heat, stirring frequently, until soft, for about 10 minutes. Process to a paste in a spice grinder;

you will probably need to process the paste in two batches.
2 Return the paste to the pan and add all the remaining ingredients. Cook, stirring from time to time, for 5 minutes. Leave to cool, then remove the kaffir lime and *salam* leaves, scraping off any bits of sambal with a spatula. Refrigerate in a covered container for 2–3 weeks. Serve with rice or noodles.

Beef Soup with Sawtooth Coriander

4 cups (1 litre) water
2 stems lemongrass, bottom 7 in
  (18 cm) only, bruised and cut in
  4–5 pieces
1 1/2 in (3 cm) galangal, thinly sliced
4–5 kaffir lime leaves, torn
4–6 bird's-eye chilies, lightly
  bruised
2 tablespoons Thai roasted chili
  paste (*nam prik pao*)
1 1/2 tablespoons fish sauce
1 medium ripe but firm tomato, cut
  in 8 wedges

1 1/2–2 tablespoons lime or lemon
  juice
7 oz (200 g) fillet or striploin
  beef, chilled in the freezer for
  30 minutes, very thinly sliced
  across the grain
Salt, to taste
4–6 sawtooth coriander leaves,
  torn, or 1/4 cup loosely packed
  coriander leaves

1 Put the water, lemongrass, galangal, lime leaves and chilies in a saucepan. Bring to a boil, lower the heat and simmer uncovered for 5 minutes. Stir in the chili paste, fish sauce, tomato and lime juice. Simmer for 1 minute, then add the beef and cook just until the beef is done.
2 Taste and add salt and more lime juice if desired. Add the sawtooth coriander leaves and serve hot with rice and other dishes.

MUSHROOMS & other fungi

Mushrooms and other types of fungi are unique in the plant world, for they grow without roots or leaves and are unable to photosynthesize by tapping the sun's energy. Although the famous French culinary bible, *Larousse Gastronomique*, states somewhat dismissively that "mushrooms can hardly be considered as food, but more as a condiment," they have always been highly esteemed in Asia. One variety, the black mushroom, or shiitake, has been

cultivated in Asia for more than 2,000 years. The ancient Romans and Greeks discovered how to cultivate mushrooms on poplar wood, and the French learned only in the late 17th century how to cultivate button mushrooms. Gathering wild mushrooms in the pine forests during autumn is as much of a passion for the Japanese as it is for continental Europeans. The right combination of heat and rainfall during the monsoon period brings many types of mushrooms popping out of the soil or sprouting on fallen logs or trees in most other parts of Asia. These wild mushrooms are generally found only in local markets, and only those which are cultivated are widely available.

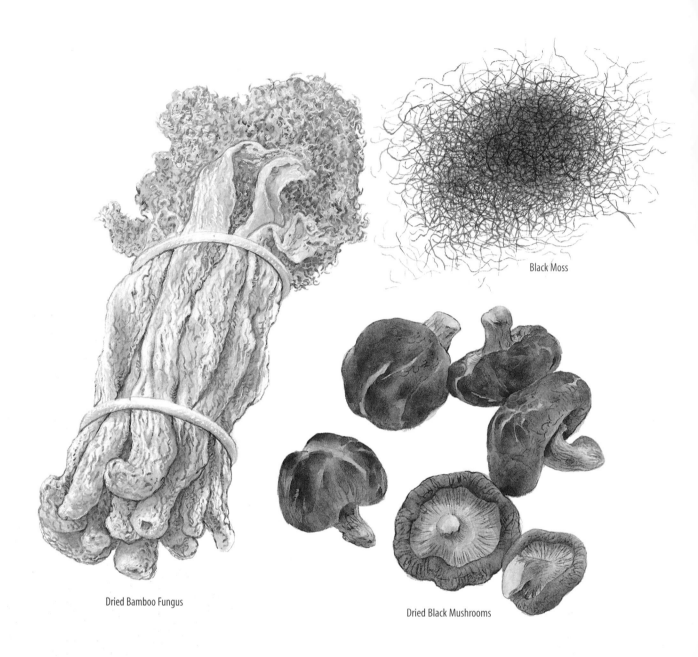

Black Moss

Dried Bamboo Fungus

Dried Black Mushrooms

Dried Bamboo Fungus, known as the "king" of all dried delicacies hailing from the mountains, is sold in packs of ten or 4-oz (100-g) pieces, usually at a high price.

Appearance & Flavor Dried bamboo fungus is eaten mainly for its pulp, which is tender and smooth. If made from ripe bamboo fungus, the vegetable adds a sweetness to dishes. **Choosing & Storing** Dried bamboo fungus should be stored in a dry, cool place. Frozen dried bamboo fungus can keep for up to 2 years. **Preparing** Before cooking, the bamboo fungus should be soaked in lightly salted water for about 20 minutes. Squeeze out all moisture. Just before using, boil the fungus for not more than 1 minute, then dip it in cold water. **Nutritional & Medicinal Properties** The pulp is rich in fibre and contains 19 amino acids, including eight that are vital for one's health. Some believe that dried bamboo fungus aids in the prevention of cancer, hypertension as well as carpulance, and it is also used as a slimming agent for abdominal fat. **Culinary Uses** Dried bamboo fungus is an ingredient in some soups, stews and gratins in Chinese, Japanese and Western cuisine.

Black Moss

Black Moss is actually neither a fungus nor a seaweed as many people believe, but a type of algae (*Gracilaria verrucosa*) which grows in springs at the edge of the Mongolian desert. This esoteric item is a must at Chinese Lunar New Year feasts as the name—*fa cai* in Mandarin or *fatt choy* in Cantonese—is a homonym for the New Year greeting, "wishing prosperity." One does indeed need to be somewhat prosperous to be able to afford this pricey ingredient. Concerns about the over-exploitation of this algae may mean that it will be increasingly rare on festive tables in the future.

Appearance & Flavor Black moss resembles a tangle of very fine black hairs. It has no appreciable flavor, but is enjoyed because of its texture and cultural associations. **Choosing & Storing** Black moss is sold in small packets which can be kept in a cupboard almost indefinitely. **Preparing** Soak in warm water until soft. **Nutritional & Medicinal Properties** The Chinese believe that black moss has a "cooling" and cleansing effect on the body. **Culinary Uses** The soaked moss is often simmered in chicken stock seasoned with Chinese rice wine, a touch of soy sauce and sugar. More commonly, it is added to mixed braised vegetable dishes such as *lo han chai*, which also contains lotus seeds, dried lily buds and dried black mushrooms. It is also an ingredient in the quaintly named "Monk Jumps Over the Wall," a dish supposedly so delicious that a Buddhist monk leapt over a wall to eat it (or, in other versions of the tale, the monk leapt over a wall with joy after eating it).

Dried Black Mushrooms

Dried Black Mushrooms are in huge demand because they develop a more intense flavor than their fresh counterpart, often known as shiitake (see page 126). Dried mushrooms are used both as a flavoring and as a vegetable in their own right. For the Chinese, the shape of the mushroom signifies an umbrella, which is seen as sheltering the entire family. Thus, dried black mushrooms must be present during important family events such as New Year family reunion dinners.

Appearance & Flavor Dried black mushrooms vary in quality, with the thick, crinkled, white-flecked caps of the so-called "flower" mushroom often preferred. Other dried black mushrooms have dark brown caps of varying thickness. The flavor is intense and somewhat meaty, and the texture pleasantly chewy. **Choosing & Storing** Generally, the thicker the mushroom cap, the better the flavor and texture. The cheaper, thinner mushrooms are adequate for slicing and using as a flavoring in rice and noodle dishes or for fillings. Inspect the mushrooms to make sure there is no brownish powder under the gills, which would indicate that they are starting to rot. Store in a cupboard in an airtight container for several months. **Preparing** Dried mushrooms should be covered with boiling water and left to soak for at least 20 minutes, or longer if the caps are thick. Remove from the water, squeeze out the moisture, then cut out the hard stem. The soaking water is often added to soups and stews, tipped slowly out of the soaking bowl so that any gritty residue remains in the bottom. **Nutritional & Medicinal Properties** Similar to fresh shiitake mushrooms (see page 126). **Culinary Uses** The soaked mushrooms are generally used whole in braised dishes, and may be shredded or halved when stir-fried with noodles or fried rice. Whole black mushrooms, filled with minced seafood and steamed, are a gourmet treat. The mushroom can also be added, whole or sliced, to stir-fried vegetable dishes and countless meat, seafood or vegetable dishes, or finely sliced and used in fillings for dumplings or spring rolls.

Button Mushrooms

Button Mushrooms were the first mushrooms to be successfully cultivated by the French. They are also the most widely used mushroom in the West, and are now grown in cooler parts of Asia. Although the flavor is milder than that of many Asian varieties, the button mushroom is a popular vegetable everywhere, from northern India to China. In fact, China exports huge quantities of canned button mushrooms.

Appearance & Flavor Small button mushrooms have an umbrella-shaped cap, which flattens out as the mushroom grows larger. The flavor is mild and the texture relatively firm even after cooking. **Choosing & Storing** Choose dry mushrooms without any sign of mold or slime. Wrap in paper towels and refrigerate in a perforated plastic bag for a few days. **Preparing** Trim the stems and wipe the caps with a paper towel, but do not wash or peel. **Nutritional & Medicinal Properties** Button mushrooms are rich in phosphorus and riboflavin, and are very low in calories. **Culinary Uses** Button mushrooms can be eaten raw with a spicy dip, but are more often sliced and added to soups, stir-fries, curries or braised dishes.

Cloud Ear or Wood Ear Fungus

Cloud Ear or Wood Ear Fungus grows wild on damp tree bark, and is also cultivated. This strange, shriveled fungus is widely available dried (see below). The highly prized albino form known as white fungus, silver fungus or white cloud fungus is more commonly found dried than fresh (see page 128).

Appearance & Flavor Fresh cloud ear fungus is wrinkled, brownish and almost translucent, and looks somewhat like an ear or an open flower. There is virtually no taste at all, and the fungus is enjoyed for its chewy texture and the color contrast it provides in many dishes. **Choosing & Storing** If fresh fungus is available, choose pieces that feel somewhat rubbery, without any traces of slime. Wrap in paper towels and refrigerate for several days. **Preparing** Wash well and discard any hard patch that may be growing in the center of the mature fungus. Blanch in boiling water for 1–2 minutes, then drain well. **Nutritional & Medicinal Properties** This fungus is rich in calcium and phosphorus, and contains about 10% protein. **Culinary Uses** Blanched cloud ear fungus can be added to soups, meat or vegetable stews and salads.

Dried Cloud Ear or Wood Ear Fungus

Dried Cloud Ear or Wood Ear Fungus is the dried version of fresh cloud ear fungus, and is widely available in Asia. It is reconstituted by soaking just before it is used, with no appreciable difference in flavor and texture to the fresh fungus.

Appearance & Flavor Two varieties of dried cloud ear fungus are available. One is smaller, thin, crinkly and uniformly black, while the larger variety is thicker with a pale gray or beige underneath. The almost negligible flavor is identical for both fungi, although the texture of the larger variety tends to be more crunchy. **Choosing & Storing** Dried cloud ear fungus is sold in plastic bags and keeps almost indefinitely in a dry cupboard. **Preparing** Soak in warm water to cover generously until the fungus softens and swells to about five times its dried size. Small, thin pieces of fungus will take about 10 minutes, while larger pieces need a little longer to reconstitute well. Drain and cut out any hard central portion, then slice or chop according to the recipe. **Nutritional & Medicinal Properties** Similar to the fresh fungus. **Culinary Uses** The soaked cloud ear fungus can be added directly to salads and fillings. It may also be added to braised and stir-fried dishes containing meat, poultry or vegetables. It gives a pleasant texture and adds visual contrast.

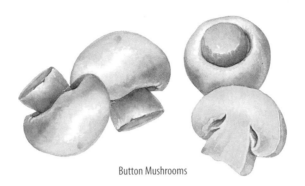

Button Mushrooms

Fresh Cloud Ear Fungus
(Wood Ear Fungus)

Dried Cloud Ear Fungus

Enokitake or Golden Mushrooms are easily cultivated, and are increasingly available fresh outside Japan. Their Japanese name comes from the *enoki*, or Chinese hackberry tree on which the mushrooms grow in the wild.

Appearance & Flavor These are very dainty little mushrooms which grow in clumps, connected at the base. They have slender, creamy white stems—usually between 3 and 5 in (8 and 12 cm) in length—with tiny golden heads. The flavor is mild and the texture pleasantly crisp. **Choosing & Storing** Fresh *enokitake* is usually sold in small amounts (around 4 oz/100 g) in plastic containers, sometimes vacuum-packed, in the cold section of many supermarkets as well as Asian and specialty stores. Left in their original packaging, they can be refrigerated up to a week. **Preparing** Cut off the root end if the mushroom stems are still joined together. Rinse under running water, then drain. **Culinary Uses** *Enokitake* is commonly used raw as an edible garnish or a salad ingredient. They can also be added to soups just before serving. They should not be overcooked or they may lose their fragrance. *Enokitake* is also added to some steamed dishes, such as Japanese savory custard.

Matsutake Mushrooms are a highly prized variety. In Japan or Korea, the mushroom is gathered wild in pine forests during the autumn season—scarcely enough is harvested to meet local demand. Only a small quantity of the fresh mushroom is carefully packed in sawdust and exported for wealthy gourmets abroad each year, although there are reports of its occasional appearance in the northwest US coast, sold as "pine mushrooms."

Appearance & Flavor *Matsutake* are beige in color, with knobbed caps and thick stems, and are usually picked before the caps have a chance to open fully. The caps can grow to an enormous size, as much as 10 in (25 cm) across. Their piney fragrance, firm texture (even after cooking), and meaty flavor make these the ultimate mushroom and invoke the same reverence among the Japanese and Koreans as truffles do among the French. **Choosing & Storing** If you are lucky enough to find fresh *matsutake*, buy them and eat almost immediately. **Preparing** Wipe the surface with a dampened paper towel. They are usually cut into thick slices for cooking. **Culinary Uses** These mushrooms are best grilled after being sliced and marinated in mirin and soy sauce. They can also be grilled whole, without any marinating. Alternatively, slice one or two mushrooms and serve them in a clear soup.

Nameko Mushrooms are somewhat slippery little Japanese mushrooms which are most commonly sold in vacuum packs, either alone or as part of mixed "forest vegetable" pickles (often containing ferns and burdock), or water-packed in jars.

Appearance & Flavor *Nameko* mushrooms have small, rounded caps, which are pale golden brown in color, with long, curved stems. The caps have a somewhat slippery coating and gelatinous texture, while the flavor is surprisingly rich and earthy. **Choosing & Storing** Fresh *nameko* are not commonly available outside Japan. Look for firm, fresh-looking mushrooms and refrigerate in a paper towel for 1–2 days. **Preparing** Rinse and drain the mushrooms, but do not remove the stems. If not adding to dishes which will be cooked, blanch for 1 minute in boiling water, then drain. **Culinary Uses** *Nameko* mushrooms can be added to soups, steamed savory custard or used as a garnish.

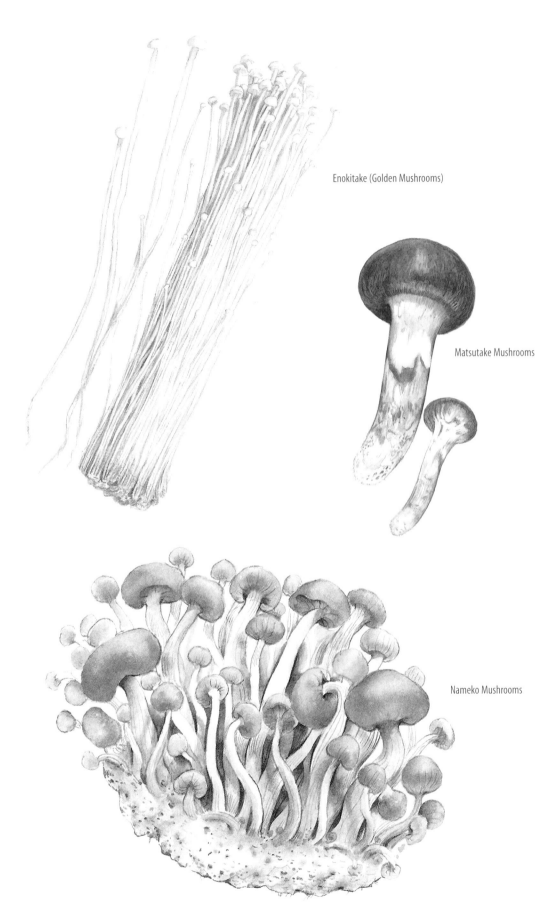

Enokitake (Golden Mushrooms)

Matsutake Mushrooms

Nameko Mushrooms

Oyster Mushrooms

Oyster Mushrooms are also known as abalone mushrooms. They are sometimes called "the shellfish of the forest," more likely because of their oval shape and often pearly gray color rather than any resemblance that their flavor might have to that famous bivalve. Oyster mushrooms taste best when small and immature. They are cultivated on organic waste such as sawdust and logs and are increasingly available outside Asia.

Appearance & Flavor There are many variations in size and color. This fan-shaped mushroom can be very small, with thin caps (around $1^1/_2$ in/4 cm in diameter), or with thick caps (around 3 in/8 cm in diameter). The color ranges from pale pink to delicate gold and silver gray. The flavor is relatively spicy when eaten raw, but becomes pleasantly mild after cooking. **Choosing & Storing** Choose and store as for fresh shiitake mushrooms. **Preparing** Discard the stems, which tend to be tough, before cooking. Smaller mushrooms can be cooked with the cap whole, although it may be advisable to halve or slice larger ones. **Culinary Uses** Oyster mushrooms can be eaten raw, although they have a rather pungent, peppery flavor and are always cooked in Asia. They are used whole, if small, or sliced and added to soups or braised dishes, and are also stir-fried. Oyster mushrooms are often added to a medley of stir-fried mushrooms (which might also include shiitake and *enokitake*), or can be simply stir-fried with spring onions and splashed with oyster sauce. To keep their pleasantly firm texture, do not overcook.

Shiitake Mushrooms

Shiitake Mushrooms in their dried form are usually referred to as Chinese mushrooms or dried black mushrooms (see page 121), but the fresh mushrooms are more commonly known by their Japanese name, shiitake. Fresh shiitake mushrooms, particularly popular in Japan, China and Korea, are increasingly cultivated in the West. Their robust flavor and firm texture make them a versatile vegetable, which can be cooked in Western recipes as well as in countless Asian dishes. Be sure to use the type of mushroom specified in recipes, as the flavor of the dried mushroom is more intense.

Appearance & Flavor Fresh shiitake mushrooms are light chestnut brown, with a relatively flat cap and cream-colored stem. They have a meaty flavor and pleasantly firm texture, even after cooking. The fresh mushrooms are used as a vegetable rather than a seasoning, unlike dried black mushrooms. **Choosing & Storing** Choose plump, firm mushrooms without any sign of mold or slime. Wrap in a paper towel and keep refrigerated in a perforated plastic bag for a few days. **Preparing** Before cooking, discard the stems and wipe the caps with a paper towel, but do not peel or wash. **Nutritional & Medicinal Properties** For many centuries, the Chinese have referred to the shiitake as "the elixir of life" and attributed special powers to it, including the ability to prolong life and enhance sexuality. Shiitake mushrooms have high levels of niacin and riboflavin. They contain an amino acid that lowers cholesterol and improves circulation, and lentinan, which stimulates the production of white blood cells essential to the immune system, and also thought to be effective in fighting hepatitis B and some types of cancer. **Culinary Uses** Shiitake mushrooms can be stir-fried, steamed with a filling, added to soups or grilled. One of the simplest ways to cook them is to stir-fry in a little oil with garlic until they are soft, then splash with oyster sauce and serve. Their full flavor can also be appreciated if they are marinated in soy sauce and mirin, then grilled. Fresh shiitake mushrooms do not adapt well to Western-style baking, unlike large brown or button mushrooms, as shiitake do not contain as much moisture as these mushrooms and the flesh tends to dry out.

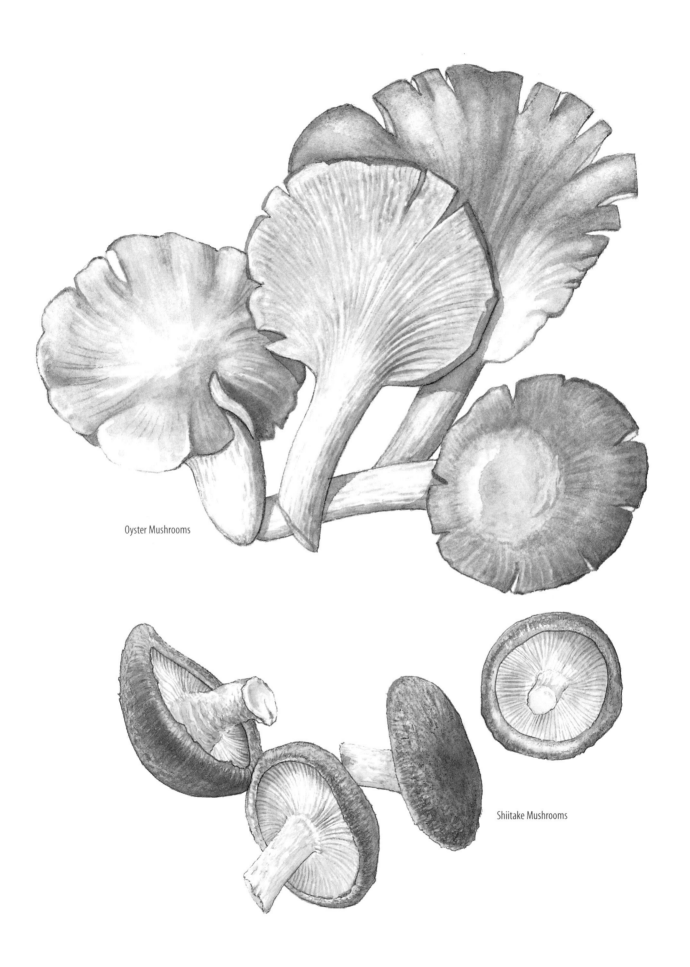

Oyster Mushrooms

Shiitake Mushrooms

Shimeji Mushrooms

Shimeji Mushrooms are much sought after in Japan, perhaps as much for their appearance (the miniature fungi being ideal as a garnish) as for their delicate flavor. Fresh *shimeji* can sometimes be found in Japanese stores. *Shimeji* mushrooms grow on trees, and are often found on beech trees, hence their English name "beech mushroom."

Appearance & Flavor *Shimeji* mushrooms grow in clumps, the slender stems merging into a solid base. The cap of each mushroom has a tiny depression in the center, almost as if a fairy had pressed her finger into them. The flavor is mild, slightly sweet and almost nutty. **Choosing & Storing** Choose fresh, springy mushrooms without slime or discoloration. Wrap loosely in paper towels and keep refrigerated in the vegetable drawer. *Shimeji* keeps better than most mushrooms, and can be stored for 1 week. **Preparing** Cut the stems from the solid base. Wipe the caps gently with a paper towel. **Nutritional & Medicinal Properties** Japanese studies indicate that this type of mushroom contains ingredients believed to help fight tumors. **Culinary Uses** *Shimeji* mushrooms are added to soups or gently simmered and served as a garnish. They are always eaten cooked, as the flavor is unpleasant when raw and difficult to digest.

Straw Mushrooms

Straw Mushrooms are widely available canned and also found in vacuum packs in the refrigerated section of some Asian stores. However, nothing matches the firm texture and flavor of the fresh mushroom. Straw mushrooms are (as the name implies) grown on rice straw in warmer parts of Asia, and are particularly popular in Thailand.

Appearance & Flavor These small, oval mushrooms are completely covered with a sheath in their immature stage, but as the mushroom matures, the sheath splits and the mushroom looks like a partially opened umbrella. Fresh straw mushrooms have a firm yet slippery texture and a delicate, woodsy flavor. **Choosing & Storing** Look for firm, fresh mushrooms, preferably those where the sheath has not yet opened, with no trace of slime, or unpleasant odor. Wrap in paper towels and refrigerate for up to 2 days. **Preparing** Rinse briefly and drain, but do not discard the stems. Large caps are often halved lengthwise before cooking. If using in salads, blanch in boiling water for 2 minutes, then drain. **Nutritional & Medicinal Properties** Straw mushrooms are high in riboflavin and niacin, and are considerably rich in phosphorus. **Culinary Uses** Straw mushrooms can be added to soups, curries (especially those with coconut milk), salads or stir-fried dishes.

White Cloud or Dried Silver Fungus

White Cloud or Dried Silver Fungus is an albino form of regular black fungus. Because of its flower-like shape and clear color after it has been soaked, it is especially appreciated by the Chinese and Japanese—to whom the aesthetics of food are almost as important as the taste—as an addition to various desserts or sweet soups.

Appearance & Flavor White cloud fungus is generally pale ivory or even pale yellow in color, and quite crinkly in appearance, somewhat like a dried flower. It has no obvious flavor and is therefore used primarily for its texture and decorative appearance. **Choosing & Storing** As for dried black fungus. **Preparing** As for dried black fungus. **Nutritional & Medicinal Properties** White cloud fungus is believed by the Chinese to be "cooling" to the body. **Culinary Uses** Soaked white cloud fungus is often simmered with a light sugar syrup and other ingredients such as lotus seeds and perhaps dried longans to make a sweet soup. This can be served hot as part of a meal, or with ice for a refreshing snack during the summer.

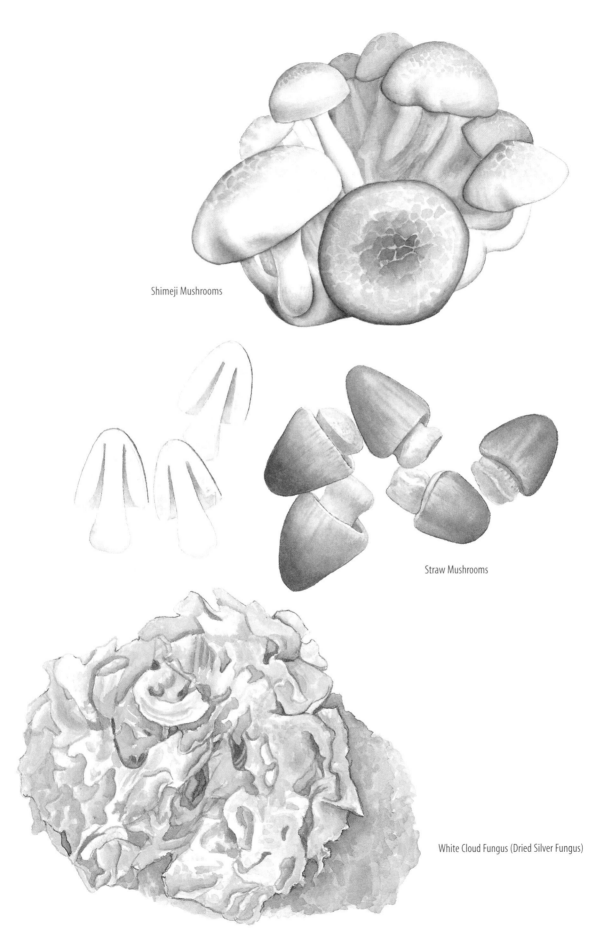

Shimeji Mushrooms

Straw Mushrooms

White Cloud Fungus (Dried Silver Fungus)

Thai Steamed Oyster Mushrooms in Banana Leaf Cups

3 large banana leaves, cut into 16 circles, each 6 in (15 cm) in diameter
1$^1/_2$ cups (375 ml) thick coconut milk
2 tablespoons Thai red curry paste
1 tablespoon fish sauce
$^1/_2$ teaspoon salt
2 eggs, lightly beaten
7 oz (200 g) oyster mushrooms, stems discarded, caps diced
3 cups (200 g) Chinese cabbage, finely chopped
$^1/_2$ cup Thai basil
$^1/_2$ red chili, julienned
2 kaffir lime leaves, sliced in hair-like shreds

1 Soften the banana leaf circles by blanching them in boiling water for about 1 minute. Drain, then place one circle on top of another. Lift up and fold two edges of the circles and staple together in the corner. Repeat on the remaining sides to form a square cup. Repeat to make eight cups.
2 Combine the coconut milk, curry paste, fish sauce, salt and eggs in a bowl, mixing well. Add mushrooms and cabbage. Put 4–5 basil leaves in the bottom of each cup. Divide the vegetable mixture between the cups and sprinkle the top of each with chili and the kaffir lime leaves.

3 Put the cups in a bamboo steamer and set over a wok of boiling water. Steam until cooked, or for about 20 minutes, adding more boiling water to the wok after 10 minutes. Serve hot or at room temperature.

Note: If banana leaves are not available, use small heatproof bowls.

Steamed Savory Custard with Nameko Mushrooms

4 small fresh prawns, peeled and deveined
4 oz (125 g) chicken breast, finely diced
$^1/_2$ teaspoon soy sauce
12 canned gingko nuts (optional)
4 oz (125 g) *nameko* mushrooms

Custard
4 eggs
2$^1/_3$ cups (600 ml) *dashi* stock
$^1/_2$ teaspoon salt
$^1/_4$ teaspoon soy sauce

1 Make the Custard by whisking the eggs, stock, salt and soy sauce together. Set aside.
2 Put the prawns and chicken breast in two bowls, and season each with $^1/_4$ teaspoon soy sauce, tossing to mix. Put 1 prawn, $^1/_4$ of the chicken, 3 gingko nuts, and $^1/_4$ of the mushrooms into each of four covered, heatproof cups or small bowls.
3 Pour the Custard gently into each cup, skimming off any bubbles

which form on top. Cover the cups or bowls with lids or aluminum foil and place inside a bamboo steamer. Set over a wok of boiling water, then steam for 10 minutes, until the custard is set. Serve hot.

Note: *Dashi* stock can be made with instant *dashi* granules or powder according to the instructions found on the jar.

Grilled Fresh Matsutake Mushrooms

4–8 fresh *matsutake* mushrooms, depending upon size
3 tablespoons mirin
3 tablespoons soy sauce

1 Wipe the mushrooms with a damp cloth to remove any dirt. Trim off the hard bottom end of each of the stem. Slice the cap and stem of the mushroom lengthwise.
2 Put the mushrooms in a bowl and sprinkle with rice wine and soy

sauce. Set aside to marinate at room temperature for about 1 hour. Grill over very hot charcoal or under a broiler for about 1$^1/_2$ minutes on each side. Brush with the marinade during cooking. Serve hot.

Thai Tom Yam Soup with Straw Mushrooms

2–4 teaspoons Thai chili paste (*nam prik pao*)
1 stem lemongrass, thick bottom part only, bruised and cut in thirds
3 kaffir lime leaves, torn at the edges
2 tablespoons lime or lemon juice
1 tablespoon fish sauce
1 teaspoon sugar
4 oz (125 g) straw mushrooms, halved
1 medium tomato, quartered
2–3 bird's-eye chilies, lightly bruised
Sprigs of coriander leaves (cilantro), to garnish

Vegetable Stock
5 cups (1$^1/_4$ liters) water
1 medium onion, diced
1 large carrot, diced
1 stalk celery, sliced
1 whole coriander plant, including roots and stems, minced
1 teaspoon black peppercorns

1 Make the Vegetable Stock by combining the water, onion, carrot, celery, coriander and peppercorns in a large saucepan. Bring to a boil, cover, lower heat, and simmer for 30 minutes, or until the liquid has been reduced to 3$^1/_2$ cups.
2 Strain the Vegetable Stock into a medium-sized saucepan and stir in the chili paste, lemongrass and lime leaves. Bring to a boil, lower heat, and simmer uncovered for 3 minutes, stirring occasionally.

3 Add the lime juice, fish sauce, sugar, mushrooms, tomatoes and chilies. Bring to a boil, reduce heat, and simmer for 3–4 minutes, or until the mushrooms are cooked. If using canned mushrooms, simmer for 3 minutes. Transfer to a serving bowl and garnish with coriander sprigs. Serve the soup hot, together with steamed jasmine rice.

Korean Mixed Mushroom Hotpot

1$^1/_2$ lbs (750 g) mixed fresh mushrooms (shiitake, brown mushrooms, oyster mushrooms and button mushrooms)
1$^1/_2$ cups (80 g) Chinese cabbage, cut in 2-in (5-cm) lengths
4–6 spring onions, cut into 2-in (5-cm) lengths
10 oz (300 g) beef sirloin, thinly sliced (optional)
6 cups (1$^1/_2$ liters) vegetable or beef stock
Salt, to taste
Ground black pepper, to taste

1 Discard the tough mushroom stems, and slice the caps. Arrange all ingredients except the stock in a heatproof casserole. Bring the stock to a boil, then add to the casserole. Bring to a boil slowly, then simmer

until the mushrooms are cooked, for about 10 minutes. Taste the soup and add salt if desired. Sprinkle with the ground pepper and serve hot with rice.

Stir-fried Mixed Mushrooms

2 tablespoons oil
2 cloves garlic, minced
$1/_2$ teaspoon finely grated ginger
7 oz (200 g) fresh shiitake mushrooms, sliced
7 oz (200 g) button mushrooms, sliced
4 oz (125 g) oyster mushrooms, sliced
2 tablespoons chicken stock or water
$1/_4$ teaspoon sugar
1 spring onion, cut into 2-in (5-cm) lengths
4 oz (110 g) *enokitake*, hard stems trimmed, mushroom left whole
1 tablespoon oyster sauce
Ground black pepper, to taste

1 Heat the oil in a wok and add the minced garlic and ginger. Stir-fry over medium–high heat for 15 seconds, then add the shiitake, button and oyster mushrooms. Stir-fry until they start to soften, then pour in the stock and sugar.
2 Add spring onion and stir-fry another few minutes, then gently stir in the *enokitake*. Continue stir-frying for 1 minute, add the oyster sauce and black pepper, stir for a few seconds, then transfer to a serving dish. Serve with rice or as a Western appetizer over grilled or pan-fried polenta.

Note: A mixture of $1^1/_4$ lbs (500 g) of almost any type of fresh mushrooms can be used, with the more delicate mushrooms added to the wok at the last minute.

Japanese Simmered Dried Black Mushrooms

8 large or 12 medium dried black mushrooms, soaked for 1 hour in warm water to soften, soaking water reserved
$1^1/_2$ teaspoons sugar
1 tablespoon soy sauce
$1/_4$ teaspoon salt
1 tablespoon mirin

1 Discard the stems and put the mushroom caps in a small saucepan. Pour in the soaking liquid, taking care to leave any sediment in the bottom of the soaking bowl. Add water if required to cover completely.
2 Add the sugar, soy sauce and salt, and bring to a boil. Cover and simmer

for 1 hour, or until the mushrooms are very tender. Add the mirin, cover, remove from the heat, and set aside for 15 minutes. Transfer to a serving bowl. Set aside to cool, and serve at room temperature.

Chinese White Fungus and Melon Balls in Syrup

1 large floret (1 oz/30 g) dried silver fungus, soaked in warm water 1 hour
$1^3/_4$ cups (125 g) rock sugar
4 cups (1 liter) water
$1/_2$ honeydew melon or cantaloupe, scooped with a small spoon or melon baller

1 Drain, then trim the fungus and discard any hard parts. Cut into bite-sized pieces and set aside. Bring the sugar and water to a boil in a large saucepan. Stir to dissolve the sugar.

2 Add the fungus and simmer over low heat for 15 minutes. Transfer to a bowl, cool, then chill. To serve, divide the syrup, fungus and melon balls among four bowls.

Thai Cloud Ear Fungus with Chicken and Ginger

2 cups (300 g) fresh or $^1/_2$ cup dried
  cloud ear fungus
2 tablespoons oil
1 medium onion, thinly sliced
4 cloves garlic, minced
14 oz (400 g) boneless chicken
  thighs, cut in bite-sized pieces
2 in (5 cm) ginger, finely sliced
2–3 spring onions, cut in lengths
1 tablespoon fish sauce
1 tablespoon soy sauce
1 tablespoon white vinegar
1 teaspoon sugar
$^1/_4$ cup (15 g) mint sprigs
$^1/_2$–1 teaspoon chili flakes

1 If using fresh fungus, wash well and discard any hard patches. Blanch in boiling water for 1–2 minutes, then drain well. Cut in bite-sized pieces. If using dried fungus, soak in warm water for about 10 minutes until soft and swollen, then remove any hard portions. Cut into bite-sized pieces and set aside.
2 Heat the oil in a wok, then add the onion and stir-fry over medium heat until slightly softened, about 2 minutes. Add garlic and stir-fry for 1 minute, then raise heat and add chicken and ginger. Stir-fry until the chicken changes color all over, then add cloud ear fungus, spring onions, fish sauce, soy sauce, vinegar, sugar and half the mint. Reduce heat and stir-fry for 3 minutes. Transfer to a serving bowl. Garnish with the rest of the mint and sprinkle with chili.

Miso Soup with Enokitake

2 tablespoons white miso
3$^1/_2$ cups (875 ml) *dashi* stock,
  heated slightly

Garnish
4 oz (125 g) *enokitake*, stem ends
  trimmed
1 spring onion or shallot, thinly
  sliced

1 Put the miso paste in a bowl and pour in $^1/_2$ cup of the *dashi* stock, blending with a wire whisk to make a smooth mixture. Put the remaining *dashi* stock into a saucepan and cook over medium heat. Gradually add the dissolved miso, stirring until completely dissolved. Heat until it almost comes to a boil, then simmer very gently for 1 minute.
2 Add the *enokitake* and simmer very gently for 1 minute. Transfer the miso soup to four soup bowls, garnishing each with some of the spring onion. Serve hot with steamed rice and other Japanese dishes.

Note: *Dashi* stock can be made with instant *dashi* granules or powder according to the instructions found on the jar.

the ONION family

The botanical genus, *Allium*, includes the world's most widely used flavoring vegetables, onion and garlic, which are also among the oldest known medical herbs. Egyptian drawings dating back some 3,000 years depict garlic, which was given to workers who built the famous pyramids, while a 2,000-year-old Indian manuscript recommends onions as a diuretic and anti-rheumatic, beneficial to the heart, eyes and digestion.

Members of the onion family—especially spring onions and leeks—may vary in size, intensity of flavor, and appearance from country to country. To add to the confusion, the names given for certain vegetables may differ among Western countries; for example, what is known as a shallot in one area may be called a spring onion in a neighboring state or country. The onion and its cousins are enjoyed throughout Asia, with a few exceptions. The Brahmin and Jains in India, and some Chinese Buddhists, do not eat onions or garlic for they are thought to inflame sexual passions (although other societies might consider the heavy flavor of garlic to have exactly the reverse effect).

Garlic

Garlic is famed for its ability to intensify and enhance the flavors of whatever it is cooked with, and since antiquity, has been renowned in both Western and Asian cultures for its medicinal value. Records show that Egyptian laborers were fed liberal amounts of garlic as they worked on the famous pyramids, and garlic also formed part of the diet of ancient Roman soldiers. With the exception of Japan and some groups in India, garlic is liberally used, both raw and cooked, throughout Asia.

Appearance & Flavor Garlic heads are covered with a papery skin ranging from creamy white to pinky purple. Within the outer skin, the cloves are arranged around a thin, central stem. The flavor of garlic is strong when raw, but diminishes after cooking, becoming almost sweet after prolonged slow cooking. Chinese stores and markets often sell heads of smoked garlic, imported from China, recognizable by brownish black patches on the skin. **Choosing & Storing** For greater freshness and keeping quality, choose whole bulbs of garlic rather than loose cloves, and make sure they are still completely covered with the outer skin. Press the cloves on the outside of a bulb gently to check if they are still firm. Avoid garlic with sprouts, and look out for tiny worms. Garlic can be stored in an open container (not plastic) in a dark, dry place for 2–3 months. **Preparing** When peeling garlic, place a clove flat on a board and cut off the blunt end with a knife. Place the knife blade flat on the clove and tap lightly to slightly crush the garlic. The cloves can then be easily removed by flicking them out with the point of the knife. **Nutritional & Medicinal Properties** The herb contains a mild antibiotic which is believed to help intestinal infection. It also helps reduce cholesterol and blood pressure, and is a cure for coughs, cold and asthma. Tests have also indicated that garlic helps reduce the incidence of colon cancer, and gastro-intestinal cancer. **Culinary Uses** In Asia, crushed garlic is often added to curry pastes and sauces, or chopped and stir-fried to flavor oil before the addition of other ingredients. Whole cloves of garlic are often used in vegetable or lentil stews and pickles, and with braised meat. Crisp fried garlic are a popular garnish for vegetable dishes, soups and noodles in Southeast Asia.

Garlic or Chinese Chives

Garlic or Chinese Chives, also known as Asian chives, have been grown in China and Japan for 3,000 years. Known as *gao choy* in Cantonese and *jiu cai* in Mandarin, they are very popular in Chinese and Korean cuisine. A pale, golden form of garlic chives known as blanched garlic chives is prized for its more delicate flavor. The strong flavor of garlic chives means that they are generally used as a flavoring herb rather than a vegetable. An exception to this is the unopened flower heads or buds of mature garlic chives, which are regarded as a gourmet treat.

Appearance & Flavor Regular garlic chives resemble coarse, flat blades of dark green grass. Blanched garlic chives have a pale yellowish color, which comes from being grown under shade. Garlic chives have a strong flavor when raw, but become more delicate after brief cooking. When flowering, garlic chives develop a spike with a pale green oval tip finishing in a sharp point. **Choosing & Storing** Select those that have a bright green color. The lower ends of the chives should be crisp and snap if bent. Flowering chives should have tightly folded buds. Chives with open flowers will taste old and tough. Wrap in a paper towel and keep refrigerated in a plastic bag for 1–2 days. **Preparing** Discard the hard ends of the stems and chop as the recipe directs. **Nutritional & Medicinal Properties** Garlic chives are rich in beta-carotene, iron and vitamin C. The Chinese believe they are good for blood circulation as well as the digestive system. **Culinary Uses** Regular garlic chives are added to noodles and stir-fried vegetables or meat, or minced and added to dumpling fillings. Blanched and flowering garlic chives are usually stir-fried and lightly seasoned with soy or oyster sauce. Because of their decorative appearance, flowering garlic chives are an ideal garnish.

Blanched Garlic Chives

Garlic Chives (Chinese Chives)

Garlic

Leeks

Leeks are grown in cooler north Asian countries, as well as in mountainous regions of tropical Asia. Like onions, they are an ancient vegetable which the Egyptians held in high esteem. The infamous Roman emperor, Nero, who was given the nickname, Porrophagus, or "leek eater," insisted on being served leek soup every day as he believed the leek improved his voice. Asian leeks are generally much smaller, sometimes only one quarter the size, of their Western counterparts in Europe and in the US.

Appearance & Flavor Leeks grow with a tightly folded white base, with dark green leaves opening out from the white portion. The flavor is mild and slightly sweet after cooking; if eaten raw, leeks are more pungent. Normally, only the white portion of the leek is used in Europe, although in Asia, part of the green leaves may also be used. **Choosing & Storing** The green portion of leeks should be crisp and bright in color. Discard most of the green portion, wrap the white part of the leeks in paper towels, and refrigerate in a plastic bag for up to a week. **Preparing** Trim off the root end, peel off any torn or dirty outer layers, and wash the leeks thoroughly to get rid of any soil. Slice thinly and use. **Nutritional & Medicinal Properties** Leeks are very rich in beta-carotene, and contain vitamin C, calcium and phosphorus. They also contain a flavonoid which is being studied for its anti-oxidant and brain-protecting properties. **Culinary Uses** In northern China, julienned raw leeks are served with Peking duck, rolled in pancakes along with the duck skin. In other parts of Asia where this vegetable is grown, leeks are used in soups and braised dishes, and stir-fried (take care they do not brown or they may become bitter).

Onions

Onions are used almost daily in cooking throughout Asia, with the surprising exception of Japan, where they are only occasionally used. Onions are eaten both cooked and raw, not just as a vegetable but also as a flavoring, a garnish, a salad and a pickle. It is hard to imagine Asian cuisine—or any cuisine—without this humble, ancient vegetable.

Appearance & Flavor There are three major types of onions used in Asian cuisine. Brown-skinned onions have a firm, dry skin and creamy white flesh which is relatively mild; red-skinned or Bombay onions whose brownish red skin covers mild, juicy, purplish red flesh; and white-skinned onions with papery white skin and white flesh with a more pungent flavor than the other varieties. **Choosing & Storing** Onions should be firm when pressed, and should not smell musty. Avoid any which are starting to sprout. Store as for garlic, and avoid putting together with potatoes as the onions may cause deterioration. **Preparing** Onions should be peeled by cutting off the root and stem ends, then pulling back the layers of skin. Onions are often halved lengthwise, then sliced thinly across for cooking or adding to salads. Cut across in this fashion, the layers of sliced onion will separate during cooking or tossing in salads. When cutting onions lengthwise into wedges for cooking, do not cut too much off the root end or the layers will separate. To remove some of the bite of raw onions, slice thinly, sprinkle with salt and refrigerate for 30–60 minutes. The onion slices are then rinsed and, if liked, tossed with lemon juice. **Nutritional & Medicinal Properties** Onion contains calcium, phosphorus, as well as compounds such as allicin, flavonoids, phenolic acids and sterols. It is taken for flu, coughs, colds, mouth infections and tooth decay, and has anti-inflammatory, diuretic, analgesic as well as antibiotic properties. **Culinary Uses** Onions are used in countless ways—puréed into a paste and used to thicken curries; stir-fried (often with garlic and ginger) to form the basic seasoning for countless simmered dishes; sliced, salted, then tossed with lemon juice to make a condiment; sliced or quartered and stir-fried with other vegetables, meat or noodles; slowly fried until crisp and used as a garnish; or julienned and used as a garnish for soups or added to salads.

Leeks

Onions

Shallots

Shallots have been cultivated for at least 2,000 years. Botanists debate whether this small-bulbed onion variety is the same species as the regular onion (*Allium cepa*), or a different species known as *Allium ascalonicum*. With their sweet flavor, delicate fragrance, and tender flesh, shallots are widely used in most of Asia, particularly in the tropics.

Appearance & Flavor Usually smaller than the brown-skinned French *eschalot*, the Asian version has reddish brown papery skin with purplish pink flesh, and grows with two or more bulbs clustered together. **Choosing & Storing** Choose and store as for onions. **Preparing** Cut off the base of each shallot and peel off the outer skin. To hold shallot slices together, slice lengthwise. If you wish the slices to separate into rings when cooked or tossed with other ingredients, slice across. **Nutritional & Medicinal Properties** Similar to onions. **Culinary Uses** The moisture content of shallots is less (per weight) than the larger red onions, so shallots are often preferred to onions as an ingredient in ground seasoning pastes (such as *masala*, *rempah* or *bumbu*) used in many Indian and Southeast Asian dishes. This paste is gently fried—the use of onions tends to make the paste simmer rather than fry. Shallots are widely used as a thickening agent and for their flavor in curry-style dishes, while crisp fried sliced shallots are a popular garnish in many cuisines, particularly Indonesian and Malay dishes. To make the garnish, slice the shallots across very thinly and pat the slices dry before deep-frying them slowly in moderately hot oil. When golden brown, drain the shallots and cool completely before storing them in an airtight jar.

Spring Onions

Spring Onions are known in some areas as bunching onions, green onions, Welsh onions, scallions or, even more confusingly, in parts of Australia, as shallots. Spring onions are actually the immature onion plant, picked before the bulb has had a chance to form and mature. The flavor, more delicate than that of mature onions, makes this a popular flavoring vegetable throughout Asia.

Appearance & Flavor Spring onions grow in bunches with a white base and green leaves. Some have a distinct bulb at the white end, while others are uniform in width. Certain varieties have a purple tinge on the outer leaves of the end. The most common type found in Asia is generally about half the diameter and length of spring onions found in the West. The flavor is mild. **Choosing & Storing** Look for spring onions with firm, bright green leaves. To store, put the root end in a glass containing a small amount of water. Cover the leaves and glass entirely with a loose plastic bag, and keep refrigerated for up to a week, wiping away any moisture that forms inside the bag every 2–3 days. **Preparing** Cut off the root end before using, peel away any damaged outer leaves and wash well. If using large spring onions, the white portion should be halved lengthwise before slicing across. A popular garnish in Chinese and Thai restaurants, spring onion brushes are made by trimming off the root end of the spring onion. Cut across about 2 in (5 cm) above where the green leaves form, then cut deep lengthwise slits along the green ends of the spring onion. Place the brush in ice-cold water for approximately 15 minutes until the green portion of the spring onion curls. **Nutritional & Medicinal Properties** Spring onions are rich in vitamin C, phosphorus, calcium and contain traces of iron. The Chinese believe that spring onions are good for the digestion, and help ward off the arrival of a cold. **Culinary Uses** Spring onions are often chopped and added raw just before serving a range of dishes, from soups to noodles to stews. They are generally added toward the end of cooking when used in stir-fried combinations so that they keep their bright color and fresh texture. They are often stir-fried with bean curd in Chinese cuisine, and are a popular garnish in both Japanese and Chinese cuisine.

Shallots

Spring Onions

Stir-fried Rice Vermicelli with Garlic Chives and Pork

5 oz (150 g) pork, sliced in thin strips
1 teaspoon rice wine or saké
1 teaspoon soy sauce
$1/2$ teaspoon cornstarch
$1/2$ tablespoon sesame oil
$1/4$ teaspoon ground white pepper
4 tablespoons oil
1 teaspoon minced garlic
8 oz (250 g) dried rice vermicelli (*bee hoon* or *mifen*), soaked in hot water to soften, drained, cut in 3-in (8-cm) lengths
4–5 garlic chives, blanched yellow variety if possible, cut in lengths

Sauce
1 tablespoon oyster sauce
$1/2$ tablespoon rice wine or saké
$1/2$ tablespoon soy sauce
$1/2$ tablespoon black soy sauce
3 tablespoons chicken stock
$1/2$ teaspoon sugar

1 Place the pork in a bowl and add the rice wine, soy sauce, cornstarch, sesame oil and pepper. Massage the meat well and set aside.
2 Prepare the Sauce by combining the oyster sauce, rice wine, soy sauces, chicken stock and sugar in a bowl, stirring to dissolve the sugar. Set aside.

3 Heat 1 tablespoon of the oil in a wok, add the garlic and stir-fry over high heat for a few seconds. Add the pork mixture and stir-fry for 2 minutes. Using a spatula, transfer the garlic and pork to a bowl.
4 Add the remaining oil to the wok and heat. Add the rice vermicelli and chives and stir-fry over high heat for 30 seconds. Lower heat, add the Sauce and continuing stir-frying over medium heat for 3 minutes. Return the pork and garlic to the wok. Stir-fry for 30 seconds, mixing well. Sprinkle with the remaining sesame oil, then transfer to a serving dish. Serve with chili sauce.

Stir-fried Beef with Ginger and Leeks

1 lb (500 g) beef fillet or striploin
1 tablespoon cornstarch
1 tablespoon rice wine or saké
1 tablespoon soy sauce
1 tablespoon oyster sauce
1 teaspoon sugar
$1/2$ teaspoon ground white pepper
$1/4$ cup (60 ml) oil
$11/2$ in (4 cm) young ginger, cut into thin strips
1 small leek, white part only, very thinly sliced
$1/2$ cup (125 ml) water
1 egg, lightly beaten

1 Chill the beef in the freezer for 15 minutes. Cut across the grain into paper-thin slices. Put in a bowl and toss to coat it with the cornstarch. Add the rice wine, soy sauce, oyster sauce, sugar and pepper, mixing well. Marinate for 30 minutes.
2 Heat the oil in a wok, then add the ginger slices and stir-fry for about 1 minute over medium heat until golden and crisp. Remove with a slotted spoon or spatula and drain on paper towels.

3 Increase heat and stir-fry the beef for 15 seconds over very high heat. Add the leeks and stir-fry for 1 minute. Add ginger slices and water, stir, then immediately pour in the egg and stir for about 5 seconds, until the egg sets. Transfer to a serving dish and serve hot with steamed white rice.

Cabbage Stir-fried with Onion and Indian Spices

$1/4$ cup (60 ml) oil
1 teaspoon cumin seeds
$1/2$ teaspoon fennel seeds
2–3 medium onions, halved and thinly sliced across
$11/4$ lbs (600 g) cabbage, sliced into shreds
Salt, to taste
$1/4$ teaspoon ground red pepper
$1/2$ teaspoon *garam masala*
1 tablespoon lemon juice

1 Heat the oil in a large wok. When the oil is moderately hot, add the cumin and fennel and cook for a few seconds until the seeds start to crackle. Add the onion and stir-fry over medium heat until it starts to brown slightly. Put in the cabbage and stir-fry over medium heat until it wilts and begins to brown, for about 5 minutes.

2 Sprinkle the cabbage with the salt and red pepper, mixing well. Reduce heat slightly and cook, stirring occasionally, over low to medium heat until the cabbage is tender, for 3–5 minutes. Sprinkle with *garam masala* and lemon juice, stir and mix well, then transfer to a serving dish.

Spicy Malaysian Vegetable Pickles

1 cucumber, skin left on, seeds removed, cut in matchstick strips
1 teaspoon salt
1 medium carrot, cut into short, thin strips
$1/3$ cup (85 ml) oil
1 tablespoon sugar
10–12 shallots
6–8 cloves garlic
$1^1/_2$ in (4 cm) ginger, finely sliced
$1/_2$ teaspoon salt
3 tablespoons white vinegar
3 red chilies, halved lengthwise, deseeded
1 tablespoon sesame seeds, lightly dry-roasted

Spice Paste
6 dried chilies, cut in lengths, soaked in hot water to soften
4 shallots, sliced
1 in ($2^1/_2$ cm) ginger
Thin slice turmeric root or $1/_2$ teaspoon ground turmeric
1 tablespoon dried prawns, soaked in hot water to soften, drained
2 candlenuts or macadamia nuts, chopped

1 Sprinkle the cucumber with salt and set aside for 10 minutes. Rinse and drain. Soak the carrot in enough water to cover for 10 minutes, then drain. Prepare the Spice Paste by processing all the ingredients in a spice grinder or blender to a smooth paste, adding a little of the oil if needed to keep the mixture turning.

2 Heat the oil in a wok and gently stir-fry the Spice Paste for 3 minutes. Add the sugar, shallots, garlic and ginger and stir-fry for 2 minutes. Add salt and vinegar and stir.

3 Add the drained carrots and stir-fry over low–medium heat for 3–4 minutes, then add the cucumber and chilies and stir-fry for 4–5 minutes. Sprinkle with the sesame seeds, stir, and allow to cool. Serve as a side dish at room temperature. The pickles can be kept refrigerated for 10 days in a covered container.

Leek and Sweet Corn Soup

4 tablespoons oil or 3 tablespoons butter
1 large onion, diced
4–5 cloves garlic, minced
$1/_2$ stalk celery, diced
$1^3/_4$ cups (250 g) white portion of leek, thinly sliced
2 cups (250 g) fresh or frozen sweet corn kernels
4 cups (1 liter) chicken stock
Salt and pepper, to taste
2 tablespoons minced coriander leaves (cilantro), to garnish

1 Heat the oil or butter in a large saucepan, add the onion and garlic and stir-fry over low to moderate heat until transparent, for about 3 minutes. Add the celery, leek and corn and stir-fry until soft, for about 4 minutes. Add the stock and bring to a boil. Cover, lower heat and simmer until the vegetables are soft, for about 20–25 minutes.

2 Blend or process the soup until smooth, then season to taste with salt and pepper. Reheat the soup slowly, then transfer to a serving bowl and garnish with coriander leaves (cilantro).

Stir-fried Spring Onions with Bean Curd

16 oz (450 g) pressed or extra firm bean curd (*tau kwa*)
3 tablespoons oil
20 spring onions, cut in short lengths to make about 2 cups
2 tablespoons soy sauce
$1/_2$ teaspoon salt

1 Drain and pat the bean curd dry with a paper towel and cut into small cubes. Heat oil in a wok and fry bean curd over high heat for 2–3 minutes, stirring frequently, until crisp and golden.

2 Add the spring onions and stir-fry until cooked, for about 2 minutes. Add the soy sauce and salt, then stir and transfer to a serving dish.

Stir-fried Chicken with Onion, Tomato and Broccoli

10 oz (300 g) boneless chicken thighs, cut in bite-sized cubes
2 teaspoons fish sauce
$1/4$ teaspoon freshly ground black pepper
2 tablespoons cornstarch
1 cup (250 ml) oil
2 teaspoons minced garlic
1 medium onion, cut in wedges
2 spring onions, cut in lengths
10 oz (300 g) broccoli, cut in small florets
$1/3$ cup (85 ml) water
1 medium tomato, cut in wedges

Sauce
2 teaspoons cornstarch
$3/4$ cup (185 ml) chicken stock
2 teaspoons fish sauce
2 teaspoons oyster sauce
$1/2$ teaspoon sugar

1 Prepare the Sauce by mixing the ingredients in a small bowl, stirring well until the sugar dissolves, then set aside.
2 Put the chicken cubes in a bowl and toss with the fish sauce and pepper. Sprinkle over the cornstarch, tossing to coat the chicken evenly. Heat the oil in a wok until very hot, add a third of the chicken, and deep-fry for about 3 minutes until golden brown. Using a slotted spatula, remove the chicken and drain on paper towels. Repeat with the remaining batches of chicken. Transfer the drained chicken to a serving dish.

3 Remove all but 1 tablespoon of oil from the wok. Heat and add the garlic. Stir-fry over medium–high heat for a few seconds, then add the onion and stir-fry for 30 seconds. Add the spring onions and stir-fry for 5 seconds.
4 Add the broccoli and stir-fry for 1 minute. Pour in the water, cover the wok, reduce heat slightly and simmer for 2 minutes. Add the tomato, stir, then pour in the Sauce, stirring for about 30 seconds, until it thickens and clears. Pour the gravy over the chicken and serve.

Chinese Garlic Chive Pancakes

$1^1/2$ cups (185 g) flour
$2/3$ cup (170 ml) boiling water
2–3 teaspoons sesame oil
$1/2$ teaspoon salt
$2/3$ cup (100 g) minced garlic chives or spring onion greens
Oil for shallow frying

1 Place the flour in a bowl and make a well in the center. Pour in the boiling water and stir with a wooden spoon to mix well. When cool enough to handle, knead on a lightly floured surface until smooth —add a little flour if the mixture is sticky—for 2–3 minutes. Rub the surface with sesame oil, put in a bowl and cover with plastic wrap. Set aside for 1 hour.
2 Divide the dough into four portions. Roll each on a floured board to make a circle about 10 in (25 cm) in diameter. Sprinkle

the top of each circle generously with salt, then scatter a quarter of the chives over the dough. Roll up into a cigar shape, then take one end and roll into a coil. Flatten with the palm of the hand, then roll the dough gently into a thin circle.
3 Heat a little oil in a frying pan until medium-hot. Add the pancakes and cook for about 3–4 minutes on each side, until golden brown and cooked through. Serve hot as a snack with Chinese tea, black Chinese vinegar and plenty of chili sauce.

Korean Spring Onion Pancakes

4 oz (125 g) lean ground beef
4 spring onions, cut into 2-in (5-cm) lengths
$1/4$ cup (60 ml) oil

Batter
1 cup (125 g) plain flour
1 egg, lightly beaten
1 teaspoon salt
Pinch of white pepper
$3/4$ cup (185 ml) water

1 To prepare the Batter, mix the flour, egg, salt and pepper, stirring in water to make a smooth, reasonably thin batter. Add the ground beef, then stir in the spring onions.
2 Heat 2 tablespoons of the oil in a frying pan and when moderately hot, add a small ladleful of batter, spreading to make a thin pancake

about 4 in (10 cm) across. Cook the pancakes for about 2 minutes, or until golden brown underneath and starting to set on top, then flip over and cook until light brown on the other side. Repeat until the mixture is used up. Serve the pancakes hot with soy sauce and minced garlic.

Indian Onion Fritters

1 cup (130 g) chickpea flour (*besan*)
1 teaspoon baking powder
1 teaspoon salt
1 teaspoon ground coriander
$1/2$ teaspoon ground cumin
$1/2$ teaspoon ground red pepper
$1/4$ teaspoon ground turmeric
1 tablespoon lemon juice
$3/4$ cup (185 ml) water
2 tablespoons minced coriander leaves (cilantro)
2 medium onions (7 oz/200 g), peeled and diced

Oil for deep-frying
Fresh Coriander and Coconut Chutney (see page 114)

1 Pour the chickpea flour into a bowl and sift in baking powder. Stir in the salt, coriander, cumin, red pepper and turmeric. Add the lemon juice and gradually stir in the water, adding enough to make a thick batter (you may need to add another 1–2 tablespoons of water). Stir in the coriander leaves and set aside for at least 10 minutes.

2 Heat the oil in a wok or saucepan. When it is hot, stir the onions into the batter. Drop the onion batter into the oil, about 1 tablespoon at a time, and fry until golden brown. Drain on paper towels and serve the fritters hot with the Coriander and Coconut Chutney (page 117) or a sour tamarind dip.

South Indian Garlic Curry

$2^1/2$ tablespoons oil
15–20 large garlic cloves (8 oz/250 g), peeled and left whole
10 shallots, peeled and left whole
4 green chilies
1 teaspoon fenugreek seeds
$1/2$–1 teaspoon ground red pepper
$1/2$ teaspoon ground turmeric
$1^1/2$ cups (375 ml) thick coconut milk
$1/2$ teaspoon salt

1 tablespoon tamarind pulp, soaked in $1/2$ cup (125 ml) warm water, squeezed and strained to obtain juice

1 Heat the oil in a saucepan and add the garlic, shallots and chilies. Stir-fry gently until just lightly colored but not brown. Remove from the pan and add the fenugreek. Stir-fry over moderate heat for about 1 minute, then add the red pepper and the turmeric. Stir for a few seconds then pour in the coconut milk. Add the salt and bring slowly to a boil, stirring frequently.

2 Add the garlic, shallots and chilies and cook uncovered, stirring from time to time, until the vegetables are soft. Add the tamarind juice and cook for another 2–3 minutes. Serve hot with rice.

Onion and Yoghurt Salad

3 medium red onions, thinly sliced
1 teaspoon salt
1 cup (250 ml) plain yoghurt
1 teaspoon finely grated ginger
2 medium tomatoes, peeled and diced
2 green chilies, deseeded and minced
2–3 tablespoons minced coriander leaves (cilantro)

1 Sprinkle the onion slices with salt. Set aside for 30 minutes. Squeeze out excess liquid but do not rinse.
2 Combine the yoghurt and ginger, then stir in the onions, tomatoes, chilies and coriander leaves. Cover and chill in the refrigerator for at least 30 minutes before serving with rice and other dishes.

PRESERVED vegetables

Many of the vegetables grown in Asia are not only eaten fresh but are preserved in a variety of ways: dried; salted and sun-dried; preserved in brine, simmered in salty water then packed in rice bran mash; or pickled with vinegar. In northern Asia, vegetables were traditionally pickled to provide a source of food during the cold winter months when almost nothing grows. In tropical countries, vegetables which are likely to deteriorate quickly without refrigeration

are often pickled to preserve them. These homemade pickles are seldom kept for more than a month, and many are not usually sold commercially. Despite the advent of modern food preservation techniques, preserved vegetables are still popular for their flavor and are a deeply entrenched part of local diets in many areas. *Kim chee* in Korea is one of the best examples of this, while Chinese living in areas where fresh vegetables are abundant throughout the year still enjoy using various types of pickled cabbage.

Preserved Chinese Cabbage is made from salted and dried Chinese or napa cabbage, although it is difficult to tell this from the appearance of the preserved vegetable when packed, as it has been coarsely chopped and is brownish in color. Preserved Chinese cabbage is normally sold in packets, which are sometimes labeled "Tianjin Preserved Vegetable," Tianjin cabbage being yet another name for this type of cabbage. It is often known by its Cantonese name, *tang choy*, and is frequently served in soups.

Appearance & Flavor The Chinese cabbage, which is shredded before pickling, turns golden brown once preserved, making it difficult to recognize what vegetable has actually been used to make the pickle. It is slightly moist, with a salty flavor and crunchy texture. Garlic is usually added to the pickle, giving it a flavor that is robust and appealing. **Choosing & Storing** Preserved Chinese cabbage can be kept at room temperature for several months. In humid climates, it is best refrigerated to avoid any mold developing, and will keep almost indefinitely. **Preparing** The preserved cabbage should not be soaked and it is not normally cooked. **Culinary Uses** Preserved Chinese cabbage is eaten as a garnish, not as a main vegetable. It is often sprinkled on rice porridge, and is sometimes used to garnish noodle dishes.

Pickled Daikon is said to have first been made by a 17th century Buddhist priest. The whole radish is left in salt for a couple of weeks, then packed in vats of rice bran mash, where it develops a distinctive flavor. The Japanese call this pickle *takuan*, and it is eaten almost daily in most Japanese households. The Chinese also have a version of this moist pickle, known as *chye poh* in Hokkien.

Appearance & Flavor The Japanese version of pickled *daikon* (*takuan*) is generally bright yellow and quite pungent, with an excellent crunchy texture. The Chinese variety is a buff or pale yellow color and lacks the distinctive flavor of the Japanese *takuan*. **Choosing & Storing** Moist pickled *daikon* is normally vacuum-packed and sold in the refrigerated section of supermarkets or Asian stores. Keep refrigerated. After opening, the pickled *daikon* should keep for about 1 month. The Chinese variety should be shred at room temperature. **Preparing** Rinse briefly in water, then slice or chop. **Culinary Uses** Pickled *daikon* is eaten as a condiment, served together with rice in Japan, where its distinctive flavor and saltiness add flavor to the bland steamed rice, which is always cooked without salt. In China, this pickle is not served as a separate condiment but is used primarily as a flavoring for rice porridge. Pickled *daikon* can also be added in small amounts to noodles and used to flavor stir-fried vegetable dishes.

Kim Chee

Kim Chee (also spelt *kim chi*) is the Korean name for salted, preserved and lightly fermented vegetables with a large amount of garlic and chili added. *Kim chee* is commonly made using Chinese cabbage, although it can also contain *daikon* radishes, cucumbers and other vegetables. Traditionally, *kim chee* was layered in ceramic pots which were buried in the earth under the house to stop them from freezing during the winter.

Appearance & Flavor Vegetables used in *kim chee* are chopped or sliced, and the pickle liberally flecked with red chili and laced with garlic, ginger and sometimes chopped spring onions. The taste is generally hot, very garlicky, salty, fermented and slightly sour. **Choosing & Storing** Jars of *kim chee* are generally sold in the refrigerated section of Asian stores in temperate climates, and should be kept refrigerated until ready to use. **Preparing** None needed. The pickle should not be rinsed before serving. **Culinary Uses** Because of its pungency, *kim chee* is eaten as a side dish or condiment rather than as a main vegetable. It can also be added sparingly to stir-fried vegetable or meat dishes and noodles as a piquant seasoning. You could even add a small amount of *kim chee* to omelettes or to Western-style stews if you desire a different accent.

Dried Lily Buds or Day Lilies

Dried Lily Buds or Day Lilies are often called "golden needles," which is the translation of the poetic Chinese name for this dried flower bud. Fresh day lilies, which have beautiful yellow-gold flowers, are frequently grown for their appearance in the garden, and have the additional charm of being edible. The buds, picked before the lily flower has fully opened, are occasionally available fresh in Asian markets, but because of their fragility, are generally sold dried. Dried lily buds are available in Chinese provision shops worldwide.

Appearance & Flavor The dried buds are long and straggly with a yellowish beige or pale brown color, rather than the bright gold of the fresh flower. The flavor is vaguely like that of mushroom, although some think they taste vaguely of onion. They add an interesting, slightly chewy texture to soups and stews. **Choosing & Storing** Dried lily buds are sold in cellophane or plastic packs, and can be stored in a cupboard for several months. **Preparing** Soak in hot water for about 10 minutes until soft. The reconstituted buds are quite long, so for the sake of neat appearance and ease of eating, they are usually tied in a knot, one by one, before cooking. The hard knob at the base should be pinched or cut off. **Culinary Uses** Soaked lily buds are added to various vegetable combinations, especially the vegetarian dish, *chap chye*, some braised meat dishes, and in soups, such as the hot-and-sour broths in Chinese cuisine. The dried buds can be cooked lightly, then used to garnish salads or soups.

Pickled Mustard Cabbage is made from bamboo or leaf mustard and is treated in the same way as Swatow or heart mustard to obtain a moist pickle. Pickled mustard cabbage is sometimes sold under the name "sour mustard pickle" or "sour mustard greens" and is popular with Chinese cooks throughout Asia.

Appearance & Flavor This cabbage pickle, called *gai choy* in Cantonese, is sold from tubs, or packed into plastic bags in Asia. Elsewhere, it is usually sold in vacuum-packed plastic containers or cans. The leaves of the bamboo or leaf mustard are left on the stems for pickling, so the whole vegetable, with the pale green stems and darker green leaves—albeit shrunken—can be seen (provided you are not buying a can, of course). The flavor is salty and slightly sour. **Choosing & Storing** If buying the cabbage from a tub, make sure it does not have an unpleasant smell. Refrigerated in a plastic bag, the pickled mustard cabbage keeps for several months. Vacuum-packed pickled mustard cabbage can be refrigerated almost indefinitely. **Preparing** Rinse the cabbage in a couple of changes of water and taste. If it seems excessively salty, soak in warm water for about 30 minutes. The pickle should be chopped coarsely if being added to soup, or can be thinly sliced for other uses. **Culinary Uses** Used in the same way as pickled Swatow mustard cabbage (see page 152). Pickled mustard cabbage is best added to cooked dishes rather than used as a condiment. Chopped pickled mustard cabbage can be steamed with minced pork or mashed bean curd.

Preserved Mustard Cabbage is relatively widely used by Chinese cooks, although it is not as well known in the West. The preserved cabbage is used largely in home-style recipes as a flavoring rather than a vegetable, and is often known by its Cantonese name, *mui choy*, or *mei cai* in Mandarin.

Appearance & Flavor Preserved mustard cabbage is made using whole bamboo or leaf mustard cabbages, which are cooked, then mixed with salt, sugar and dried. Preserved mustard cabbage is very soft and pliable, and is golden brown in color with white salt crystals usually clearly visible on the leaves. The taste is pleasantly mild, thanks to the addition of the sugar. **Choosing & Storing** Preserved mustard cabbage is normally sold in sealed plastic bags, which can keep for several months if unopened. Once the package has been opened, the cabbage can be stored refrigerated in an airtight container for about 6 months. **Preparing** Rinse the cabbage in a couple of changes of water, then squeeze to remove excess moisture. Some cooks recommend blanching the preserved mustard cabbage in boiling water to remove the odor, and draining well before use. **Culinary Uses** Preserved mustard cabbage is commonly used as a seasoning, often cooked with minced pork or bean curd and steamed. It can also be added to stir-fried and braised dishes—one popular way of eating the vegetable in Southeast Asia is to cook it with braised fatty pork, served with plain rice porridge. Preserved mustard cabbage is very seldom eaten alone as a vegetable.

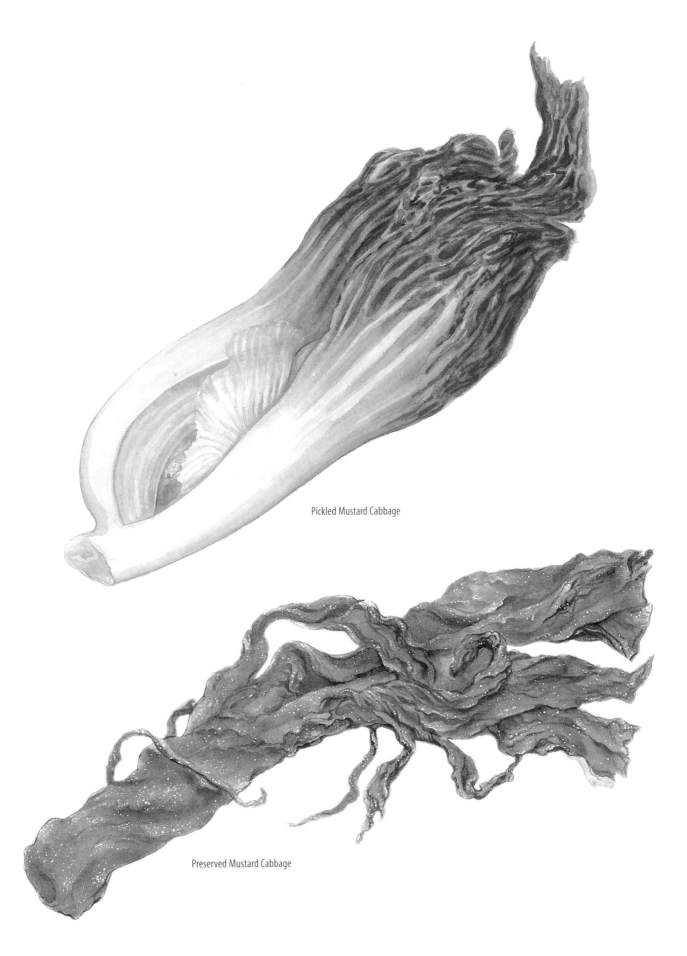

Pickled Mustard Cabbage

Preserved Mustard Cabbage

Sichuan Pickled Vegetable is also known as *zha cai* in Mandarin, and is a popular Chinese pickle with a spicy flavor. It is sometimes claimed that this pickle is made from Chinese radish or kohlrabi although others swear that the particular vegetable used to make it is only found in China and has no common English name.

Appearance & Flavor Sichuan pickled vegetable is preserved with salt, garlic and plenty of hot chili. The whole vegetable is about the size of a closed fist, and pale olive green with red chili flakes usually visible on the surface. It has a spicy, pungent flavor and firm texture. **Choosing & Storing** This is sometimes sold loose or vacuum-packed in plastic bags, but is also available in cans outside Asia. It is generally labeled "Sichuan Preserved Vegetable" or "Sichuan Mustard Pickle." After opening, keep refrigerated in a closed container for several months. **Preparing** When using Sichuan pickled vegetable, do not rinse off the spicy coating, but simply slice or chop the pickle. **Culinary Uses** Use Sichuan pickled vegetable sparingly in stir-fried dishes with pork or chicken, or slice thinly and add to soups. The pickle can also be served as a condiment with rice porridge.

Pickled Swatow Mustard Cabbage, often known by its Cantonese name, *ham suen choy*, the Hokkien *kiam chye*, or the Mandarin *xian cai*—which means "salted vegetable"—is a sour and salty vegetable and is frequently used in soups. There are two main types of mustard cabbage: the very bitter Swatow or heart mustard cabbage described here, and the milder, long-leaf wrapped or bamboo mustard cabbage (see page 150). The pickling process helps reduce their inherent bitterness.

Appearance & Flavor Pickled Swatow mustard cabbage is a wet, salty pickle. The vegetable is blanched in water and then pickled with salt and a touch of vinegar. In Asia, it is often sold from tubs, but is more commonly sold in vacuum packs elsewhere. Generally, a large portion of the leaves have been removed, so the pickle consists mostly of the cabbage heart and the thick stems, which are pale green in color. The taste is salty and very sour, with just a hint of bitterness. **Choosing & Storing** If buying the cabbage from a tub, make sure it does not have an unpleasant smell. Refrigerated in a plastic bag, the swatow mustard cabbage keeps well for several months. Vacuum-packed pickled Swatow mustard cabbage can be stored refrigerated almost indefinitely. **Preparing** Rinse the pickle in a couple of changes of water and taste. If it seems excessively salty, soak in warm water for about 30 minutes. The pickle should be chopped coarsely if being added to soup, or can be thinly sliced for other uses. Pickled Swatow mustard cabbage is always added to cooked dishes, rather than served alone as a condiment. **Culinary Uses** This pickle is very often added to soups, and is an excellent foil to more strongly flavored ingredients such as duck—the soup made from the carcass of Peking duck almost invariably contains pickled Swatow mustard cabbage. One or two tablespoons of shredded pickled Swatow mustard cabbage adds flavor to many noodle and stir-fried vegetable dishes, and can also be added to fillings for dumplings.

Sichuan Pickled Vegetable

Pickled Swatow Mustard Cabbage

Vegetarian Bean Curd Skin Rolls

6 sheets dried bean curd skin,
   6 x 8 in (15 x 20 cm)

Filling
2 tablespoons oil
1 large clove garlic, minced
A handful of dried black moss,
   soaked in warm water to soften,
   drained and coarsely chopped
2 tablespoons dried black fungus,
   soaked in warm water to soften,
   shredded, soaking water reserved
1$^1/_4$ cups (100 g) bean sprouts,
   straggly tails removed
1 small carrot, cut into thin shreds
$^1/_2$ stalk celery, cut into thin shreds
1 spring onion, minced

3 water chestnuts, minced
1 tablespoon rice wine or saké
1 tablespoon soy sauce
$^1/_2$ teaspoon salt
White pepper, to taste
1 teaspoon cornstarch

1 To make the Filling, heat the oil in a wok and then add the garlic and stir-fry for a few seconds. Add the black moss, fungus, bean sprouts, carrot, celery, spring onion and water chestnuts and stir-fry over high heat for 1 minute. Add the rice wine, soy sauce, salt and pepper. Combine the cornstarch with $^1/_4$ cup of the liquid reserved from soaking the dried fungus, then add to the wok and stir until the mixture thickens and clears. Transfer to a plate to cool.
2 Moisten the bean curd skin by wiping it with a clean, damp cloth. Divide the Filling into 6 portions and spoon one portion along the middle of each bean curd skin, pressing to shape it into a roll. Fold the end of the bean curd skin nearest you over the Filling, then fold in both ends, and roll up firmly into a cigar shape.
3 When all rolls are prepared, place them in a steamer and steam over high heat for 10 minutes. Serve hot with rice.

Stir-fried Chicken and Sichuan Pickled Vegetable

2 tablespoons oil
2 cloves garlic, minced
1 teaspoon minced ginger
1 red chili, minced
8 oz (250 g) chicken, cut into thin
   strips
2 heaped tablespoons Sichuan
   pickled vegetable, cut into thin
   strips
1 small carrot, cut into matchsticks
1 stalk celery, cut into matchsticks
3 spring onions, cut in lengths
1 tablespoon rice wine or saké
$^1/_4$ cup (60 ml) chicken stock
White pepper, to taste

Sauce
2 teaspoons cornstarch
$^1/_2$ cup (125 ml) chicken stock
1 tablespoon oyster sauce
1 teaspoon soy sauce
1 teaspoon rice vinegar
1 teaspoon sugar
1 teaspoon rice wine or saké
$^1/_4$ teaspoon sesame oil

1 Prepare the Sauce by combining all the ingredients in a small bowl. Stir well and set aside.
2 Heat the oil in a wok and add the garlic, ginger and chili. Stir-fry for a few seconds, then add the chicken and stir-fry for 1 minute. Add the pickled vegetable, carrot, celery and spring onions and stir-fry for another 30 seconds. Pour in the rice wine and the chicken stock and continue to cook until the vegetables are just done. Pour in the Sauce and stir until it thickens and clears. Sprinkle with pepper and serve.

Chilled Tofu with Dried Prawns and Preserved Sichuan Vegetable

16 oz (500 g) chilled soft or silken
   tofu, drained
2 tablespoons dried prawns, soaked
   in warm water, to soften, drained
2$^1/_2$ tablespoons finely diced
   preserved Sichuan vegetable
1 tablespoon salted soy bean paste
   (*tau cheo*), mashed
$^1/_2$–1 teaspoon dried chili flakes or
   minced red chili
1 tablespoon sesame oil
1 spring onion, thinly sliced

1 Carefully put the tofu in a colander and dip the colander in a large bowl of cold water for 1 minute. Lift out colander, drain and repeat twice, using fresh water each time. Drain the tofu thoroughly and transfer to a cutting board. Cut the tofu into large cubes and arrange on a serving plate. Chill in the refrigerator for a short while, about 30 seconds.
2 Grind the dried prawns in a spice grinder or blender until coarsely flaked; do not grind to a fine powder. Transfer to a small bowl. Add the preserved Sichuan vegetable, soy bean paste and chili to the prawns and stir to mix thoroughly. Spread the mixture evenly over the tofu, then scatter with the spring onion. Serve immediately.

Pickled Mustard Cabbage with Beef

3 tablespoons oil
7 oz (200 g) sirloin, sliced into strips
1 heaped tablespoon very finely shredded ginger
1½ cups (185 g) finely sliced celery
9 oz (250 g) pickled mustard cabbage, rinsed and drained, thinly sliced
¼ cup (60 ml) chicken stock
1 tablespoon rice wine or saké
White pepper, to taste

Sauce
1 tablespoon cornstarch
¾ cup (185 ml) chicken stock
1½ tablespoons oyster sauce
1 tablespoon rice wine or saké

1 Prepare the Sauce by mixing all the ingredients in a small bowl. Set aside.
2 Heat 1 tablespoon of the oil in a wok and add the beef. Stir-fry just until it changes color, then remove from the wok and set aside. Add the rest of the oil to the wok and when very hot, add the ginger and stir-fry for a few seconds. Add the celery and pickled cabbage and stir-fry over high heat for 1 minute. Add the chicken stock and beef and stir for 1 minute, then add in the wine and sprinkle with pepper. Pour in the prepared Sauce mixture and stir until it thickens and clears, then serve.

Preserved Mustard Cabbage with Pork

7 oz (200 g) preserved mustard cabbage (*mei cai*), washed in several changes of water, soaked in fresh water for 30 minutes
14 oz (400 g) lean ground pork
2 in (5 cm) ginger, very finely grated, pressed to extract juice
1½ tablespoons oyster sauce
4 teaspoons rice wine or saké
4 teaspoons thick black soy sauce
2 teaspoons sugar
1 teaspoon oil
½ teaspoon white pepper

1 tablespoon cornstarch
⅓ cup (80 ml) water
1 spring onion, minced (optional)

1 Squeeze the soaked mustard cabbage to expel as much moisture as possible. Slice thinly and put into a bowl with the pork, ginger juice, oyster sauce, rice wine, soy sauce, sugar, oil and pepper, stirring to mix well. Sprinkle in the cornstarch and water. Stir to mix well with the pork.

2 Spoon the mixture into a heatproof dish (such as a pie plate) that will fit into a steaming basket, pressing the mixture gently with the back of the spoon to smooth the surface.
3 Place the dish into a bamboo steaming basket and cover. Place the steamer over boiling water in a wok. Steam for 15–20 minutes, or until cooked, adding extra boiling water after 10 minutes. Garnish with the spring onion, and serve hot with steamed rice.

Pickled Swatow Mustard Cabbage and Bean Curd Soup

½ cup (2½ oz/75 g) lean pork loin, thinly sliced
4 cups (1 liter) chicken stock
4 oz (125 g) pickled Swatow mustard cabbage (*kiam chye*), thinly sliced
1-in (2½-cm) slice ginger, bruised
1 tablespoon rice wine or saké
1 tablespoon rice vinegar
1 tablespoon soy sauce
8 oz (250 g) silken bean curd, cubed
White pepper, to taste
2 tablespoons minced coriander

leaves (cilantro) or spring onion greens, to garnish

Marinade
1 teaspoon cornstarch
2 teaspoons oyster sauce
1 teaspoon soy sauce

1 Put the pork in a bowl and toss with the cornstarch. Add the rest of the Marinade ingredients, toss and leave to marinate for 15 minutes.

2 Put the chicken stock, pickled cabbage, ginger, rice wine, vinegar and soy sauce in a pan and bring to a boil. Lower heat and simmer partially covered for 5 minutes. Add the pork and simmer 1 minute, then put in the bean curd and cook 1 minute. Sprinkle with the pepper and coriander leaves or spring onion greens. Serve hot.

Braised Mixed Vegetables with Dried Lily Buds (*Chap Chye*)

3 teaspoons oil
2 teaspoons minced garlic
2 teaspoons finely grated ginger
1 teaspoon salted soy bean paste (*tau cheo*), mashed
6 dried black mushrooms, soaked in hot water to soften, liquid reserved, stems removed, discarded, caps halved
2 tablespoons cloud ear fungus, soaked in hot water to soften, liquid reserved, sliced
10 dried lily buds, soaked in hot water to soften, liquid reserved
4 dried bean curd skin, soaked in hot water to soften, cut into 2-in (5-cm) lengths
1 teaspoon soy sauce
$1/2$ teaspoon salt
$1/4$ teaspoon chicken stock granules (optional)
$1/4$ teaspoon ground white pepper

$1/2$ head Chinese cabbage (1 lb/ 500 g), cut in chunks
4 oz (125 g) canned bamboo shoots, drained and thinly sliced
2 teaspoons cornstarch
1 tablespoon water
1 oz (30 g) bean thread noodles or glass noodles (*tung hoon*), soaked in warm water until soft, cut into 3-in (8-cm) lengths
1 spring onion, thinly sliced

1 Heat the oil in a wok and stir-fry the garlic and ginger over low heat for 30 seconds. Add the bean paste and stir-fry for another 30 seconds. Measure the reserved soaking liquids and add enough water to make 2 cups (500 ml). Add the mixture, mushrooms, fungus, lily buds, bean curd skin, soy sauce, salt, chicken stock granules and pepper to the pan. Bring to a boil, cover, lower heat, and simmer 15 minutes. Add the cabbage and bamboo shoots, mixing well. Cover the wok and simmer for about 15 minutes, until the cabbage is tender.
2 Combine the cornstarch and water in a small bowl, then add to the pan and cook for 30 seconds, until the mixture thickens and clears. Add the glass noodles and spring onion, stir thoroughly and transfer to a serving dish.

Korean Kim Chee Stir-fried with Pork

2 tablespoons oil
14 oz (400 g) pork loin, thinly sliced
4 dried black mushrooms, soaked in warm water to soften, stems discarded, caps sliced
1–2 red chilies, deseeded and sliced
1–2 green chilies, deseeded and sliced
1 small onion, thinly sliced
4 oz (125 g) *kim chee*, squeezed dry and finely chopped
1 tablespoon sesame seeds, toasted and coarsely crushed while warm

Seasoning
4 tablespoons Korean chili paste (*gochu jang*)
1–2 teaspoons ground red pepper
2 cloves garlic, minced
1 teaspoon finely grated ginger
2 tablespoons water
$1^1/2$ tablespoons soy sauce
1 tablespoon sugar
2 teaspoons rice wine or saké
2 teaspoons sesame oil

1 Prepare the Seasoning by mixing all the ingredients in a small bowl, stirring until the sugar has dissolved.
2 Heat the oil in a wok and add the pork. Stir-fry over high heat for about 30 seconds, then add the mushrooms, chilies, onion and *kim chee*. Stir-fry for 1 minute, then add the Seasoning and continue stir-frying for about 3 minutes, or until the pork is cooked. Sprinkle with the sesame seeds and serve hot.

Sushi with Tuna and Pickled Daikon

1¹/₂ cups (300 g) raw Japanese rice
2 cups (500 ml) water
1 small piece konbu sea kelp
  (optional)
16–18 sheets nori seaweed (6 x 6 in/
  15 x 15 cm)
6–8 lettuce leaves, torn in 3¹/₂-in
  (9-cm) squares
2 teaspoons wasabi paste
7 oz (200 g) fresh tuna, thinly sliced
7 oz (200 g) pickled daikon, cut into
  matchsticks
7 oz (200 g) Japanese cucumber, cut
  into matchsticks

Dressing
3 tablespoons rice vinegar
3 tablespoons sugar
1 tablespoon mirin
1¹/₂ teaspoons salt

1 Put the rice, water and konbu in a pan, cover and bring to a boil. Discard the konbu and cover the saucepan, leaving the lid slightly open. Cook over moderate heat until the water is completely absorbed. Cook over minimum heat for 10 minutes. Remove from heat and set aside for 10 minutes. Prepare the Dressing by stirring the vinegar, sugar, mirin and salt in a small bowl until the sugar is dissolved.
2 Transfer the cooked rice to a wide bowl and toss gently with a wooden spoon, gradually pouring the Dressing over the rice. Toss frequently for 5 minutes. Set aside until the rice is completely cold, which will take about 20 minutes.

3 Put a piece of nori diagonally on a board. Line with a piece of lettuce. Shape about 2 tablespoons rice into a rectangle as long as the lettuce squares, and place in the center. Smear with wasabi and add a piece of tuna, some pickled daikon, and cucumber. Fold over the end facing you, then wrap in both sides to form a cone shape. Place 2–3 grains of rice under the edge of the nori and press gently to seal. Repeat with the rest of the pieces of nori and filling. Serve the sushi with the pickled ginger slices, grated fresh daikon, wasabi and soy sauce.

Rice Porridge with Preserved Chinese Cabbage

1 cup (200 g) raw rice, washed and
  drained
4 cups (1 liter) water
4 cups (1 liter) chicken or
  vegetable stock
1 medium sweet potato, peeled
  and diced
2 tablespoons preserved Chinese
  cabbage
1 century egg, peeled and diced
  (optional)
3 tablespoons minced coriander
  leaves (cilantro) or spring onions
2 tablespoons crisp fried shallots
1 tablespoon finely shredded
  young ginger
White pepper, to taste
1 teaspoon sesame oil
Soy sauce for serving

1 Put the rice, water and chicken stock in a large saucepan and bring to a boil, stirring from time to time. Partially cover the pan and simmer over low heat for 45 minutes, stirring occasionally. Add the sweet potato and continue cooking until the vegetable is tender for 10–15 minutes.

2 Transfer the rice porridge to four bowls. Garnish each with some of the preserved cabbage, century egg (if using), coriander leaves or spring onion greens, crisp shallots, ginger, pepper and sesame oil. Serve with a bit of soy sauce.

SEAWEEDS

Seaweeds belong to a group of primitive plants known as algae, and can be divided into three groups: brown, green and red algae. Kelp is a term used to cover various types of brown algae. Laver, a green algae, is very important in Korean and Japanese cuisine. Red algae are used to produce the very important agar agar, which is used as a vegetable form of gelatin throughout Asia.

In Asia, seaweeds have been highly prized for centuries for their nutritional value and flavor, used primarily in the colder northern countries of Japan, Korea and China, as well as eaten in the coastal parts of Southeast Asia, particularly the Philippines. Fresh seaweeds are seldom found in major markets in Asia (apart from Japan and Korea), and only a few varieties are sold fresh in Western countries. A number of dried seaweeds, however, are available in Asian stores and many supermarkets. Some seaweeds which have already been prepared and seasoned are ready for eating, and are sold in plastic packs in the refrigerated section of Japanese and Korean specialty stores.

Hijiki, as it is known in Japan, does not have a common English name. Its scientific name is *Cystophyllum fusiforme*. The seaweed is most commonly found in Japan, where it is sold dried, and is usually used in braised dishes.

Appearance & Flavor *Hijiki*, which looks rather like short, fine black wires, retains its crunchy texture after soaking and simmering. The flavor of the seaweed, somewhat bitter and salty, is usually dominated by the seasonings with which it is cooked, generally soy sauce and sweet rice wine or mirin. **Choosing & Storing** *Hijiki* is dried and sold in plastic packets. Like all other dried seaweeds, *hijiki* can be stored in an airtight container in a cupboard almost indefinitely. In a humid tropical or subtropical climate, it is best kept refrigerated in an airtight container after opening. **Preparing** *Hijiki* should be soaked in cold water until softened, or for about 1 hour. It will swell to about two or three times its dried size. **Nutritional & Medicinal Properties** *Hijiki* contains valuable nutrients, including niacin, calcium and protein. It is also a source of lignans, which help fight against cancer—it is thought that the low incidence of breast cancer among Japanese women can be attributed to their consumption of seaweed and soy bean products. *Hijiki* is also totally fat free and hardly contains any calories. **Culinary Uses** Soaked *hijiki* can be simmered with seasonings for about 10 minutes, and kept refrigerated for several weeks to be used as an edible garnish. It can also be added to soups or Teochew rice porridge with sliced fish.

Konbu or Dried Kelp (*Laminaria japonica*) is sometimes known as sea tangle or sea belt. In Japan, it is called *konbu* or *kombu*. The seaweed is harvested in the cold waters of northern Japan, and can grow up to 12 in (30 cm) in width and several meters in length. The leaves are sun-dried before cutting, folding and packaging. *Konbu* contains glutamic acid, which acts as a natural flavor intensifier.

Appearance & Flavor *Konbu* or dried kelp is stiff and dark greenish black in color, with a whitish, salty bloom on it. It is not normally eaten directly, but is used to give a subtle marine flavor and pleasant aroma to many dishes. After adding to water, the kelp swells to about twice its dried size. Pickled *konbu* (*su-konbu*) is sold in plastic packets and is used as an edible garnish. The crunchy strips have an appealing sweet-sour flavor. **Choosing & Storing** *Konbu* is dried and cut into strips before being packed, usually in cellophane. It is often labeled "*konbu*" or "*kombu*" without the English name. Store *konbu* as you would *hijiki*. **Preparing** Dried *konbu* should not be rinsed before using or its flavor and nutrition will be diminished. Wipe with a clean dry cloth and cut with scissors to the required size. Some Japanese cooks recommend scoring the laver slightly to release the glutamic acid more effectively. **Nutritional & Medicinal Properties** *Konbu* contains iodine, calcium, iron, magnesium, calcium and folitates. **Culinary Uses** *Konbu* is used with dried bonito flakes (*katsuobushi*), to make the basic Japanese stock, *dashi*. *Konbu* is also added to sauces or placed under steamed fish for flavor. It is sometimes sold in shredded form, for deep-frying as a garnish.

Hijiki

Konbu (Dried Kelp)

Nori or Dried Laver

Nori or Dried Laver (*Porphyra spp.*) derives its English name from the Latin, meaning "water plant." However, it is increasingly known in the West by its Japanese name, *nori*. A similar type of laver growing along the rocky coasts of northern Europe used to be eaten in places like Wales and Scotland. In Korea, where laver is almost as popular as it is in Japan, it is known as *keem*. Laver is cultivated in shallow waters, and after gathering is washed in fresh water and dried in paper-thin sheets. It was once grown in the bay of Tokyo, until pollution forced an end to its collection.

Appearance & Flavor *Nori* or dried laver can be dark green, purplish black or dark brown, and is sold in varying sizes. The flavor intensifies after toasting. Much of the packaged *nori* has already been toasted. It is also sometimes seasoned with a soy sauce before toasting. **Choosing & Storing** Sheets of *nori* come in several sizes, with the most common measuring 8-in (20-cm) square. Sheets this size are often marked with small rectangles, which are cut for wrapping around rice. However, if using for this purpose, it is easier to buy small packets containing strips of *nori* about 3 in (8 cm) in length. There is also a type of finely shredded *nori* sold in a small bottle for shaking over rice dishes or soups as a condiment. Choose the size of *nori* depending upon the intended usage, and store in an airtight container in a cupboard, away from direct light. After opening, *nori* is best kept refrigerated in an airtight container. **Preparing** No preparation is needed, unless large sheets of *nori* are used—these need cutting to size for wrapping sushi. Use scissors rather than a knife to do this. **Nutritional & Medicinal Properties** As for other seaweeds. **Culinary Uses** Use the *nori*, which is fairly flexible, to wrap sushi rolls, individual bite-sized sushi or small rice balls. To seal the edges, moisten the end of the *nori* lightly with a finger dipped in water, taking care not to use too much water. Sheets of seasoned toasted *nori* can be eaten as a nutritious snack, or shredded and sprinkled over rice. For an interesting accent to Western-style soups or vegetables, combine shredded *nori*, sea salt and black peppercorns in a grinder and twist to sprinkle over food.

Wakame is the Japanese name for a type of kelp scientifically known as *Undaria pinnatifida*. It does not have any common English name. In Korea, it is known as *miyuk*, and in China as *lai wu xi ca*. *Wakame* is seldom available fresh outside north Asia, and even there, only in the spring and summer. *Wakame* comes in two forms: the dried form and the moist, salted variety. Both have a very good flavor and texture.

Appearance & Flavor Both the fresh and the moist, salted *wakame* are bright green and resemble narrow ribbons. When dried, *wakame* looks like shriveled black strands, yet regains its original color and texture after a brief soaking. Japanese and Korean *wakame* has an appealing crisp texture and mild vegetable flavor. The Chinese also prepare coarse sheets of a similar type of dried kelp. The flavor is close to that of Japanese *wakame*, although the color is purple-black after soaking, and because the seaweed is not as thick, the texture is not quite as springy. The Chinese product is usually sold pressed into thick squares or ovals; it is very mild in flavor and somewhat like strands of firm jelly in texture. **Choosing & Storing** Moist, salted *wakame* is sold in plastic packs in the refrigerated section of Japanese stores. Keep refrigerated until using. Dried *wakame* is either dark greenish black, purplish black or brown. The former is of a better quality. Dried *wakame* can be stored in its original package in a cupboard almost indefinitely, but after opening must be kept in a tightly closed container, preferably in the refrigerator. **Preparing** Moist, salted *wakame* needs to be rinsed. Put it in a colander or sieve under running cold water for a few seconds, drain and squeeze gently. Dried *wakame*, which swells to around five times its volume, should be soaked in warm water just until softened. Do not soak too long or the slightly chewy texture will be lost. The amount of time this takes will depend on the thickness of the *wakame*, but 10 minutes is usually sufficient. Drain immediately. If there is any hard central rib, cut away using a pair of scissors or a sharp knife and discard. **Nutritional & Medicinal Properties** *Wakame* is highly nutritious and calorie-free. In Korea, a soup of *wakame* or *miyuk* seaweed and oysters is traditionally eaten every day for seven weeks to restore the health of women after childbirth. **Culinary Uses** With its decorative appearance and excellent texture and flavor, *wakame* is a popular addition to salads. It is often combined with sliced cucumber and a lightly vinegared dressing. It is also added to miso and other Japanese soups.

Smoked Salmon and Cucumber Rolls Wrapped with Nori

7 oz (200 g) thinly sliced smoked salmon, cut into strips (2 x 5 in/ 5 x 12 cm)
1^1/$_2$ tablespoons wasabi paste
1 cucumber, quartered lengthwise, seeds removed, cut into 1^1/$_2$-in (4-cm) lengths
^{1}/$_4$ cup sliced pickled ginger
5 nori sheets, cut into 20 small rectangles, each about 2 x 4 in (4 x 10 cm)

Dipping Sauce
^{1}/$_4$ cup (60 ml) soy sauce
^{1}/$_4$ cup (60 ml) thick black soy sauce or tamari
^{1}/$_4$ cup (60 ml) water
2 tablespoons mirin
1 tablespoon dried bonito flakes (katsuobushi)

1 Make the Dipping Sauce by mixing both types of soy sauce, water, mirin and bonito flakes in a small sauce-pan. Bring to a boil while stirring constantly, then remove the Sauce immediately from the heat and strain through a fine sieve. Transfer to four small sauce bowls.
2 Lay several pieces of smoked salmon on a flat surface. Dip your finger in the wasabi paste and make a vertical smear down the middle of each piece of salmon. Place a strip of cucumber and a slice of ginger vertically on each piece of salmon, then roll up firmly.

3 Moisten the end of a piece of nori with a wet finger. Place the salmon roll at one end, then roll up firmly, pressing to seal. Repeat until all ingredients are used up. Transfer the rolls to four individual serving plates. Place a small mound of horseradish on each plate. Serve with the Dipping Sauce at room temperature as an appetizer or first course.

Egg and Nori Rolls

4 eggs
^{1}/$_4$ teaspoon salt
1 packet nori seaweed, in small strips or rectangles
1 tablespoon oil
Japanese seven-spice mixture (shichimi togarashi) or dried chili flakes (optional)

1 Break the eggs into a bowl and add the salt. Beat lightly. Heat a frying pan, preferably non-stick, with about 1 teaspoon of the oil, swirling it around to coat the bottom of the pan. Pour in ^{1}/$_3$ of the egg, swirling the pan to coat the bottom with a thin layer. Cook just until the top starts to set. Cover the egg with pieces of nori, then use a couple of spatulas to roll the egg away from you. Leave the roll to cook for about 1 minute, then turn out and leave to cool. Repeat to make 3 rolls.
2 When the rolls are cool, cut into bite-sized pieces and serve, sprinkled with the chili flakes or spice mixture (if using). Serve with cocktail forks or toothpicks.

Korean Simmered Wakame

Large handful dried wakame
1 tablespoon oil
1 teaspoon sesame oil
1 tablespoon minced garlic
^{1}/$_4$ teaspoon salt
1 teaspoon sesame seeds, toasted and coarsely crushed

1 Put the wakame in a bowl and cover with a generous amount of warm water. Soak until it swells and softens slightly, about 10 minutes. Drain and put in a saucepan with all the remaining ingredients. Bring to a simmer, cover, and cook gently for 5 minutes. Remove the lid and cook, stirring frequently, over medium heat for 5 minutes. Serve hot, or cool then chill and serve cold.

Fresh Tuna Baked in Konbu

3/4 cup white miso paste
3 tablespoons rice wine or saké
3 tablespoons mirin
1 1/2 tablespoons sugar
4 strips dried *konbu*, each about
    3 x 6 in (8 x 15 cm)
10 oz (300 g) fresh tuna fillet,
    coarsely sliced
4 spring onions, thinly sliced
2 teaspoons finely grated ginger
4 tablespoons finely diced green
    bell pepper

1 Put miso, saké, mirin and sugar in a small saucepan and cook over low heat, stirring occasionally, for 20 minutes. Allow to cool completely. Soak the pieces of *konbu* in warm water until soft. Cut two very narrow and long strips from each piece to use as a tie. Pinch the ends of each piece of *konbu* together and tie so that they form an oval "boat" for the tuna mixture.

2 Combine the cooled miso with tuna and all the other ingredients, mixing well. Put 1/4 of the tuna mixture into each *konbu* boat and bake at 180 °C (350 °F) for about 15 minutes. Serve hot.

Seaweed and Crabmeat Salad

1/4 cup dried *wakame*
4 oz (125 g) fresh or canned
    cooked crabmeat, flaked
1 1/2 tablespoons soy sauce
2 teaspoons rice vinegar
2 teaspoons sesame seeds, dry-
    roasted until golden brown,
    coarsely crushed while still warm
1 1/2 teaspoons sesame oil
Ground red pepper or *sansho*
    pepper, to taste

1 Soak the seaweed in warm water until it softens and expands to about 5 times its original size; this will take about 10 minutes. Drain and chop the seaweed coarsely, then transfer to a bowl. Add the crabmeat flakes.

2 Combine the soy sauce, vinegar, sesame seeds, sesame oil and red pepper or *sansho* pepper in a bowl, mixing well, then pour over the crab and seaweed and toss. Chill in the refrigerator before serving.

Braised Hijiki

1 slice deep-fried Japanese bean
    curd (*aburage*)
2 tablespoons sesame oil
1 cup dried *hijiki*, soaked in warm
    water for 30 minutes, drained
2 medium potatoes, peeled and
    cubed
1/2 cup (125 ml) *dashi* stock
    (made with instant *dashi*
    granules), or water

2 tablespoons rice wine
    or saké
1 tablespoon mirin
1 tablespoon soy sauce
1 tablespoon sugar

1 Put the deep-fried bean curd in a pan of boiling water and cook for about 1 minute. Drain, and cut into bite-sized pieces.

2 Heat the sesame oil in a wok or wide saucepan and add the drained *hijiki*. Stir-fry for 1 minute, then add the bean curd and potato and stir-fry for 2 minutes. Add all the other ingredients, cover the pan, and simmer until the potato is soft.

TOFU & other soy products

The soy bean is the richest plant source of protein, and is also an important source of vitamins A and B, calcium, niacin and thiamin, as well as minerals such as iron, magnesium and potassium. The humble soy beans contain phytoestrogens, which have been proven to be very beneficial to women undergoing hormonal changes. The best known soy products (apart from various soy sauces) include the many different forms of bean curd, dried bean curd

skin and protein-rich cakes of fermented soy beans widely known as *tempeh*. (The small squares of soft bean curd, fermented with Chinese wine and sold in jars, are used solely as a flavoring and therefore are not discussed here.) All soy products have similar health benefits, although the protein content varies depending on the product.

Bean Curd or Tofu

is the most common soy product and is soft in texture. Bean curd is made by adding a coagulant to soy milk, the nutritious liquid extracted from boiled and crushed soy beans. This liquid is left to separate into curds and whey, then the curds are drained and allowed to set. When compressed to reduce the water content, they become hard or "pressed" bean curd (see page 171).

Appearance & Flavor Bean curd has a creamy white color, and is generally made into blocks 2–3 in (5–7 cm) thick. The flavor is fairly neutral. Pasteurized bean curd in plastic packs does not have quite the same flavor as fresh bean curd, but is still highly acceptable. **Choosing & Storing** In the West, bean curd is most commonly pasteurized and water-packed in plastic tubs or cartons. In Asia, metal trays of freshly made bean curd cut into squares are more common. If buying fresh soft bean curd, make sure it has a pleasant smell. Packaged bean curd should be refrigerated after purchase. If it does not have a printed expiry date, use within 1 week of purchase. Fresh soft bean curd can be refrigerated for up to 1 week. Cover with water and change daily. **Preparing** Bean curd can be cut but should be handled carefully as it is more fragile than pressed bean curd. It is best drained on several sheets of paper towels for 10 minutes before slicing, then diced or cut into large squares. **Nutritional & Medicinal Properties** The protein content is around 11%, and the fat content is 5%. Like all forms of bean curd, this is an excellent substitute for meat in a vegetarian diet. **Culinary Uses** Bean curd is cubed and added to soups; sliced and layered with a filling of minced pork or fish, then steamed with fish, ginger, spring onions and preserved sour plums. Bean curd is also braised, fried or scrambled with chili and minced meat.

Deep-fried Bean Curd

is popular in both Chinese and Japanese cuisine, and is available in several shapes and sizes. In Japan, it is made by pressing fresh bean curd briefly to reduce its water content, then deep-frying it in very hot oil until crisp on the outside and meltingly soft inside. In China and Taiwan, the much firmer pressed bean curd is used for frying, resulting in a dryer form that keeps well even without refrigeration.

Appearance & Flavor Deep-fried bean curd is available in rectangles, small cubes or triangles, as well as in a flattened, thin form (*aburage* in Japanese). Deep-fried bean curd has a more definite flavor than other types of bean curd, and is almost nutty. **Choosing & Storing** Deep-fried bean curd sold loose can be kept refrigerated for about a week. Several forms of Japanese *aburage* are sold in vacuum packs. **Preparing** To remove some of the oiliness of Chinese-style squares of deep-fried bean curd, drop it in boiling water for about a minute, rinse and drain before inserting a filling or adding to other ingredients. Japanese *aburage* does not need this treatment, although some cooks would recommend it. **Nutritional & Medicinal Properties** The protein content is almost 19%, and the fat content, about 31%. **Culinary Uses** Thick pieces of deep-fried bean curd (especially the Chinese variety, known as *tau pok*) are added to soups, noodles and braised dishes. The bean curd becomes spongy and very tasty as it absorbs the liquid during cooking. The Japanese sometimes simmer cakes of dried deep-fried bean curd in a soy-flavored broth before filling them, and also add smaller cakes to simmered or steamed dishes containing vegetables or meat.

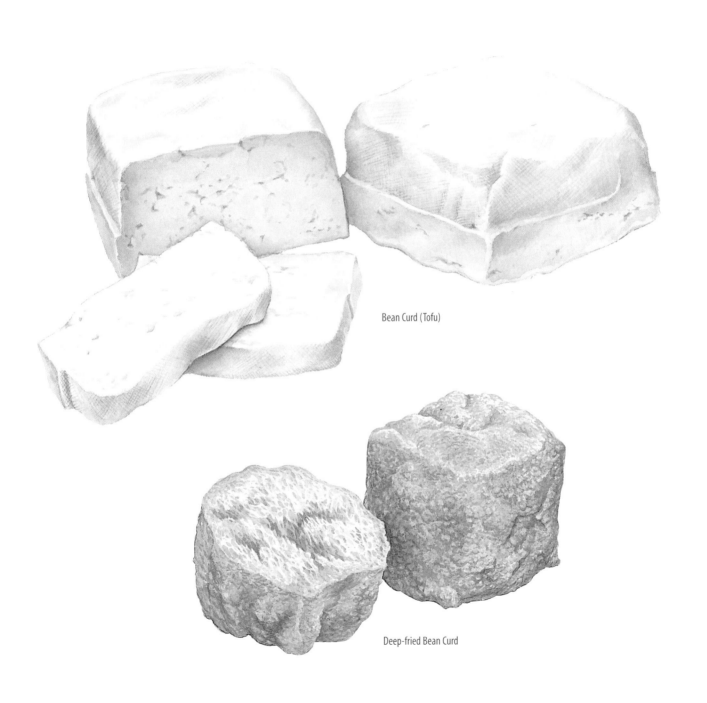

Bean Curd (Tofu)

Deep-fried Bean Curd

Grilled Bean Curd

Grilled Bean Curd is known in Japanese cuisine as *yakidofu*, and is made by grilling both sides of lightly pressed bean curd over very high heat or under a broiler. It is thought to be one of the earliest ways of preparing tofu in Japan. Grilled bean curd was traditionally cooked over open coals in country farmhouses.

Appearance & Flavor This form of bean curd is easily recognized by its light brown speckling. It is usually packed in water in rectangular plastic containers. The flavor of grilled bean curd is more pronounced than regular bean curd. **Choosing & Storing** Keep refrigerated until the date indicated on the package. **Preparing** Remove from the package, rinse and pat dry. Slice or cube as required. **Nutritional & Medicinal Properties** The protein content of grilled bean curd is roughly 9% and it has approximately 5% of fat. Like other tofu products, grilled bean curd is a low-calorie, low-cost alternative to meat that is easy to digest. **Culinary Uses** As it contains very little water, grilled bean curd absorbs the flavor of other ingredients which makes it ideal for soups, stews and one-pot dishes (*nabemono*) such as sukiyaki. It has the added advantage of not falling apart during slow cooking. Grilled bean curd is also popular skewered and grilled, often with a miso paste. In the Kanto region of Japan, grilled bean curd is cooked together with sweet soy sauce to make *nishime*, a popular dish eaten during the Japanese New Year.

Pressed Bean Curd or Tau Kwa is available loose or packed in plastic

tubs. According to Chinese tradition, the method of making soy milk and bean curd was discovered by a philosopher and scholar, Lord Liu An, in 164 BC. In the intervening centuries, many variations of the basic soft bean curd have been developed, including pressed bean curd, which has been compressed to expel most of the moisture.

Appearance & Flavor Pressed bean curd usually resembles a solid, ivory-colored cake. Sizes vary, but pressed bean curd is often about 3 in (8 cm) square and 1 in (2$\frac{1}{2}$ cm) thick. **Choosing & Storing** If sold in vacuum packs or plastic tubs, keep sealed and refrigerate. Use before the expiry date. After opening, cover with water and keep refrigerated. Loose pressed bean curd, which will be fresh and not pasteurized like the bean curd sold in plastic tubs, should be covered with water in a container. It can be refrigerated for up to a week. **Preparing** Pat the bean curd cakes thoroughly dry with a paper towel before deep-frying, otherwise the oil will splatter. The bean curd can be left whole, diced, or sliced. **Nutritional & Medicinal Properties** The protein content of pressed bean curd is 22%, and the fat content, 11%. **Culinary Uses** As pressed bean curd holds its shape well, it is particularly good for deep-frying. Often the whole cake is deep-fried for 2–3 minutes on either side, until crisp and golden, then drained on paper towels and sliced or diced. It can then be added to noodles, soups, salads or combined with stir-fried vegetables. To reduce the fat intake, brush it with oil on both sides and cook under a hot grill until golden brown. Deep-fried bean curd cakes are also slit horizontally and raw vegetables such as bean sprouts and shredded carrot inserted in the pocket. This type of bean curd can also be added to braised dishes.

Silken Bean Curd is the softest type of bean curd. It gets its name from the Japanese *kinugoshidofu*, which translates as "silk-strained bean curd", referring to the fine texture. The curds of coagulated soy milk are not drained, resulting in a very delicate, soft bean curd.

Appearance & Flavor Silken bean curd has a very fine texture and is usually white in color. However, pale creamy yellow silken bean curd, which has added egg, is popular with many Chinese. Silken bean curd has a very delicate flavor and a faint fragrance. **Choosing & Storing** This is often available in plastic containers, with a clear plastic sheet on top, or in lined cardboard cartons, which should be refrigerated and used before the printed expiry date. Silken bean curd is also sold in small plastic tubes or rolls, often weighing around 7 oz (200 g). Plastic tubes of silken bean curd keep well unopened, and can be refrigerated for 2–3 weeks. After opening, the silken bean curd can be stored for a few days. **Preparing** Plastic tubes or rolls of silken bean curd are particularly convenient to use. Lay the tube on a board and cut across the end with a sharp knife. Grasp one end of the plastic, squeeze slightly, and the bean curd roll will slide out easily. For hot bean curd, just put the entire plastic tube in a saucepan of boiling water and simmer for 5 minutes. Cut open and slice before serving. Other types of silken bean curd should be handled carefully, and diced or sliced across only just before using. **Nutritional & Medicinal Properties** The protein content is 6%, and the fat content, around 3%. **Culinary Uses** Silken bean curd can be sliced and steamed, or diced and added to soups. It is also popular chilled in the summer months, served with a soy-based sauce garnished with dried bonito flakes (*katsuobushi*) or grated ginger in Japan, or served with preserved ("hundred year") egg and shredded ginger in China. Silken bean curd can also be blended with fresh fruit and a little low-fat milk and ice to make a healthy drink or smoothie (although this is a Western invention that is not found in Asia). Silken bean curd can also be blended with mustard, salt, a little crushed garlic and lemon juice as a fat-free mayonnaise substitute.

Bean Curd Skin or Yuba contains the highest percentage of protein of all soy bean products. The skin forms on top of vats of boiling soy milk, just like the skin on boiled dairy milk, and is lifted off, drained and then dried. Fresh bean curd skin is widely used as a meat substitute in Chinese vegetarian cuisine. However, in most countries, only dried bean curd skin is available, sold in plastic packs.

Appearance & Flavor Bean curd skin is sold in several forms, the most common being fine sheets. Thicker strips of dried bean curd skin, usually somewhat twisted, are sold in lengths of about 6–10 in (15–25 cm). It is also possible to find rolls of bean curd skin, made by tightly rolling up the fresh bean curd skin before drying it. They are often tied with a string. All forms of bean curd skin have a very subtle flavor. **Choosing & Storing** These products are sold in plastic packs and can be stored at room temperature for several months. After opening, keep in an airtight container or cover with plastic wrap and refrigerate. **Preparing** Sheets of dried bean curd skin should be lightly moistened with a damp towel to make them pliable before cutting into shape. Strips of bean curd skin are normally deep-fried until crisp, then added to braised dishes. Rolls of bean curd skin retain their shape when unwrapped. Remove any string and deep-fry before adding to braised dishes or soups. **Nutritional & Medicinal Properties** The protein content of bean curd skin is 52%, the fat content, 24%. **Culinary Uses** Sheets are generally used as a nutritious food wrapper, much like spring roll skins. Both strips and rolls of bean curd skin are generally added to soups and braised vegetable or meat dishes. Fried bean curd strips make a tasty snack, either plain or with a dip.

Silken Bean Curd

Bean Curd Skin (Yuba)

Soy Milk

Soy Milk is made in different ways in China and Japan. The Chinese soak the protein-rich dried soy beans until soft, then purée and squeeze them to obtain the liquid. This liquid is boiled to destroy a substance which prevents the release of protein. In Japan, the soaked beans are boiled before being puréed, then strained and boiled again. Soy milk and the products made from it are highly digestible and nutritious. Some processed forms of soy milk contain fats from the emulsifier added to thicken the milk, although fat-reduced forms are now widely available.

Appearance & Flavor Soy milk is white in color, and the flavor relatively neutral. However, the Chinese frequently add a flavoring such as almond or, in Southeast Asia, pandanus leaf, as well as sugar. **Choosing & Storing** Both fresh and packaged soy milk (sold in bottles or cartons) can be kept refrigerated for several days. **Preparing** Not needed. **Nutritional & Medicinal Properties** The protein content is about 4%, the fat content a minimum of 2%. Because soy milk contains plant oestrogens, it is increasingly popular in the West for women undergoing menopause. **Culinary Uses** Soy milk is normally consumed as a beverage in Asia (or used commercially to make various types of bean curd). It is sometimes used as as a substitute for dairy milk in Western countries.

Tau Fa or Tofu Custard

Tau Fa or Tofu Custard is formed by mixing soy milk with a coagulating agent which makes it set into a type of junket. It is sometimes called "tofu pudding," and also often known by its Mandarin name, *dou hua*, or its Hokkien name, *tau hway*. It makes a nutritious and easily digested snack, often eaten for breakfast with pickles and soy sauce or enjoyed with a sugar syrup.

Appearance & Flavor The custard is very soft and creamy white in color, with a delicate flavor and texture reminiscent of silken bean curd. Additional flavoring is often added to the sugar syrup which is frequently sold with the tofu custard. **Choosing & Storing** Keep tofu custard refrigerated for 2–3 days in a covered container. **Preparing** No preparation needed. **Nutritional & Medicinal Properties** Tofu custard has a protein content of around 4% and a fat content of 2%.

Culinary Uses Tofu custard is normally sold hot in markets and street stalls in Asia, scooped out of huge metal tubs into a bowl and eaten with savory pickles at breakfast, especially in China, or more commonly as a sweet, nutritious and easily digested snack in parts of Southeast Asia, with sugar syrup sometimes flavored with almond essence or fragrant pandanus leaves. It can also be chilled and served with syrup, or with lychees, longans and other kinds of fruit.

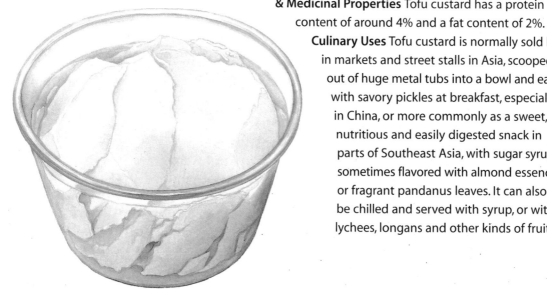

Tempeh

Tempeh was first developed in Indonesia and is made from soaked and boiled soy beans mixed with a bacteria which encourages them to ferment and mold to form a solid cake. *Tempeh* is easily digestible and is, like other fermented soy bean products, such as miso paste, one of the few non-meat sources of vitamin B12.

Appearance & Flavor Fresh *tempeh* has an edible, whitish bloom, a result of the fermentation caused by *Rizopus* mold which binds the beans together. Fresh *tempeh* cakes are white, with the pale yellow soy beans clearly visible, and smell and taste somewhat like nutty mushrooms. In Asia, *tempeh* is often sold in its traditional wrapper (a piece of leaf), or in a plastic bag. Outside Asia, *tempeh* is generally vacuum-packed and sold in the refrigerated section of Asian or health food stores. It does not develop the characteristic white bloom of the Indonesian product, and is generally light brown in color. Seasoned *tempeh* has been developed especially for a Western market, and it is now possible to find, for example, barbecue- or Mexican-flavored *tempeh*. **Choosing & Storing** If buying fresh *tempeh*, make sure that the mold on the cake is not starting to turn black. Refrigerate wrapped in a piece of paper towel in a covered container for up to 1 week. Vacuum-packed *tempeh* should be refrigerated and used before the printed expiry date.

Preparing No advance preparation is necessary.

Nutritional & Medicinal Properties The protein content of *tempeh* is 18%. *Tempeh* also contains riboflavin, niacin and thiamin.

Culinary Uses *Tempeh* can be deep-fried and is often added to other ingredients such as peanuts, prawns, soft bean curd or vegetables. Cakes of *tempeh* can be simmered in seasoned liquid or added to soups and stews. In Indonesia, very thinly sliced *tempeh* is often seasoned with crushed garlic, salt and coriander and sun-dried before being deep-fried to make a savory and nutritious snack. *Tempeh* also makes a tasty vegetarian substitute for meat in dishes requiring stir-fried minced chicken or beef pieces.

Steamed Silken Bean Curd with Vegetables

1 lb (500 g) silken bean curd, cubed or sliced
1/2 small carrot, very thinly sliced, blanched in boiling water 3 minutes
6–8 fresh or canned straw mushrooms, rinsed and drained, halved lengthwise
2 teaspoons cornstarch
1/2 cup (125 ml) chicken or vegetable stock
2 teaspoons oyster sauce
1 teaspoon fish sauce
1/2 teaspoon sugar
1/4 teaspoon white pepper
2 teaspoons oil

1 teaspoon minced garlic
4 baby *bok choy*, halved lengthwise, blanched in boiling water for 2 minutes, drained

1 Place the bean curd slices in a single layer in a shallow heatproof bowl. Put one slice of carrot half on top of each piece of bean curd, then arrange one mushroom half on top of the carrot.
2 Combine the cornstarch, stock, oyster sauce, fish sauce, sugar and pepper in a small bowl, stirring to dissolve the sugar.

3 Heat oil in a small saucepan and stir-fry the garlic over low heat for 10 seconds. Add the stock mixture, bring to a boil, and stir for 1 minute, until the mixture thickens and clears. Spoon over each piece of bean curd.
4 Place dish in a bamboo steamer and put into a wok of boiling water. Cover and steam for 5 minutes. Then remove the dish. Dip the *bok choy* in boiling water to reheat, drain well and place around the bean curd before serving.

Pork and Prawn Rolls in Bean Curd Skin

3 large sheets dried bean curd skin
Oil for deep-frying

Filling
10 oz (300 g) lean ground pork
10 oz (300 g) fresh prawns, peeled and deveined
4 shallots or 1/2 medium onion, minced
2 spring onions, minced
6 water chestnuts, minced
1 1/2 tablespoons cornstarch
1/2 teaspoon salt

White pepper, to taste
1 egg
1/2 cup (60 g) grated carrot, blanched 2 minutes in boiling water

1 Put the egg in a shallow bowl. Wipe the bean curd skin with a damp towel to moisten and make supple. Cut in 6-in (15-cm) squares.
2 To make the Filling, grind the pork and prawns in a food processor or blender until fine. Add the shallots, spring onions and water chestnuts

and continue to process. Add the remaining ingredients and blend to a smooth paste.
3 Put about 2 tablespoons of the mixture in the center of each bean curd sheet, shaping into a roll. Tuck in the ends, then both sides, and roll up to make a cigar shape. When all the rolls are prepared, heat the oil in a wok and deep-fry, a few at a time, until golden brown and crisp. Serve with chili or plum sauce for dipping.

Indonesian Spiced Tempeh with Palm Sugar and Sweet Soy Sauce

Oil for deep-frying
6 oz (180 g) unseasoned *tempeh*, diced
3–4 shallots, minced
3 cloves garlic, minced
1 red chili, minced
2–3 bird's-eye chilies, minced
3 tablespoons sweet Indonesian soy sauce (*kecap manis*)
2 tablespoons oyster sauce
1 tablespoon shaved palm sugar or soft brown sugar

1 teaspoon salt
2 heaped tablespoons tamarind pulp, soaked in 1/2 cup (125 ml) warm water, squeezed and strained to obtain juice
2 stems lemongrass, tender inner part of bottom third only, bruised

1 Heat oil in a wok, then add *tempeh* and deep-fry over medium heat for 4–5 minutes, until golden brown

and cooked. Drain on paper towels. Discard all but 2 tablespoons of the oil. Reheat and add the shallots, garlic and chilies and stir-fry for 3 minutes over low–medium heat. Return the *tempeh* to the wok and add all other ingredients, mixing well. Simmer until the liquid dries up, stirring frequently. Serve at room temperature as an accompaniment to rice and vegetables.

Deep-fried Bean Curd with Bean Sprouts and Peanut Sauce

Oil for deep frying
14 oz (400 g) pressed or grilled bean curd, cut in 4 slices, dried with paper towels
1 small cucumber
2 teaspoons salt
2 cups (160 g) bean sprouts, washed and drained

Peanut Sauce
4 shallots, minced
2–3 red chilies, deseeded
2 tablespoons finely shaved palm sugar
$1/3$ cup (80 g) chunky peanut butter
4 teaspoons black soy sauce

1 tablespoon tamarind, soaked in $1/4$ cup (60 ml) water, squeezed and strained to obtain juice
$1/4$ teaspoon salt
$1/4$ cup (60 ml) water

1 Prepare the Peanut Sauce by processing the shallots, chilies and palm sugar in a spice grinder until finely ground, adding a little water if necessary to keep the mixture turning. Transfer to a bowl and stir in the peanut butter, soy sauce, tamarind juice and salt, mixing well. Gradually pour in water to make a thick sauce, then set aside.

2 Heat the oil in a wok. When very hot, add the bean curd and deep-fry for 4 minutes, or until golden brown and crisp on both sides. Drain on paper towels, then slice. Rake the skin of the cucumber with a fork, then rub firmly with salt. Cut into even slices and arrange on a serving dish. Place the bean curd on top of the cucumber slices and scatter with bean sprouts. Pour the Peanut Sauce over the bean curd and vegetables and serve immediately.

Fried Bean Curd with Garlic, Black Pepper and Coriander

8 oz (250 g) firm bean curd, drained, cut in 8 triangles each about $1/2$ in ($1^1/2$ cm) thick
1 teaspoon black peppercorns
2–3 cloves garlic
1 teaspoon coriander root or stems
$1/2$ teaspoon sugar
1 tablespoon fish sauce
$1/4$ cup (60 ml) oil
1 small onion, very thinly sliced
1–2 firm, ripe tomatoes, sliced
1 small cucumber, skin raked with a fork, sliced
Coriander leaves, to garnish

1 Put the bean curd pieces in a single layer on one end of a towel, then fold over the towel and pat gently to absorb any moisture. Leave in the towel while preparing the marinade.
2 Grind the peppercorns to a coarse powder in a spice grinder. Add the garlic, coriander root and sugar and process to a smooth paste. Add the fish sauce and pulse a couple of times to blend.
3 Transfer half the marinade to a plate and place the bean curd on it

in a single layer. Spread the top of the bean curd with the rest of the marinade and set aside at room temperature for 30 minutes.
4 Heat the oil in a large frying pan. When hot, drain the bean curd and add to the pan. Fry until golden brown, about 2–3 minutes. Turn and fry the other side, then drain on paper towels. Transfer to a serving dish and surround with the slices of onion, tomato and cucumber. Sprinkle with a few sprigs of fresh coriander and serve hot.

Stir-fried Bean Curd with Cashews

$1/4$ cup (60 ml) oil
2 cloves garlic, minced
1 lb (500 g) pressed bean curd, dried with a towel, cubed
1 teaspoon finely grated ginger
4 spring onions, cut into $1^1/2$-in (4-cm) lengths
3 tablespoons soy sauce
2 teaspoons oyster sauce (optional)

$1/4$ teaspoon ground white pepper
$1/3$ cup (45 g) cashew nuts, lightly toasted until golden

1 Heat oil in a wok for 30 seconds, then add garlic and stir-fry for a few seconds. Add the bean curd and stir-fry over medium–high heat until crisp and golden all over, for about

3 minutes. Add the ginger, the spring onions and the remaining ingredients and stir-fry for 30 seconds. Add the cashew nuts and stir to mix well. Transfer to a serving dish and serve hot with steamed white rice.

TUBERS, stems & roots

Wild edible roots and tubers have provided people all over Asia with food for thousands of years. Now widely cultivated, they are eaten in many ways: cooked as vegetables; used for desserts; drinks and cakes; dried and ground to make flour. The leaves of many root vegetables are also edible simmered or blanched and enjoyed with savory dips. Most root vegetables and their leaves are high in nutritional value.

Some of the roots and tubers which replace rice as the staple in arid parts of Asia (such as cassava or tapioca) are native to the region, while others (sweet potato and yam bean) were introduced from the Americas. Some roots (more correctly termed rhizomes), such as the lotus root, have been grown in Asia since time immemorial.

Arrowhead is a crisp, white-fleshed tuber very similar in size and shape to the more familiar water chestnut, and like that vegetable, grows in ponds and paddy fields. Arrowhead —which should not be confused with a similarly named vegetable, arrowroot—is widely cultivated in China and Japan, and exported from southern China to countries with large Chinese communities during the Chinese New Year period (January/February).

The arrowhead (which is sometimes referred to as caladium) gets its name from the arrow or boomerang-shaped leaves which grow above the starchy corm. Arrowheads are sometimes put at the neck of a container of water so that they will send down roots and the shoots will grow decorative green leaves.

Appearance & Flavor Arrowheads look somewhat like a small onion, spherical in shape and covered with a thin, brownish skin, with a couple of horizontal lines running around the bulb. The top end tapers into a shoot. Arrowheads are starchy and have a pleasant flavor. **Choosing & Storing** Look for corms that have short shoots, preferably no more than 1 in ($2^1/_2$ cm) in length, as these are younger and sweeter. Wrap in paper towels and keep refrigerated in a plastic bag for a few days. **Preparing** The corm or bulb is covered with a pale outer skin, and unlike the sweet water chestnut, must be cooked to remove bitterness. Cut off the shoot and peel the papery brown skin, then leave whole if adding to braised dishes, or slice for use in stir-fried dishes. **Nutritional & Medicinal Properties** Perhaps surprisingly, arrowheads are higher in protein, minerals, and fiber than the common potato. **Culinary Uses** Whole arrowheads are added to braised meat or vegetable dishes, toward the end of cooking time as they need only around 15 minutes cooking. They are also good stir-fried, preferably with other vegetables such as black mushrooms and snow peas or green bell peppers for a range of colors, textures and tastes.

Arrowroot is best known outside of Asia for the highly digestible starchy flour that is extracted from the tuber. Originally from Central America, arrowroot is also occasionally eaten as a vegetable in some Asian countries, particularly Japan and China. There are many varieties of arrowroot with differing appearances. Some resemble tubers, some look like small bamboo shoots, while others have a more generic root-like appearance. Arrowroot starch is commonly used as a thickener, in the same way as cornstarch.

Appearance & Flavor Arrowroot has fresh white flesh and a pleasant aroma and texture. **Choosing & Storing** Look for firm, fresh-smelling tubers. Wrap in kitchen paper and keep refrigerated for several days. **Preparing** Wash the arrowroot thoroughly and remove any fibrous scales. Because the flesh tends to be somewhat fibrous as well, it is best to grate the peeled root. **Nutritional & Medicinal Properties** Arrowroot helps relieve acidity, stomach cramps and indigestion, and is mildly laxative. **Culinary Uses** Arrowroot can be added to soups, steamed, braised or stir-fried, and can be substituted for bamboo shoots in most recipes.

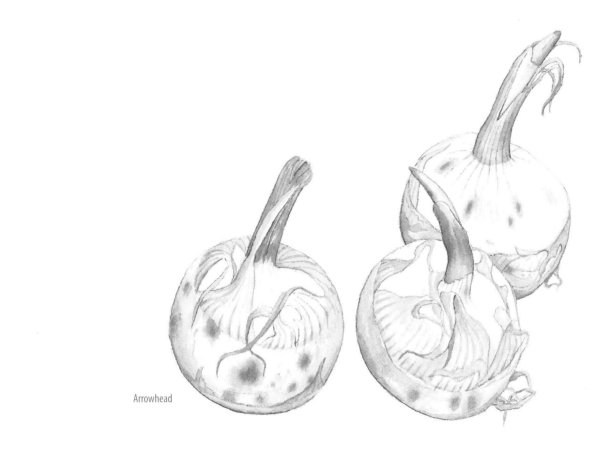

Arrowhead

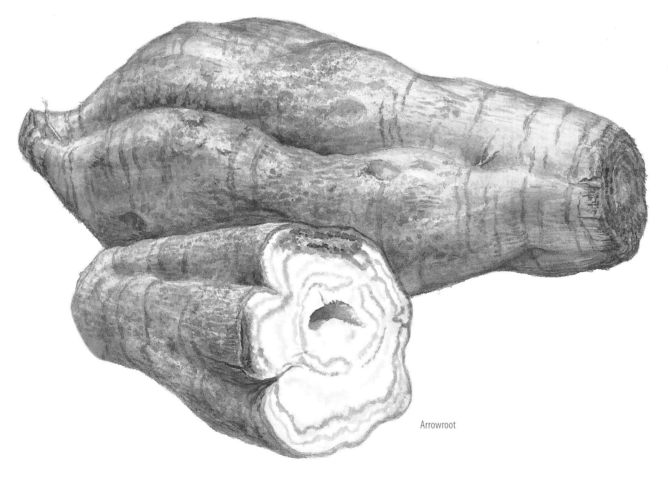

Arrowroot

Bamboo Shoots

Bamboo Shoots fall into three major categories, the most delicious being the small, tender "winter" bamboo shoots dug from the soil before they have emerged into the light. There are also "spring" bamboo shoots, cut when the shoot has grown to about 10 in (25 cm) in length above the ground. "Summer" bamboo shoots are derived from a particular variety of bamboo which produces very thin, almost asparagus-like shoots. While vacuum-packed or canned bamboo shoots are acceptable, nothing matches the flavor and texture of the finest fresh shoots, which have inspired ancient Chinese poets to pen lines of praise.

Appearance & Flavor Fresh bamboo shoots, normally sold with the outer brownish husk removed, have an earthy flavor and a firm texture. **Choosing & Storing** Make sure the shoots smell fresh and do not show any discoloration. Keep refrigerated for up to 2 weeks. If the shoots have already been peeled, store for 1–2 days. Shredded bamboo shoots should be used on the day of purchase. They can also be deep-frozen and kept for up to 3 months. Vacuum-sealed packs of boiled bamboo shoots are often available in the refrigerated section of Asian stores. **Preparing** If unpeeled fresh bamboo shoots are available, cut a ring around the bottom of the stem and pull off the outer layer of the husk, then work up the stem to remove all the layers. Put in a saucepan, add water to cover, bring to a boil, then discard the water. Repeat this twice to remove all traces of hydrocyanic acid, which gives bamboo a bitter taste. Add fresh water, then simmer until the shoots are tender. The shoots can then be sliced or cut according to the recipe. The prepared shoots can also be deep-frozen for up to 3 months. Canned bamboo shoots, although cooked, should be simmered in water for 10 minutes, then drained before using in any recipe—this removes any metallic taste the canned shoots sometimes have. **Nutritional & Medicinal Properties** Bamboo shoots are relatively low in nutritional value, although they contain some phosphorus, calcium and beta-carotene. **Culinary Uses** Because of their mild flavor, bamboo shoots are best cooked with other ingredients. In Asia, they are added to fillings for savories such as spring rolls, simmered in soups, braised dishes and stews, stir-fried and made into pickles. Young bamboo shoots are sometimes basted with soy sauce or miso paste and grilled in Japan. Fresh bamboo shoots are also good julienned and stir-fried with red-roasted Chinese pork (*char siew*).

Banana Stem

Banana Stem, or at least that portion removed from the inner part of the banana trunk, is an inexpensive vegetable found everywhere from Bali to Burma. This is a practical way of using the banana plant once it has borne fruit (bananas fruit only once, so are felled after fruiting to allow the young plants or suckers, which grow from the mature palm, to flourish). Some Asian cultures even have stories about ghosts reputed to haunt old bamboo trees, a sure incentive for gardeners to chop them down immediately after they fruit.

Appearance & Flavor The banana stem is made up of very thick layers containing a sticky sap, which is removed after blanching or boiling. The stem has very little flavor but has a pleasant texture. **Choosing & Storing** Generally, only a short section (about 12 in/30 cm) of the tender inner portion of the stem is sold. If cutting your own banana stem after felling the entire plant, use an oiled knife to cut out the top part of the stem just where the stems and leaves branch out. Peel off the outer layers to get the crisp center of the stem. Wrap in paper towels and keep refrigerated for 3–4 days. **Preparing** Discard two or three of the outer layers, then use an oiled knife to slice the inner stem across. Soak in cold water for 2 hours, then pull away the sticky sap from the slices. **Culinary Uses** Banana stem is simmered in soups and vegetable stews often enriched with coconut milk. It can also be blanched and eaten with a spicy dip.

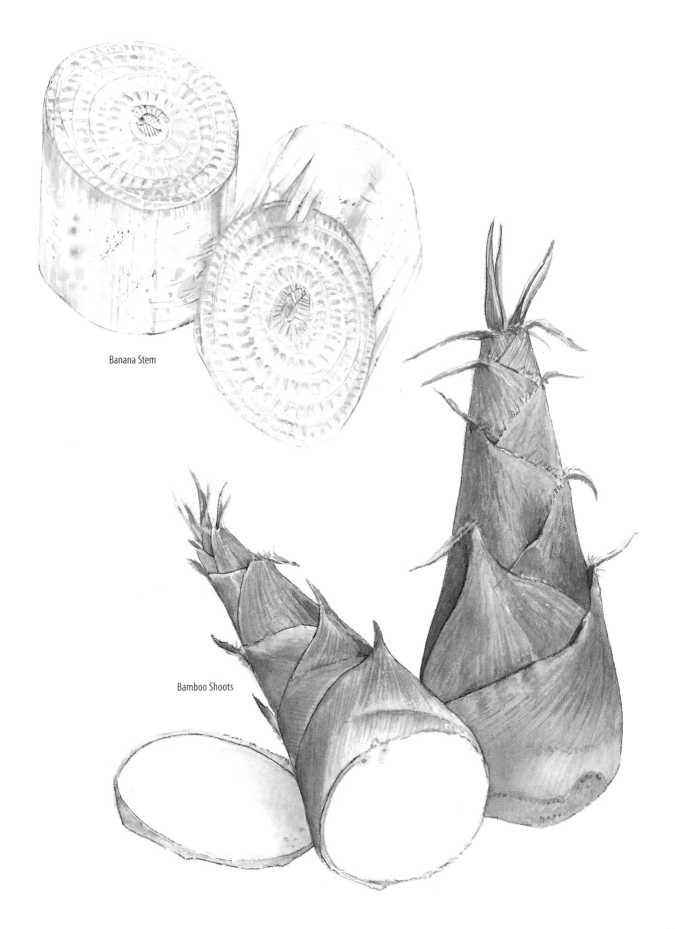

Banana Stem

Bamboo Shoots

Burdock

Burdock is a very long and very thin root generally associated with Japanese cuisine (and known there as *gobo*), although it is native to both Europe and Asia. Even the famous English herbalist, Culpeper, included burdock in his famous 17th-century work. The Chinese have used burdock both as a vegetable and a medicine for centuries. The crunchy texture and medicinal properties of burdock make it a popular vegetable in China and Japan.

Appearance & Flavor Burdock root looks rather like a thin, woody stem (sometimes only 1 in/2$^1/_2$ cm in diameter) with a rough, brown surface. The flavor of burdock, which can grow up to 30 in (75 cm) or even more in length, is somewhat earthy and sweet, and is vaguely reminiscent of Jerusalem artichokes. The texture is somewhat sticky. Burdock root is ideal in slow-cooked dishes because it absorbs the flavors of other ingredients. **Choosing & Storing** Burdock is so long that it is usually cut into more manageable lengths for sale in markets. Two or three cut lengths of root are usually wrapped in plastic and kept in the refrigerated section of Asian stores. Fresh burdock should look dry and be firm with no soft spots when pressed. Wrap in plastic if bought loose and keep refrigerated for up to 2 weeks. **Preparing** Do not peel the skin (which has a good flavor) but scrub with a brush to clean well and trim off any rootlets. Cut the root into 12-in (30-cm) lengths and immediately put into a bowl of cold water with a few drops of vinegar to prevent discoloring. Soak for 10 minutes, then slice as directed in the recipe. **Nutritional & Medicinal Properties** Burdock is a diuretic and is believed to be one of the best blood purifiers. It is also believed to help cleanse the body of waste products and toxins, and is considered helpful for boils and skin problems. In addition, Western research shows that it has antibiotic properties. **Culinary Uses** Shredded burdock can be added to soups and any braised or simmered dishes.

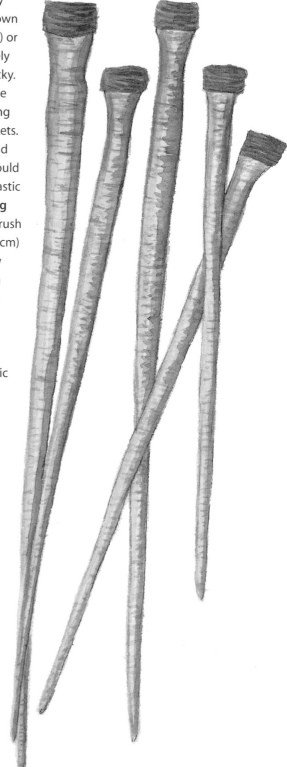

Cassava or Tapioca

are two different names for the same vegetable; the starch extracted from cassava root is commonly sold as tapioca flour, or shaped into small balls known as "tapioca pearls." Mature cassava is boiled as a vegetable, while very young roots are grated and used in cakes and savories. The young leaves are also used as a vegetable.

Appearance & Flavor Cassava root, which ranges in length from about 6–16 in (15–40 cm), has a fairly thick, wrinkled brown skin, with slight horizontal markings every few inches. The flavor is rather bland and starchy. **Choosing & Storing** Choose small, young roots as the texture will be better. Make sure they smell fresh and do not have any traces of mold. Cassava can be wrapped in plastic and refrigerated for 2–3 days, but is best used as soon as possible. **Preparing** Cassava root contains hydrocyanic acid which must be destroyed by boiling or baking. Wash and peel, then cook whole or grated. The tough green leaves should be boiled in two changes of water until soft. **Nutritional & Medicinal Properties** Although low in protein, cassava is relatively high in carbohydrates and is easily digested. The young leaves are exceptionally rich in beta-carotene, calcium and phosphorus. **Culinary Uses** To cook cassava, cut the roots into 2–3-in (6–8-cm) lengths and boil in water (with a little salt and turmeric added if liked). Cassava root can also be simmered in coconut milk, with leafy greens added if liked. Boiled cassava can be mashed and then made into savories. Be sure to remove any of the rather fibrous strings often found in the center of the root. Chunks of boiled cassava dipped in freshly grated coconut or wild honey are a popular breakfast dish in many rural areas of Southeast Asia. At other meals, a spicy sambal or dip is served together with the boiled cassava. Young cassava root can be grated, mixed with sugar and coconut milk, and baked or steamed to make a type of cake, especially in Malaysia and the Philippines. The boiled leaves can be chopped and mixed with seasoned, freshly grated coconut to make a type of salad, or added to spiced coconut milk.

Daikon or White Radish

grows in the ground like a root vegetable, although it is actually a member of the same botanical family as the cabbage. *Daikon* is a popular vegetable in Japan, and is more often known in the West by its Japanese name than its English name, long white radish. The Japanese, however, are not the only Asians who enjoy this crunchy, peppery-tasting vegetable, for from Nepal and India right through Southeast Asia to China and Korea, *daikon* is eaten raw, cooked and pickled. The flavor of the Asian radish is somewhat similar to that of the common European radish.

Appearance & Flavor The radish varies considerably in size, ranging from the mild-tasting vegetables as small as 5 in (12 cm) in length up to monsters of 35–40 cm (14–16 in). The smaller the *daikon*, the less peppery the taste and less fibrous the texture. After long cooking, however, the radish develops a very palatable, almost sweet flavor. The color of this radish is not necessarily white for in China, purple and green varieties can be found. **Choosing & Storing** Look for small, firm radishes, as the younger and smaller the radish, the milder the flavor and better the texture. **Preparing** Wash and trim off the stem end. The skin is very thin and soft, so there is no need to peel the radish. If being served raw, *daikon* is often grated or sliced and sprinkled with salt to reduce the peppery tang, and after about 10 minutes, rinsed and squeezed dry. The Japanese, however, omit this salting when using *daikon* as a garnish. The radish can also be cut into larger pieces for adding to braised dishes. **Nutritional & Medicinal Properties** *Daikon* contains vitamin C and diastase, an enzyme which aids digestion. The leaves also contain vitamin C and are rich in iron and calcium. **Culinary Uses** In Japan, finely shredded *daikon* is served unsalted as a garnish in many dishes. *Daikon* is ideal in braised mixed vegetable dishes, and is also made into pickles or *kim chee* in Korea. Although the leaves are edible and nutritious, they are seldom used, but may be stir-fried or shredded and added to soups or braised dishes.

Galangal

is used as a seasoning rather than eaten on its own as a vegetable. A member of the prolific ginger family, galangal grows in Southeast Asia and is widely used for its distinctive flavor and fragrance. The ginger goes by various names, including blue ginger, greater galangal, *laos* in Indonesia, *kha* in Thailand and *lengkuas* in Malaysia. Water-packed galangal sold in jars is an acceptable substitute for the fresh ingredient.

Appearance & Flavor Galangal rhizomes look somewhat like ginger, generally a pale cream color with the younger portions a pretty blush pink. The flavor is reminiscent of jungles, somewhat spicy and quite different to common ginger. **Choosing & Storing** Look for fresh, unwrinkled rhizomes. Wrap in paper or a cloth and keep refrigerated for 1–2 weeks. Alternatively, slice thinly and store in a sealed plastic bag in the deep-freeze almost indefinitely. **Preparing** Scrape off the thin skin and slice across. If using galangal to make a spice paste, mince before pounding or processing as mature galangal is very tough. **Nutritional & Medicinal Properties** Some Chinese believe that galangal is effective in ridding the body of "wind"; the Nonyas of Penang in Malaysia pound it together with toasted dried shrimp paste and serve the resulting sambal as confinement food to mothers in the month after childbirth. **Culinary Uses** Galangal is generally considered too spicy to be eaten raw. It is commonly pounded and then stir-fried or simmered as part of a seasoning paste, particularly in Indonesia, Malaysia, Thailand, Laos and Cambodia. Bruised slices of galangal are frequently added to fish curries, chicken dishes and soups.

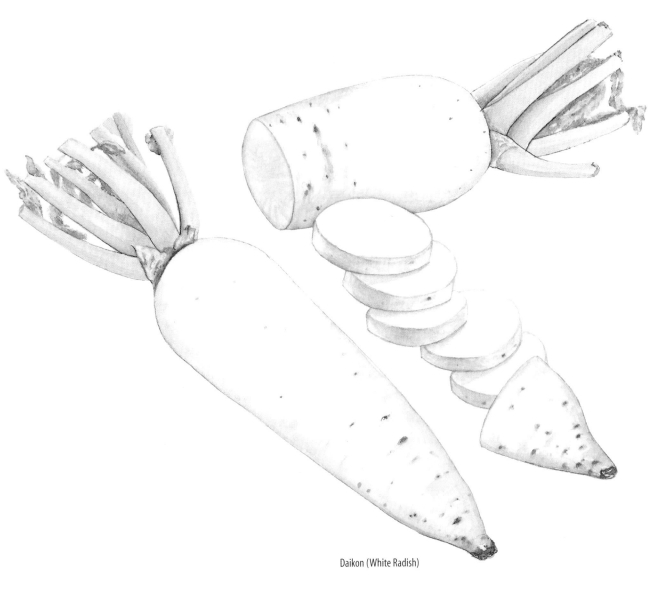

Daikon (White Radish)

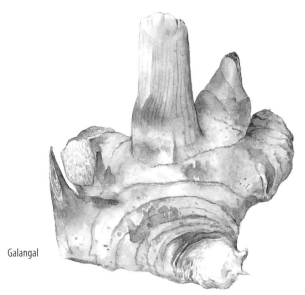

Galangal

Ginger is perhaps the most widely used seasoning throughout Asia. It has a spicy, somewhat lemony flavor and wonderful fragrance. It is highly esteemed not just for its culinary magic but for its health properties. Confucius mentioned the beneficial effects of ginger around 500 BC, and in the 1st century AD, a noted Greek physician also extolled its virtues. The ginger family is indigenous to Southeast Asia and includes at least 400 species.

Appearance & Flavor Fresh ginger looks like a bunch of knobbly sections which resemble fingers. In Asia, both the young and mature root are sold; young ginger is lighter in color and less "spicy" than the mature rhizome, and sometimes has pink tips with sections of the stem left intact. **Choosing & Storing** Ginger should look plump and firm. Store ginger whole in an open container in a dry place. If a regular supply is not available, slice the ginger and store it in the freezer. **Preparing** Using a knife, scrape off the skin, then slice or shred. Chinese bamboo and Japanese ceramic ginger graters are particularly effective to reducing ginger to a pulp. Sometimes ginger juice is required for marinades. Grate, then transfer it to a fine sieve and press down with the back of a spoon to extract the ginger juice. If using drier mature ginger, it may be necessary to add water to the ginger and mix it before straining. **Nutritional & Medicinal Properties** Ginger contains high levels of potassium, anti-oxidants, magnesium, calcium and phosphorous. It is good for nausea, and is also anti-inflammatory and antiseptic. Ginger eliminates flatulence, promotes circulation and helps alleviate the common cold. **Culinary Uses** It is almost easier to list the different types of food where ginger does not appear than to describe the multitude of its culinary uses. It is sliced or pounded and used in everything from dips and marinades to soups, stews, curries and drinks. Pickled ginger is used as a condiment, especially by the Chinese and Japanese.

Jicama or Bangkuang are crisp, sweet-fleshed tubers. The common English name for this vegetable, yam bean, is somewhat puzzling, for it is neither a yam nor does it resemble a bean. It is perhaps better known by its Mexican name in the US and in some other Western countries. To add to the confusion, some Chinese refer to jicama as a "turnip" because of its shape, although the flavor and appearance of the two are totally different.

Appearance & Flavor The tubers are shaped rather like a bulbous spinning top, and are covered with a beige-colored skin which thickens as the tubers age. Vertical indentations also develop as the jicama matures. Very young jicama can be roughly the size of an egg, while mature ones are often the size of a grapefruit or larger. The smaller and younger the jicama, the sweeter the flavor and finer the texture. The taste of jicama can perhaps be described as resembling a cross between an apple and a potato, while the texture is similar to that of water chestnuts, although less dense. **Choosing & Storing** Buy the smallest tubers available, as these are likely to be sweeter and have a less fibrous texture than more mature jicama. Check them carefully for worm holes. Keep jicama refrigerated for 2–3 weeks. **Preparing** Wash and pull off the easily removed skin with a knife. Slice, shred or grate and use raw or cooked, according to the recipe. **Nutritional & Medicinal Properties** Jicama is not high in nutritional value, containing 10% carbohydrates and traces of calcium, phosphorus and vitamin C. **Culinary Uses** Small, young jicama is often eaten raw, cut into wedges and dipped in a savory sauce or just salt. The larger vegetables are enjoyed both raw and cooked, and can at a pinch be used as a substitute for water chestnuts in recipes calling for these. Chunks or strips of raw jicama can be used in many Asian mixed salads. Jicama is also good in stir-fried vegetable combinations, adding a pleasant crisp texture and mild flavor.

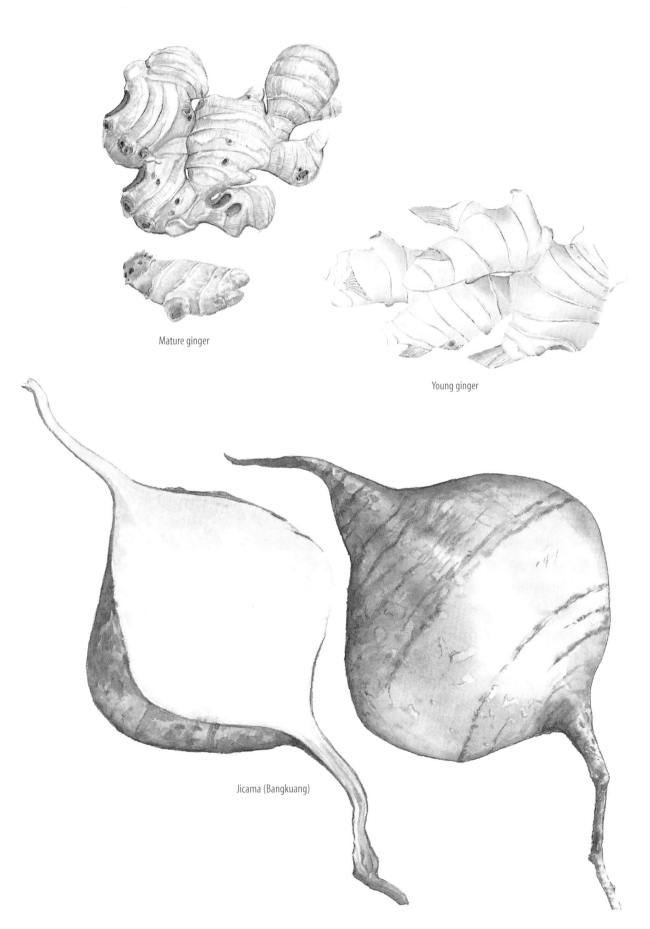

Mature ginger

Young ginger

Jicama (Bangkuang)

Kencur or Aromatic Ginger is a member of the ginger family. The fragrance of this rhizome is reminiscent of camphor, and it adds a distinctive aroma to some dishes in Indonesia, as well as other parts of tropical Asia. The broad leaves of *kencur* have much of the flavor and aroma of the rhizome, and are quite often finely shredded and used as a herb or eaten whole with a dip. *Kencur* is its Indonesian name; the rhizome is known as *pro hom* in Thailand and *cekur* in Malaysia.

Appearance & Flavor Young *kencur* rhizomes are usually bright white in color, although they may be yellowish brown when mature. The flavor is distinctive, with an aroma of camphor. **Choosing & Storing** Look for fresh, plump rhizomes; they will keep better if the leaves are still attached. Wrap in paper or a cloth and refrigerate for up to 1 week. **Preparing** Wash thoroughly and dry. Slice or chop before pounding or processing to a paste. **Nutritional & Medicinal Properties** Like galangal, *kencur* is considered to be good for mothers after childbirth, and is widely used in Indonesian herbal medicines (*jamu*). **Culinary Uses** Pounded *kencur* is added to seasoning pastes for many cooked dishes, and can also be eaten raw. The fresh leaves of the *kencur* plant are often shredded and added to Malay herb rice or *nasi ulam*, while in Thailand, they are popular as part of a platter of raw leaves and fruits served with a pungent dip.

Krachai or Chinese Keys gets its common English name from its peculiar appearance, which is thought to resemble a bunch of keys. Because it is used more commonly in Thai cuisine than that of any other Asian country, it is most often known by its Thai name, *krachai*. Fresh *krachai* is not widely available outside of Asia, although water-packed *krachai* (often referred to simply as "rhizome" on the label) exported in jars from Thailand makes a satisfactory substitute.

Appearance & Flavor *Krachai* looks far more like a bunch of slender yellowish brown carrots or even fingers than keys. The flavor is quite spicy, with an emphatic aroma. **Choosing & Storing** Look for firm, smooth rhizomes and wrap in paper or a cloth; they keep well refrigerated for up to a month. **Preparing** Wash and scrape off the skin before using. **Nutritional & Medicinal Properties** *Krachai* is believed to help relieve colic and expel wind. It is also widely used as a cure for diarrhea and dysentery. In some areas, a poultice of pounded *krachai* is used to reduce swelling and to heal wounds. **Culinary Uses** *Krachai* is sometimes eaten raw in salads, and is also added to curries and vegetable dishes. It is thought to have a particularly affinity with fish and other seafood.

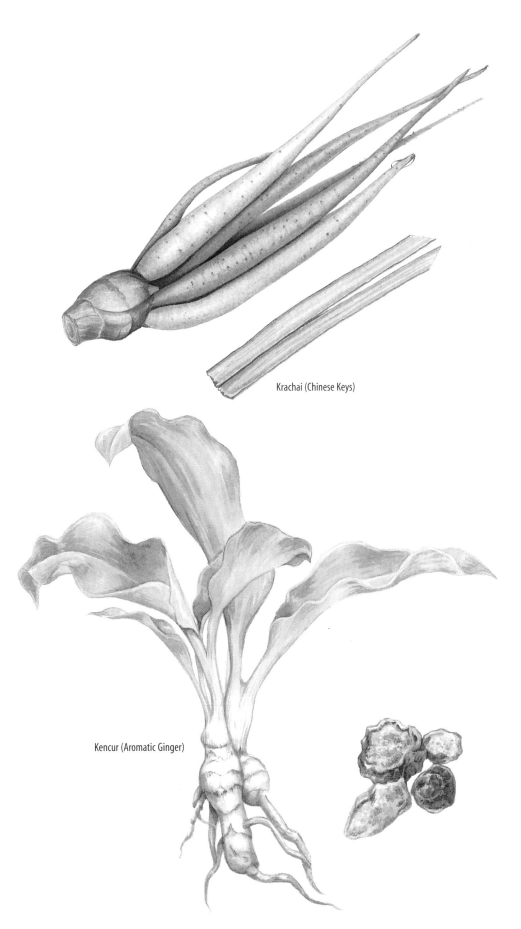

Krachai (Chinese Keys)

Kencur (Aromatic Ginger)

Lotus Roots have been cultivated by the Chinese, along with the rest of the lotus plant, for at least 3,000 years. Lotuses consist of rhizomes buried in the mud, with the stems, leaves and flowers rising above the surface of the water. All parts of the plant are edible: the ivory-colored rhizome, the leaves, the immature green seeds and the dried ripe seeds, as well as the flowers. Fresh lotus root should·be eaten while young and sweet. Young green lotus seeds are normally only available if you happen to have your own lotus pond, but the mature seeds are sometimes available fresh in vacuum packs, and are also readily available dried. Dried lotus leaves, used to give flavor when wrapped around food, are normally sold in Chinese stores.

Appearance & Flavor The lotus root consists of a number of linked segments, from around 4–8 in (10–20 cm) in length. When sliced, the crisp flesh reveals a series of hollow chambers. The decorative qualities of this vegetable are matched by its crisp texture and delicate, sweet flavor. **Choosing & Storing** Look for short, firm roots without any soft spots or black streaks. Wrap in kitchen paper and keep refrigerated for up to 1 week. **Preparing** Wash thoroughly, peel, slice and drop into water with a few drops of vinegar or lemon juice to prevent discoloring. When using dried lotus seeds (sometimes called lotus nuts), use a toothpick to push out the bitter central core if this has not already been removed. Dried lotus leaves should be soaked in boiling water to soften. **Nutritional & Medicinal Properties** Lotus root has appreciable amounts of vitamin C and phosphorus, and also contains some calcium. **Culinary Uses** In China, young lotus root is often eaten raw, sprinkled with salt and a few grains of sugar. If serving in this way, taste a little of the root first to check it is still palatable; otherwise, blanch the slices for 30–45 seconds, drain, and cool in iced water before sprinkling with salt and sugar if desired. Sliced lotus root can be added to soups, stir-fried, stuffed (fiddly but spectacular when the segment is later sliced), or dipped in batter and deep-fried as for tempura. The Chinese also use the root and the seeds in sweet soups and other savory dishes. The seeds are sometimes simmered and added to desserts. Dried lotus leaves are wrapped—after having been soaked—around whole chickens or special mixed rice dishes for steaming or baking. Fresh lotus stalks are sliced and then added to soups.

Palm Hearts

are from the center portion of any type of edible palm tree trunk, eaten as a vegetable in tropical Asia. Coconut palm heart is the best known, and is exported in cans, but many other palms have succulent, edible hearts. To obtain the palm heart, it means sacrificing the entire tree to reach its core. Most coconut palm hearts are sold when the trees have been cleared from old plantations or felled by typhoons, although some trees are specially grown and cut when young, before the coconut has had time to bear fruit. In forested areas where palms grow wild, palm heart is a common vegetable among local folk.

Appearance & Flavor The edible portion of the palm heart comes from the upper portion of the main stem or trunk, and consists of creamy white, tightly folded immature leaf stems tucked inside a tougher, fibrous cylinder. The portion containing the heart can range from about 12 to 32 in (30 to 80 cm) in length. Fresh palm heart has a crisp, dense texture and a delicate, sweet flavor. **Choosing & Storing** Some varieties of palm heart are often sold sliced, with the non-edible portion removed. This saves time, but sliced palm heart should be used on the day of purchase. If whole palm heart is available, refrigerate for 2–3 days or cut into manageable proportions, put in a container, cover with water, and refrigerate for up to 1 week. **Preparing** Some palm hearts (although not coconut and oil palm) turn brown after being exposed to the air, so trim the heart only just before eating. Use a sharp knife to cut away any tough portion of the stem to reveal the inner heart, which can then be sliced. To check if the thickened base under the portion where the immature stems are folded is edible, cut off a slice and chew to ensure that it is not too fibrous. **Nutritional & Medicinal Properties** Coconut palm heart contains around 4% protein, and also has reasonable amounts of calcium and phosphorus. **Culinary Uses** Palm heart is good raw, generally eaten as a salad tossed with an Asian-style dressing such as seasoned coconut milk, or with mayonnaise. Sliced raw coconut palm heart is the basic ingredient of the famous Filipino spring roll, *lumpia*. Palm heart can also be simmered in seasoned coconut milk as a hot vegetable dish.

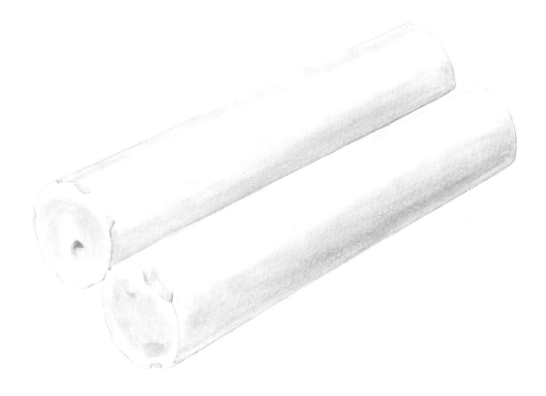

Sweet Potatoes

Sweet Potatoes originated in tropical America, and were introduced to Europe by Columbus. The vegetable also spread westward across the Pacific, brought to Asia by 15-century Chinese explorers. The sweet potato contains sugars which are released by cooking, and in Asia it is used often in desserts and cakes and as a savory vegetable. Sweet potato leaves are a popular vegetable in rural areas of Asia.

Appearance & Flavor Sweet potatoes vary somewhat in shape and size, from relatively smooth ovals to large, contorted potatoes which are difficult to peel. The color varies from purple to white, orange and creamy yellow. **Choosing & Storing** Look for uncut sweet potatoes without any broken flesh or signs of rot. If you have the option, purchase the purple or orange-fleshed varieties for maximum flavor and a moist texture. Pale yellow or white-fleshed sweet potatoes tend to be dry. They are best kept refrigerated rather than stored as for regular potatoes, and can be kept for up to 1 week. If buying sweet potato leaves, choose those which look fresh, wash well, then simmer until tender. **Preparing** Scrub the skin gently with a brush to clean. **Nutritional & Medicinal Properties** The orange-fleshed variety contains significantly higher amounts of vitamin A and beta-carotene than the white or purple. Sweet potato leaves are rich in beta-carotene, phosphorus and calcium. **Culinary Uses** In Asia, sweet potatoes are simmered in savory stews; cooked in seasoned coconut milk, often with leafy greens, or simply boiled in salted water then mashed and used to make savories. They can also be sliced and deep-fried to make crisps, or added to sweetened coconut milk, with other ingredients such as sago pearls, slices of banana, and pieces of jackfruit to make a dessert. Boiled sweet potato is sometimes mashed with sugar and egg yolk, and shaped into balls for a traditional Japanese New Year treat. The blanched leaves are sometimes added to dishes that contain coconut milk, or boiled until soft and tossed with coconut milk, ground dried prawns with chili and other savory ingredients.

Taro

Taro is also known as cocoyam or dasheen, and is one of the best root vegetables in terms of flavor and texture. Sometimes referred to as the "potato of the tropics," taro is such an ancient plant that scientists claim New Guinea natives were harvesting it some 30,000 years ago. The stems of the taro plant are used as a vegetable in some parts of Southeast Asia, particularly in Vietnam, Cambodia and Laos, where they are added to soups.

Appearance & Flavor Taro, which grows in around 200 varieties, looks somewhat like a large, narrow top covered with brownish skin. The flesh is either pinkish purple, beige or white. **Choosing & Storing** Choose dry, firm tubers and store in a cool, dry place for several days. **Preparing** Both the leaves and tubers contain highly irritating calcium oxalate crystals and so must be thoroughly boiled before eating. Do not wash before peeling, as the taro becomes slimy and irritating when wet. Peel, rinse, then blanch in boiling water for 5 minutes to remove any stickiness and calcium oxalate crystals. Drain, then proceed as directed in the recipe of your choice. **Nutritional & Medicinal Properties** Taro tubers contain appreciable levels of calcium, phosphorus as well as iron. The leaves are extremely rich in beta-carotene and calcium, and also contain significant amounts of vitamin C. **Culinary Uses** Chinese chefs like to make a "basket" of shredded taro, which is deep-fried and often used to hold stir-fried mixed vegetables. They often add taro to somewhat oily dishes, such as steamed sliced pork belly, as the taro tends to soak up the juices and flavors of other ingredients. Taro can also be braised, boiled and mashed or added to desserts. The tubers can be thinly sliced and deep-fried, and the young leaves used as a vegetable. They must be boiled in two changes of water, and need a total of around 45 minutes to become really tender. Taro leaves are also blanched and used as a food wrapper, mainly in Pacific cuisines.

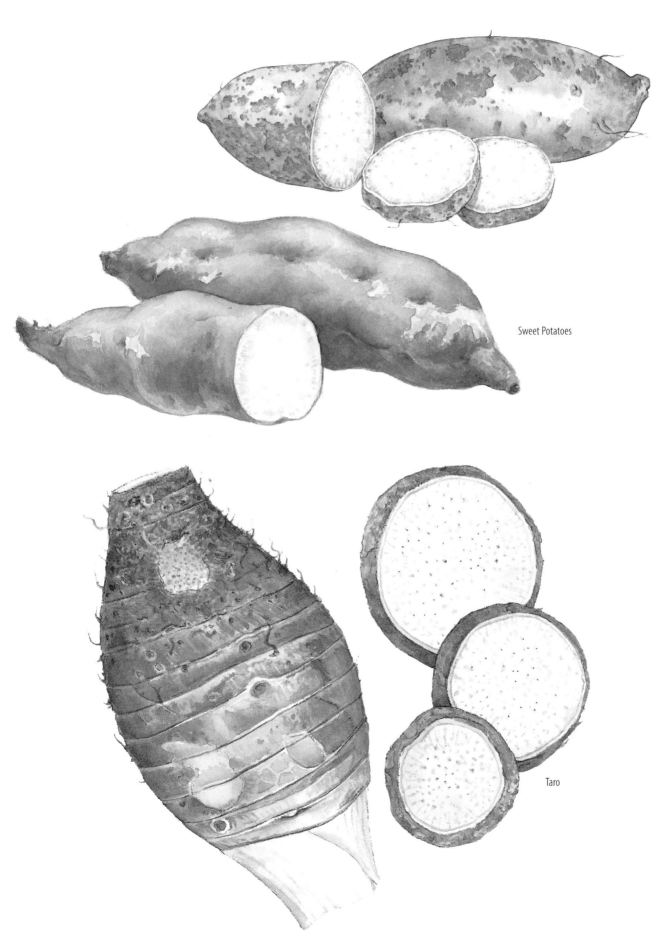

Sweet Potatoes

Taro

Torch Ginger

Torch Ginger is so called because this edible flower bud (a beautiful pale pink in color) is thought to resemble a flaming torch. This Indonesian native, also known as ginger flower or *Etlingera elatior*, is referred to as *combrang* in Indonesia, and now grows widely throughout Southeast Asia, although it is most commonly used as a herb in Singapore, in Thailand (where it is known as *kaalaa*) and in Malaysia, where it is known as *bunga kantan* or *bunga siantan*.

Appearance & Flavor Left in the wild, this ginger can grow up to 16 feet (5 meters) in height and the pale pink bud blossoms into a particularly beautiful flower, but for culinary uses, the bud is picked while it is still tightly folded. Torch ginger bud has a fresh flavor and a pleasant, distinctive taste reminiscent of polygonum or laksa leaves. **Choosing & Storing** Once predominantly gathered wild for sale, torch ginger is nowadays cultivated for commercial markets. Choose fresh-looking buds with no sign of wilting or browning at the edges. Wrap in paper or a cloth and refrigerate for a few days, or keep in the freezer almost indefinitely. **Preparing** Wash the bud and discard the stem. Halve or slice finely as specified in your recipe. **Culinary Uses** Although torch ginger is believed to be a native of Java, it is rarely used in Javanese cuisine. In fact, the use of torch ginger seems to be restricted to Thailand, Singapore and Malaysia. Torch ginger bud is added to a number of salads, particularly rice salads in southern Thailand and northern Malaysia. The separated petals of the mature flower is sometimes eaten raw with a spicy dip, such as *nam prik* in Thailand and in Singapore *rojak*. Torch ginger bud is also halved and added to piquant fish curries or *gulai*, particularly those prepared by Straits Chinese or Nonya cooks in Singapore and Malaysia. The stems are sometimes chopped and grated, then used as an tangy ingredient to flavor laksa broth.

Turmeric is widely used in India and outside Asia in its dried, powdered form—but in Southeast Asia, the fresh rhizome is preferred for its fragrance, flavor and bright yellow color. This member of the ginger family has also been used traditionally and commercially as a natural dye for food and fabrics.

Appearance & Flavor Turmeric rhizomes are much smaller than common ginger, covered with a thin brownish skin that lets the bright orange-yellow show through. Some varieties in Thailand have lemon-yellow flesh and is known as *khamin* ("turmeric") *kao* ("white"). **Choosing & Storing** Choose firm, fresh-looking and unwrinkled turmeric and wrap in paper or a cloth. It can be kept refrigerated for about 2–3 weeks. **Preparing** Scape off the fine skin and slice or chop before processing. Take care not to get the juice on clothing as it will stain permanently. **Nutritional & Medicinal Properties** Turmeric has anti-bacterial and anti-fungal properties, helps reduce inflammation, prevent blood-clotting, and is believed to help with osteoarthritis and rheumatism. **Culinary Uses** Fresh turmeric is used (generally in very small amounts) to give color and flavor to curries and pickles. The flower is edible (and is often cooked with egg) while the fresh turmeric leaves are used as a herb, particularly in West Sumatra in Indonesia. Do note that even though some southern Indian or Sri Lankan recipes call for saffron, what they really mean is turmeric. The two are not interchangeable either in terms of taste or color—food cooked with turmeric has a yellow color whereas saffron gives an orange tone.

Wasabi is a cultivated rhizome known botanically as *Wasabia japonica*. Because of the insufficient supply in recent years, the "wasabi" sold in powder or paste form is not genuine wasabi but actually a mixture of Western horseradish (*Armoracia rusticana*), mustard and green food coloring (although at least one brand of "wasabi" paste also contains some of the genuine rhizome).

Appearance & Flavor Wasabi rhizomes grow to about 4–6 in (10–15 cm) in length, have slender stems and attractive edible green leaves. The flavor of fresh wasabi is aromatic and pungent. **Choosing & Storing** Look for firm rhizomes with minimal brown patches. Rinse in cold water, wrap in paper towels and refrigerate for up to a month, rinsing in cold water once a week. **Preparing** Wash the wasabi rhizome and brush lightly to remove any dirt. Scrape away dark edges, then grate in a circular motion on a fine grater. Return any unused portion to the refrigerator. Bruise the grated wasabi with the blunt side of a knife to release maximum flavor, then roll into a ball and set aside for about 10 minutes for the flavor to develop. **Nutritional & Medicinal Properties** Wasabi is believed to contain an antidote to food poisoning, which is why it is often served with raw fish in the form of sashimi and sushi. **Culinary Uses** Wasabi is served with sushi, sashimi, buckwheat noodles (soba) and mild tofu dishes. It is best smeared onto food before it is dipped into soy sauce. Some prefer to mix wasabi with the soy sauce, but this dissipates the flavor. Wasabi can be added to mayonnaise and mashed potatoes in Western cuisine.

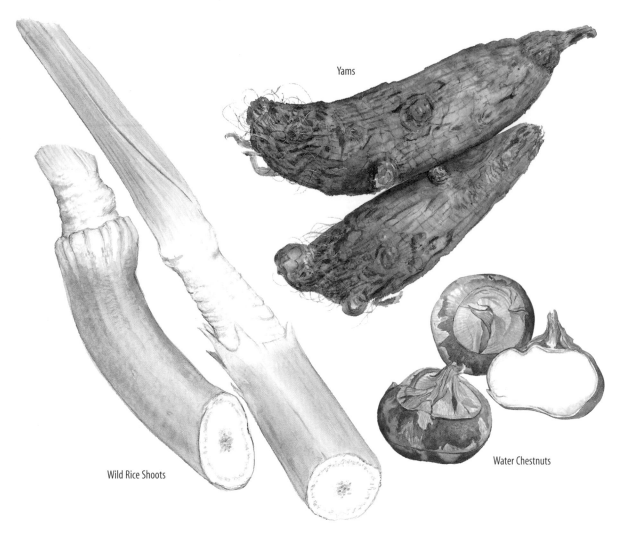

Yams

Wild Rice Shoots

Water Chestnuts

Water Chestnuts

Water Chestnuts are a gourmet's delight because of their almost milky sweetness and crisp, white flesh. They are cultivated in Japan and China (where they have been eaten for more than 3,000 years), and exported to Asian countries with large Chinese populations.

Appearance & Flavor Water chestnuts are about the size of a small plum, with dark brown skin, often with some dried mud still clinging. Traces of papery covering cling to the concentric circles around each water chestnut, while the top has some of the dried brown stalk still remaining. The flavor of fresh water chestnuts makes these one of the sweetest, most succulent vegetables imaginable and the flesh retains its delightfully crisp texture even after cooking. **Choosing & Storing** Press each water chestnut and discard any with spongy portions. It is wise to buy a few extra, because there are often one or two which reveal yellowish decaying spots when peeled, and which should be discarded. Place in a plastic container lined with a paper towel and keep refrigerated for a few days. **Preparing** Water chestnuts are very fiddly to peel, but well worth the effort. Rinse well to remove any dirt before peeling and put into cold water immediately to avoid discoloring. **Nutritional & Medicinal Properties** Water chestnuts have appreciable amounts of starch and phosphorus. The Chinese consider it a "cooling" vegetable and therefore an antidote to too much rich or fried foods. **Culinary Uses** Water chestnuts are sliced and eaten raw (especially in Thailand), and also finely chopped and added to give texture and flavor to many fillings in Chinese cuisine. Water chestnuts are sometimes made into a flour, or are popular stir-fried, for they add a crunchy texture and their sweetness intensifies after cooking. Diced water chestnuts are used in many Thai desserts and sweetmeats.

Wild Rice Shoots

are rarely found outside of Asia, and even there, they are not common. The name is somewhat misleading, for these shoots are not the normal rice plant (*Oryza sativa*) but the shoots of an aquatic plant (*Zizania acquatica*) which is harvested by native North Americans for its grain. Terminology aside, these pithy, swollen shoots—the swelling is caused by a fungus—are found in parts of China, Japan and Taiwan and are noted for their excellent taste.

Appearance & Flavor The swollen, ivory-colored shoots look somewhat like slender bamboo shoots, tapering from a broad base to a leafy tip. They have a firm texture and a delicious, delicate flavor reminiscent of the best winter bamboo shoots or heart of palm. **Choosing & Storing** Wild rice shoots are generally sold with the coarse outer leaves removed and the lower portion of the stems cut off. Black spores become visible sometimes—the Chinese consider these shoots the most desirable. Wrap wild rice shoots in a paper towel and keep refrigerated for 3–4 days. **Preparing** Peel off any outer sheaths to reach the tender, white center of the shoot. Slice across or julienne before using. **Nutritional & Medicinal Properties** Wild rice shoots contain iron, phosphorus and a small amount of beta-carotene and vitamin C. **Culinary Uses** The shoots are added to fresh spring rolls (*popiah*) in southern China, and stir-fried with mushrooms. They can also be stir-fried with meat or poultry, or added to soups.

Yams

are somewhat of an ugly duckling, not only in appearance but also from a culinary point of view as the flavor can be rather uninteresting. The yam is also subject to confusion, as sweet potatoes are often referred to as yams in the southern states of the US, and the cocoyam, or taro (see page 194), is also often confused with yam. Fortunately in Asia, yams are more simply classified. Although a number of yams are found in Asia, they fall into two main categories, known simply as the greater yam and the lesser or Chinese yam.

Appearance & Flavor The greater yam is an unevenly shaped, large, bulbous tuber weighing 1 lb (2 kg) or more. It sometimes has a deep purple skin and pale purple flesh. The lesser yam is much smaller in size, usually measuring around 3–4 in (6–8 cm) in length, and either rounded or elongated in shape, with soft, white flesh. This variety is preferable from a culinary point of view. **Choosing & Storing** Buy yams that do not have discolored patches, and store in a cool, dry place. **Preparing** Peel before boiling. If using the greater yam, dice before cooking. Lesser yams can be boiled whole. **Nutritional & Medicinal Properties** Yams are starchy vegetables, containing about 24% carbohydrates. They contain some phosphorus as well as calcium and vitamin C. **Culinary Uses** The greater yam is popular in the Philippines for use in desserts, such as *bubor cha cha* and even in ice cream. The lesser yam is boiled and made into savory snacks.

Thai Duck and Galangal Soup

1 small fresh duck, about 4 lbs
  (2 kg)
1 teaspoon salt
20 thin slices (about 2 oz/60 g)
  galangal root
3 tablespoons fish sauce
5 cups (1$^1/_4$ liters) chicken stock
8–10 shallots, thinly sliced
4–6 cloves, garlic, thinly sliced
1 teaspoon sugar
1 cup (250 ml) thick coconut milk
$^1/_4$ teaspoon freshly ground black
  pepper
1 spring onion, finely sliced
2 tablespoons minced fresh
  coriander leaves (cilantro)
Lime juice, to taste

1 Cut off and discard the tail of the duck and remove as much of the skin and fat as possible. Use a cleaver to chop the duck into about 14 pieces. Remove the fine bones of the rib cage but leave the other bones intact.
2 Place the duck pieces, salt and galangal in a dry saucepan with a heavy base and stir-fry over low heat until the meat changes color and loses its raw appearance. Splash over the fish sauce and stir for about 1 minute, then add the stock, shallots, garlic and sugar. Bring to a boil, then reduce the heat and simmer gently with the pan uncovered for about 1 hour, until the duck is tender.

3 Add the coconut milk and bring almost to a boil, stirring constantly. Sprinkle with black pepper, then transfer to a serving bowl and garnish with spring onion and coriander. Serve with rice; everyone puts a piece of duck on their plate and spoons the liquid over their rice or sips it from time to time from an individual small soup bowl. Add lime juice if desired.

Thai Water Chestnut Salad

15–20 fresh water chestnuts,
  peeled and sliced, or 1 can water
  chestnuts, drained and sliced
1 cup cucumber, peeled and sliced
2 cups jicama (*bangkuang*), peeled
  and cut into slivers
1 cup sour green mango or 1 sour
  green apple, peeled and diced
1 small stalk celery, thinly sliced
5 oz (150 g) cooked prawns, peeled,
  halved lengthwise, or 4 oz (110 g)
  cooked chicken, shredded
2 tablespoons minced coriander
  leaves (cilantro)

2 fresh or frozen kaffir lime leaves,
  finely sliced in hair-like shreds
1 tablespoon crisp fried shallots
1 red chili, deseeded and thinly
  sliced (optional)

Sauce
3 tablespoons lime or lemon juice
1$^1/_2$ tablespoons fish sauce
1 tablespoon sugar
$^1/_2$ teaspoon dried chili flakes

1 Prepare the Sauce. Put the lime juice, fish sauce, sugar and dried chili flakes in a small bowl, stirring to dissolve the sugar. Set aside.
2 Put the water chestnuts, cucumber, jicama, mango, celery, prawns and coriander and kaffir lime leaves in a large bowl. Toss to mix well. Pour the Sauce over the vegetables and mix again. Transfer to a serving bowl and sprinkle with the crisp fried shallots and chili (if using) immediately before serving. Serve at room temperature.

Filipino Cassava Cake (*Bibingka*)

2 eggs
1 cup (250 g) sugar
1 cup (250 ml) coconut milk, or
  canned evaporated milk
1 cup (250 g) grated cassava
3 tablespoons grated cheddar
  cheese
2 tablespoons melted butter, to
  grease
1 egg yolk
1 tablespoon superfine caster sugar

1 Beat the eggs and sugar together until frothy. Stir in the coconut milk, cassava and cheese. Line a square or rectangular baking dish with a few banana leaves (softened over a gas flame) or baking paper. Pour in the mixture and bake at 180 °C (350 °F) until the cake has risen and is almost done, or for about 1–1$^1/_4$ hours.

2 Beat the egg yolk, then use a brush to spread it over the top of the cake. Sprinkle with sugar and return to the oven until the top is golden brown. Leave to cool before cutting into serving pieces.

Chinese Jicama and Carrot Salad with Prawns

2 tablespoons oil
2 cloves garlic, minced
5 oz (150 g) small fresh prawns, peeled and deveined
7 oz (200 g) jicama (*bangkuang*), peeled and cut in matchstick pieces
1 medium carrot, peeled and cut in matchstick pieces
$1/3$ cup (85 ml) chicken stock
2 tablespoons soy sauce
White pepper, to taste
1 head iceberg lettuce, leaves washed and dried
1 tablespoon Hoisin sauce

1 Heat the oil in a wok and stir-fry the garlic for a few seconds. Add the prawns and stir-fry until they change color and turn pink.
2 Put in the jicama and carrot. Stir-fry until the vegetables start to wilt. Pour in the stock and simmer, stirring occasionally, until all the vegetables are soft and the liquid has dried up.

3 Add soy sauce and pepper, stir, then transfer to a bowl and set aside to cool. Serve at room temperature with the lettuce leaves and a small saucer containing the Hoisin sauce. To eat, smear a little Hoisin sauce inside a lettuce leaf, then add some of the vegetable mixture and roll up.

Malaysian Bubor Cha Cha Dessert

4 cups (1 liter) coconut milk
1 small yam (4 oz/125 g), peeled and cubed, boiled in water for 5 minutes
1 small sweet potato (4 oz/125 g), peeled and cubed
2 tablespoons sago pearls, soaked in cold water 10 minutes, drained
2 pandanus leaves, raked with a fork, or a few drops of pandan essence

3 tablespoons sugar
Pinch of salt
1 large banana, halved lengthwise, then sliced

1 Put the coconut milk, yam, sweet potato, sago pearls, pandanus leaves or pandan essence, sugar and salt in a saucepan. Bring slowly to a boil, stirring occasionally, then lower heat and simmer uncovered until the

yam and sweet potato are soft and the sago pearls turn transparent, which should take approximately 10–12 minutes.
2 Add the banana slices and simmer for another 3 minutes. Remove the pandanus leaves. Serve hot, at room temperature, or chilled in bowls.

Long White Radish and Carrot Salad

1 cup (100 g) finely shredded long white (daikon) radish
1 cup (100 g) finely shredded carrot
1 tablespoon salt
1 tablespoon sugar
$1/4$ cup (60 ml) rice or white vinegar
$1/4$ cup (60 ml) water

1 Put the radish and carrot in a bowl and sprinkle with the salt. Rub, then set aside for 10 minutes. Squeeze to remove as much moisture as possible. Place the vegetables in a sieve under running water for a few seconds, then squeeze again and

drain well. Transfer the vegetables to a bowl, add sugar, vinegar, and water, stirring to mix well. Refrigerate for around 30 minutes before serving. Drain off the liquid before serving with noodle dishes, rice or barbecued meats.

Burmese Banana Stem Fish Soup

12 in (30 cm) fresh banana stem, sliced, or 1 large tin bamboo shoots, sliced
1 lb (500 g) mackerel or other strongly flavored fish
3 cups (750 ml) water
1 stalk lemongrass, bruised
3 tablespoons fish sauce
$1/2$ teaspoon ground turmeric
2 tablespoons oil
3 medium onions, thinly sliced
4 cups (1 liter) thin coconut milk
3 tablespoons chickpea flour (*besan*), fried in a dry pan until golden brown
1 tablespoon lime or lemon juice
10 oz (300 g) dried rice vermicelli (*bee hoon* or *mifen*), soaked in hot water to soften

Spice Paste
$1^1/_2$ in (4 cm) ginger, sliced
4–6 cloves garlic
2 large red chilies
1 teaspoon dried shrimp paste

Garnish
2–3 dried chilies, sliced, and fried until crisp
Lime or lemon wedges
3 tablespoons crisp fried shallots
4–6 cloves garlic, fried until golden brown and crisp
1 spring onion, minced
2 tablespoons minced coriander leaves (cilantro)
$1/4$ cup (30 g) chickpea flour (*besan*), dry-fried until golden brown

1 Soak the banana stem in salty water for 3–4 hours. Drain, then pull away any sticky strands. Set aside. Put the fish, water, lemongrass, fish sauce and turmeric powder in a pan and simmer uncovered until the fish is cooked. Drain, reserving the fish stock. Flake the fish and set aside.
2 Prepare the Spice Paste by processing all ingredients in a spice grinder until smooth, adding a little of the oil if needed to keep the mixture turning. Heat the oil in a large pan and stir-fry the onions over low–medium heat for 2–3 minutes, then add the Spice Paste and stir-fry for 3–4 minutes, until fragrant. Add the fish stock and coconut milk, bring to a boil stirring constantly, then reduce heat and simmer uncovered for 2 minutes. Add the sliced banana stem or bamboo shoots and simmer about 15 minutes until tender (5 minutes for bamboo shoots).
3 Mix the chickpea flour with water to make a paste, then add to the soup and stir until it starts to thicken. Add the fish and lime juice. To serve, divide noodles and soup among four to six bowls. Garnish to taste.

Simmered Arrowheads and Mixed Vegetables

4 oz (125 g) arrowheads, outer leaves peeled off, cubed
$1/2$ carrot, peeled and cubed
1 small potato, peeled and cubed
1 cup (100 g) canned bamboo shoots, drained and cubed
4 oz (125 g) chicken breast, cubed
4 dried black mushrooms, soaked to soften, stems discarded, quartered
$1/2$ cup (50 g) snow or sugar peas, tips, tails and strings removed

Stock
2 cups (500 ml) water
1 teaspoon instant *dashi* granules
$1/2$ cup (170 ml) Japanese soy sauce
3 tablespoons mirin
2 tablespoons sugar

1 Heat about 2 cups of lightly salted water in a saucepan. When boiling, add the arrowheads and simmer for 2 minutes. Lift out with a slotted spoon and cool in iced water. Drain and set aside. Use the same water to blanch the carrot, potato and bamboo shoots separately in the same manner and set aside. Blanch the chicken in the same water for just 30 seconds, then drain and set aside.
2 To make the Stock, combine all ingredients in a saucepan and bring to a boil. Add the cooked vegetables and chicken and simmer gently with the pan covered until tender. Add the mushrooms and snow peas and simmer for 2 minutes. Serve in a bowl with the Stock, rice and dishes.

recipe ingredients

Dried shrimp paste is sold wrapped in paper or plastic in a dried brick. It should be toasted before use. This can be done in several ways: by dry-frying in a pan, by placing the *belacan* on the back of a spoon and toasting it above a flame, or wrapping it in foil and grilling it.

Bonito flakes are shavings of dried, smoked and cured bonito tuna, sold in fine or coarse flakes in small plastic packs. Fine flakes are used as a garnish and coarse flakes to make *dashi* fish stock. Refrigerate unused flakes in an airtight container or plastic bag.

Chinese rice wine is used in Chinese-inspired recipes and sometimes added to marinades in local dishes. The best Chinese rice wine is from Shao Hsing in China. Chinese rice wine may be substituted with dry sherry or saké.

Chicken stock is widely available canned. You can make your own using chicken stock cubes or cubes. To make the stock using cooked chicken, heat 1 teaspoon of oil in a large pan, then add 1 clove garlic (minced) to the pan and stir-fry over low heat until golden brown. Discard the garlic. Place 2 chicken carcasses or $1/2$ a chicken (with the skin and fat removed) and pour 10 cups ($2^1/_2$ liters) of water into the pan, bring to a boil and simmer for 10 minutes. Skim the surface, then add 1 medium onion (chopped), 2 spring onions (chopped), 4 thin slices of ginger, 10 peppercorns and $1/2$ teaspoon salt. Simmer, but do not boil. Strain the stock into a large bowl and chill for a few hours in the refrigerator. Skim off any fat that solidifies on the surface. If not using immediately, cover and refrigerate or freeze for longer storage.

Coconut cream and **coconut milk** are used in many Asian desserts and curries. To obtain fresh coconut cream (which is normally used for desserts), grate the flesh of 1 coconut into a bowl (this yields about 3 cups of grated coconut flesh), add $1/2$ cup of water and knead thoroughly a few times, then squeeze the mixture firmly in your fist or strain with a muslin cloth or cheesecloth. Thick coconut milk is obtained by the same method but by adding double the water to the grated flesh (about 1 cup instead of $1/2$ cup). Although freshly pressed milk has more flavor, coconut cream and milk are now widely available canned or in packets that are quick, convenient and tasty. Canned or packet coconut cream or milk comes in varying consistencies depending on the brand, and you will need to try them out and adjust the thickness by adding water as needed. In general, add 1 cup of water to 1 cup of coconut cream to obtain thick coconut milk.

Crisp fried shallots are a common garnish in many Asian dishes. They are available in packets and jars in supermarkets. To make your own, peel, wash and slice 6–8 shallots into thin strips. Heat $1/2$ cup (125 ml) oil in a saucepan over medium heat, and fry the shallots until golden brown, taking care not to over-brown the shallots as this makes them taste bitter. Remove the fried shallots with a spatula or slotted spoon, and drain on paper towels. If not using immediately, then store in a dry, airtight jar to preserve their crispness.

Dashi stock is a basic Japanese soup stock made from dried kelp (*konbu*) and dried bonito flakes. Instant *dashi* stock powder (*dashi-no-moto*) is sold in many supermarkets and the *dashi* prepared according to instructions; generally, use $1/2$ teaspoon of powder with 1 cup water.

Dried prawns are best kept refrigerated if keeping in a humid climate. Look for brightly colored, plump prawns. Soak for 5 minutes to soften before chopping or grinding.

Fenugreek seeds are almost square, hard yellowish brown seeds that are strongly flavored and generally used whole in southern Indian dishes and frequently in pickles and fish curries.

Five-spice powder is a blend of sweet, fragrant spices including star anise, cinnamon, cloves, fennel and Sichuan pepper. Five-spice powder is a popular seasoning in Chinese food as well as some Vietnamese and Thai dishes.

Fish sauce adds a salty, pungent tang to Asian dishes, and is used either in cooking or sparingly as a seasoning. Sold in bottles, the sauce ranges from almost clear to golden. Vietnamese brands are stronger flavored than Thai brands. Fish sauce keeps almost indefinitely in the cupboard.

Garam masala is a spice mixture sold in Indian foodstores. Make your own by gently roasting $1/2$ cup cumin seeds, 10 cloves, 4 whole star anise, 2 tablespoons coriander seeds, 4–5 black cardamom pods (bruised) and 10–12 green cardamom pods (bruised), 3–4 blades of mace, 5 bay leaves and 1 tablespoon black peppercorns until fragrant. Set the spices aside to cool, then grind the mixture to a fine powder in a blender, spice grinder or mortar and pestle. Store the spice paste in an airtight container.

Ghee is a rich, clarified butter and is widely used in Indian cooking. It is available ready made in Indian foodstores and supermarkets. For a healthier alternative, substitute ghee with vegetable oil and other unsaturated fats.

Korean gochu jang, a type of soy bean chili paste used in spicy Korean dishes, is available in supermarkets. If you prefer to make your own paste, you can do so by mixing $1^1/_2$–2 tablespoons of salted soy bean paste (*tau cheo*), $^1/_2$ teaspoon sugar and $^1/_4$–$^1/_2$ teaspoon ground red pepper. Stir the mixture until the sugar dissolves, then transfer to a sauce bowl.

Mirin is a sweet liquid made by fermenting steamed glutinous rice with *shoju* (a distilled spirit similar to vodka). Mirin adds a beautiful glaze to grilled foods and is used to flavor soup stocks, marinades and dressings.

Miso is a fermented paste made from soy beans and wheat. **Red miso paste** is red to brown in color, higher in protein content and saltier than the milder, sweeter **white miso paste**. Miso is used to enhance the flavor of soups, stocks and dressings and as a grilling baste for meat and fish. Never allow miso paste to boil as it loses its flavor and digestive properties. Miso is usually sold in packets in supermarkets. Store unused miso paste in a refrigerator.

Oyster sauce is a Chinese seasoning sauce that does not actually taste of oysters. (Check the label to see that you are buying real oyster sauce and not "oyster-flavored" sauce.) Oyster sauce intensifies the flavor of food and is often splashed liberally on cooked vegetables, or used in marinades—oyster sauce is surprisingly salty, so taste before adding. Vegetarian alternatives are available in most supermarkets.

Japanese rice is a short-grain variety that is slightly more starchy than Thai or Chinese long-grain rice. Available from most supermarkets, Japanese rice can be substituted with any short-grain rice.

Palm sugar is less sweet than white sugar, and has a rich, maple syrup flavor and ranges in color from golden brown to dark brown. It is used in many Southeast Asian desserts. If palm sugar is unavailable, substitute with maple syrup or brown sugar mixed with a bit of coconut cream.

Rice vinegar is a mild, faintly fragrant vinegar. Chinese brands are inexpensive and widely available, whereas Japanese rice vinegar used in sushi is slightly sweeter and milder. Although red vinegars are also available, most recipes in this book call for distilled white vinegar.

Saké, also known as Japanese rice wine, can be substituted with sherry or Chinese rice wine.

Soy sauce is brewed from wheat, salt and soy beans. **Black soy sauce** gives a smoky and slightly sweet flavor to a dish and is not as salty as the thinner regular or light soy sauce.

Seven-spice mixture or *shichimi togarashi* is a Japanese blend of ground chili and other seasonings such as *sansho* pepper, mustard and sesame seeds.

Tamarind juice is obtained by soaking 1 tablespoon of tamarind pulp in $^1/_4$ cup (60 ml) warm water, then straining the mixture. Tamarind pulp is sold dried in the pod or in compressed blocks. The juice is often used to add a tangy flavor to dishes.

Salted soy bean paste (*tau cheo*) is sold in jars and used as a salty seasoning. The bean paste is made from salted and fermented soy beans that are black to brownish in color. Some brands are golden-brown and are labeled "yellow bean sauce." "Sweet" and "hot" salted soy beans have added sugar and chili.

Sesame oil is used sparingly as a seasoning and is generally mixed with vegetable oil when stir-frying. It has a strong, nutty flavor and fragrance.

Star anise is a dried brown flower with eight woody petals. Each of these petals contains a seed. Star anise tastes of aniseed and cinnamon. Use whole and discard the spice before eating.

Thai red or green curry paste is used as a seasoning paste as well as in curries. Buy the packaged varieties or make your own paste. Dry-fry 1 tablespoon of coriander seeds with 1 teaspoon cumin seeds in a skillet over low heat for 5 minutes. Using a blender or mortar and pestle, grind the seeds to a powder together with 5 dried red chilies (slit lengthwise, deseed and soak in hot water first for 15 minutes), 3 tablespoons sliced shallots, 8 cloves smashed garlic, 2–3 slices galangal root, 2 tablespoons sliced lemongrass (tender portion of lower third only), 2 teaspoons grated kaffir lime rind, 10 black peppercorns and 1 tablespoon minced coriander root. Add 1 teaspoon dried shrimp paste and grind to a smooth paste. Transfer to a covered container and refrigerate.

Thai roasted chili paste or **nam prik pao** is most often sold in jars, and is widely available. To make your own *nam prik pao*, cook 3–4 whole dried chilies, 2–3 unpeeled shallots and 2–3 unpeeled cloves of garlic under a hot grill, broiler or in a dry wok until the chilies are crisp but not burnt (this happens very rapidly, so be sure to turn the chilies frequently). Remove the chilies and continue to cook the shallots and garlic until soft and the skin starts to blacken. Set aside to cool. Spread $^1/_2$ tablespoon of dried shrimp paste on a thin layer of aluminum foil, wrap to enclose, then grill on both sides until fragrant. Remove the stem ends of the chili. Repeat for the garlic and shallots, and remove the skins. Soak $^1/_2$ heaped tablespoon of tamarind pulp in $^1/_8$ cup (30 ml) warm water, then squeeze to obtain juice. Place the chili, shallots, garlic, tamarind juice, $^1/_2$ tablespoon of shaved palm sugar and $^1/_4$ teaspoon salt in a spice grinder and blend to fine. Heat 1 tablespoon of oil in a small pan. Add the paste and cook over low–medium heat, stirring frequently, until fragrant, about 4–5 minutes. Cool, then transfer to a covered jar and refrigerate. Makes $^1/_2$ cup.

recipe list

Angled gourd soup 93
Balinese fern tips with garlic and pepper 56
Banana flower salad with coconut cream 76
Bean sprout and green bean salad 28
Beef soup with sawtooth coriander 117
Blanched water spinach and tofu with spicy peanut sauce 59
Braised hijiki 165
Braised mixed vegetables with dried lily buds (chap chye) 156
Burmese banana stem fish soup 202
Burmese stir-fried chayote 95
Cabbage stir-fried with onion and Indian spices 142
Chestnuts with Chinese cabbage 77
Chicken deep-fried in pandanus leaves 117
Chicken pot roast with lemongrass 116
Chilled tofu with dried prawns and preserved Sichuan vegetable 154
Chinese celery, cashews and barbecued pork 114
Chinese garlic chive pancakes 144
Chinese jicama and carrot salad with prawns 201
Chinese spinach with tangy soy and sesame dressing 58
Chinese white fungus and melon balls in syrup 132
Chinese winter melon soup 94
Claypot rice with chestnuts and chicken 74
Cucumber and pineapple salad 93
Cucumber shoots in crabmeat sauce 58
Deep-fried bean curd with bean sprouts and peanut sauce 177
Egg and nori rolls 164
Eggplant stir-fried with basil 92
Eggplant tamarind curry 92
Filipino cassava cake (bibingka) 200
Fish and Vietnamese mint parcels 116
Fresh coriander leaf and coconut chutney 114
Fresh tuna baked in konbu 165
Fried bean curd with garlic, black pepper and coriander 177
Fuzzy melon with black mushrooms 95
Green chili lassi 74
Grilled fresh matsutake mushrooms 130
Indian chickpeas in spicy tomato sauce 30

Indian cucumber raita 94
Indian fried eggplant with yoghurt sauce 94
Indian mixed vegetables with coconut and yoghurt 92
Indian onion fritters 145
Indian vegetable fritters (pakhora) 29
Indonesian sambal bajak 117
Indonesian spiced tempeh with palm sugar and sweet soy sauce 176
Indonesian vegetable tamarind soup 29
Japanese simmered dried black mushrooms 132
Korean blanched soy bean sprouts with sesame 28
Korean kim chee stir-fried with pork 156
Korean mixed mushroom hotpot 131
Korean simmered wakame 164
Korean spring onion pancakes 144
Leek and sweet corn soup 143
Lettuce with bean curd and mushroom 59
Long beans with fermented bean curd 31
Long white radish and carrot salad 201
Malay rice salad with herbs and salted fish 114
Malaysian bubor cha cha dessert 201
Malaysian-style cabbage stewed in coconut milk 56
Miso soup with enokitake 133
Mustard cabbage stir-fried with ginger 58
Onion and yoghurt salad 145
Pea shoots with black mushrooms 30
Pickled mustard cabbage with beef 155
Pickled swatow mustard cabbage and bean curd soup 155
Plantains in coconut milk 76
Poached eggplant salad 93
Pork and prawn rolls in bean curd skin 174
Preserved mustard cabbage with pork 155
Rice porridge with preserved Chinese cabbage 157
Sambal belacan 75
Sambal kangkung (kangkung tumis belacan) 57
Seaweed and crabmeat salad 165
Simmered arrowheads and mixed vegetables 202
Smoked salmon and cucumber rolls wrapped with nori 164
Sour fish curry with bilimbi 75

South Indian garlic curry 145
South Indian-style snake gourd 95
Southern Indian dosai 31
Spiced breadnut slices 77
Spiced Indian cauliflower 57
Spiced Indian kidney beans 29
Spicy Malaysian vegetable pickles 143
Sri Lankan breadfruit curry 75
Steamed savory custard with nameko mushrooms 130
Steamed silken bean curd with vegetables 176
Stir-fried bean curd with cashews 177
Stir-fried beef with ginger and leeks 142
Stir-fried chicken and Sichuan pickled vegetable 154
Stir-fried chicken with lemongrass 116
Stir-fried chicken with onion, tomato and broccoli 144
Stir-fried kailan or choy sum with oyster sauce 57
Stir-fried loofah with oyster sauce 94
Stir-fried mixed mushrooms 132
Stir-fried rice vermicelli with baby corn 76
Stir-fried rice vermicelli with garlic chives and pork 142
Stir-fried snow peas with mushrooms and scallops 31
Stir-fried spring onions with bean curd 143
Stir-fried sugar peas and pumpkin 28
Stir-fried Thai minced beef and basil 115
Sushi with tuna and pickled daikon 157
Sweet Chinese azuki bean pancakes 30
Sweet mung beans with coconut 28
Thai cloud ear fungus with chicken and ginger 133
Thai duck and galangal soup 200
Thai hot sour green papaya salad 75
Thai mango and cashew salad 77
Thai steamed oyster mushrooms in banana leaf cups 130
Thai tom yam soup with straw mushrooms 131
Thai water chestnut salad 200
Thai wild pepper leaf parcels 115
Vegetarian bean curd skin rolls 154
Vietnamese peperomia salad 115
Vietnamese shredded chicken and cabbage salad 56
Young jackfruit and prawns in coconut milk 74

index

Entries with capital letters denote main entries in this book. Names of recipes appear in boldface.